SCREENING

Lisa Hopkins | # SCREENING THE GOTHIC

 UNIVERSITY OF TEXAS PRESS
Austin

First edition, 2005

Requests for permission to reproduce material from this work should be sent to Permissions, University of Texas Press, P.O. Box 7819, Austin, TX 78713-7819.

∞ The paper used in this book meets the minimum requirements of ANSI/NISO Z39.48-1992 (R1997) (Permanence of Paper).

LIBRARY OF CONGRESS
CATALOGING-IN-PUBLICATION DATA
Hopkins, Lisa, 1962–
Screening the gothic / by Lisa Hopkins. — 1st ed.
p. cm.
Includes bibliographical references and index.
ISBN 0-292-70645-6 (cl. : alk. paper) —
ISBN 0-292-70646-4 (pbk. : alk. paper)
1. English literature — History and criticism. 2. Gothic revival (Literature) — Great Britain. 3. English literature — Adaptations — History and criticism.
4. Horror tales, English — Film and video adaptations.
5. English literature — Film and video adaptations.
6. Horror films — History and criticism. 7. Film adaptations. I. Title.
PR408.G68H67 2005
820.9'11 — dc22

2004024535

For Chris and Sam

CONTENTS

$\mathcal{A}$CKNOWLEDGMENTS

$\mathcal{I}$ would like to thank Andrew Berzanskis and Jim Burr for their help in getting this project off the ground; the two anonymous readers of the manuscript; and Richard McCarter for help far beyond the call of duty with the illustrations. Earlier versions of some of the chapters have appeared in the following journals and book, and I am grateful for permission to reproduce them here: part of chapter one as " 'Denmark's a Prison': Branagh's *Hamlet* and the Paradoxes of Intimacy," *EnterText* 1.2 (Spring 2001); part of chapter four as "The Red and the Blue: *Jane Eyre* in the 1990s" in *Classics in Film and Fiction,* edited by Deborah Cartmell, I. G. Hunter, Heidi Kaye, and Imelda Whelehan (London: Pluto, 2000), 54–69; and parts of chapter five as "Returning to the Mummy" in *Postmodern Culture* (January 2002) and in my *Giants of the Past: Literature and Evolution* (Lewiston: Bucknell University Press, 2004) and "Harry Potter and the Acquisition of Knowledge" in *Reading Harry Potter: Critical Essays,* edited by Giselle Liza Anatol (Greenwood Press, 2003), 25–34.

$\mathcal{T}$HE GOTHIC
Towards a Definition

*W*hat is the Gothic? In literary studies, the term is generally applied primarily to a body of writing produced in England between about 1750 and about 1820. Often set in ancient, partially ruined castles or mansions haunted by the real or apparent threat of a supernatural presence, its cast of characters typically includes a mysterious and threatening older man, a vulnerable heroine, and a character who is poised ambiguously between good and evil. Although early Gothic novels were often set abroad, the sense of unease and the obsession with doubling that characterise the form also typically include the fear that it also had something profound to say about the reader's own condition. Its principal characteristics are a concern with the fragmented and often doubled nature of the self—Robert Miles remarks that "in its inarticulate way, Gothic worries over a problem stirring within the foundations of the self"[1]—and a concentration on the gloomy, the mysterious, and the ruined:

> Gothic signifies a writing of excess. It appears in the awful obscurity that haunted eighteenth-century rationality and morality. It shadows the despairing ecstasies of Romantic idealism and individualism and the uncanny dualities of Victorian realism and decadence. Gothic atmospheres—gloomy and mysterious—have repeatedly signalled the disturbing return of pasts upon presents and evoked emotions of terror and laughter.[2]

Many of these characteristics are present in the films which I discuss in this book and label "Gothic," but I shall be suggesting that, above all, the classic genre marker of the Gothic in film is doubleness, for it is the dualities typically created by the Gothic that invest it with its uncanny ability to hold its darkly shadowed mirror up to its own age.

Fittingly enough, this emphasis on doubling can work in two ways.

In the first place, Gothic tends to create polarities: extreme good is opposed to extreme evil, extreme innocence to extreme power, and very often extreme youth to extreme age. An aesthetic of violent contrasts in all possible fields seems to prevail in both Gothic books and Gothic films: think, for instance, of the classic scene from Bram Stoker's novel *Dracula* in which an enormously aged and utterly evil man in black preys on a very young, innocent girl in white, in the cliff-top grounds of a ruined abbey and by the light of the moon. Where a film adaptation has introduced such polarization into literary texts which previously lacked it, I have therefore identified this as a Gothicizing tactic. And yet, at the same time, there is an uncanny sense that the polarizations so beloved of the Gothic are not in fact as absolute as they seem—that things which appear to be opposite can actually be frighteningly, uncannily similar. In that famous scene in *Dracula,* for instance, the innocent-looking young girl secretly dreams of being allowed to have three husbands, just as Dracula apparently has three wives, and she grows more and more like him as the book progresses. For this reason, I claim that the blurring of previously secure polarities is as much a genre marker of Gothic as the introduction of radical polarization. This is not tricksiness or bad faith, but an attempt to allow for the complex, shifting nature of the Gothic and the fact that some of its most troubling effects arise precisely from such uncertainties about identity and the relationship of one thing to another.

One of the most notable results of this emphasis on doubling is that much criticism of and commentary on the Gothic has preferred psychoanalytic approaches to historicizing or materialist ones, a trend fed by the fact that, as Linda Bayer-Berenbaum points out, the Gothic tends "to portray all states of mind that intensify normal thought or perception. Dream states, drug states, and states of intoxication have always been prevalent in the Gothic novel because repressed thoughts can surface in them."[3] The idea of repression takes us straight to the terrain of classical Freudian psychoanalysis, and this approach has been often and fruitfully deployed in reference to Gothic texts. Thus, David J. Skal introduces his account of *Dracula* in *Hollywood Gothic* by observing, "Modern psychoanalytic theory on the subject, as classically argued by Ernest Jones in *On the Nightmare,* finds the genesis of vampire legend in the universal experience of the nightmare."[4] Ernest Jones was Freud's disciple, so it is no surprise to find him echoing his master's assumption that the dream is the royal road to meanings locked in the unconscious.

The link between the Gothic and psychoanalysis is by no means accepted as an universal truth. In *The Biology of Horror: Gothic Litera-*

ture and Film, Jack Morgan treats the horror generated by the Gothic as essentially physical and indeed biological in origin, and Markman Ellis, in his recent *The History of Gothic Fiction,* announces that "the gambit of this book is to offer an account of gothic fiction without recourse to the language or theory of psychoanalysis."[5] However, Ellis's use of the word *gambit* clearly registers the unusualness of what he thus proposes. It is true not only that the Gothic has often been held to have a particular affinity with psychoanalysis, particularly with Freudian psychoanalysis, but also, I think, that while Ellis is right that the Gothic existed without psychoanalysis, psychoanalysis might well not have existed without the Gothic.[6] It was to Gothic literature that Freud turned for some of his key ideas and phrases, and I am concerned here not with what the Gothic originally meant but with what it means in these adaptations. One of the central planks of my argument in this book is that many of the adaptations I discuss have introduced the motifs and discourse of psychoanalysis (usually, but not always, specifically Freudian psychoanalysis) to the stories they treat, even where — indeed particularly where — the original books on which they were based preferred to frame the events they represented in clearly materialist terms. This is, perhaps, an inevitable consequence of filmmakers' desire to ensure that the ensuing work can continue to speak to a contemporary audience, without being bound to the conditions of its own time. It does, however, often have the additional effect of introducing Gothicizing elements where none had been before.

All of the book's chapters discuss films which have been adapted from novels and which have had changes made to them in the process. The literary texts discussed were either originally written as consciously Gothic or have been adapted in a Gothic mode. My central claim is that, paradoxically, those texts whose affiliations with the Gothic were originally the clearest become the least Gothic when they are filmed. As I suggest in the book, this is partly because locating the origins of events in the mind rather than within society ensures a sense of the narrative's continuing relevance. It is also partly because cinema's focus on the face of the individual inevitably leads to an emphasis on the individual rather than the group, while its traditional language of visual symbolism causes things to be read in terms other than their own; this produces a modal affinity with both the Gothic and with the strategies of psychoanalytic interpretation, which is also manifested in the cinematic Gothicizing of a number of Shakespeare texts and in the paradoxical genre of family-oriented Gothic, which I explore in the last chapter. However, for a text which has already pre-empted these preferred filmic strategies by being obviously Gothic in the first place, other approaches become necessary, leading to an over-compensatory emphasis on backstory and consequences, since the psy-chologizing is felt to be already performed. The effect is generally that the Gothic logic of the original narrative becomes submerged under details and additions which often distract from the pattern of the original rather than complementing it.

The book has five chapters. The first, "Gothic Revenants: A Tale of Three Hamlets," looks at the three most recent film adaptations of *Hamlet,* directed by Franco Zeffirelli, Kenneth Branagh, and Michael Almereyda. In this chapter, I argue that although it was written long be-fore the development of the Gothic mode proper, *Hamlet* nevertheless has many Gothic features. It is set in a gloomy and mysterious castle haunted by a ghost, it has a fragile young heroine who eventually runs mad and dies, and its plot centers on murder and incest. It is also riddled with doubles, with Laertes, Fortinbras, Lucianus, and Pyrrhus all offering comparators and analogues for Hamlet and Claudius and old Hamlet threatening to leach uncannily into each other. I argue, however, that in these three film adaptations of *Hamlet,* the greater the prominence given to the outward trappings of the Gothic, the less Gothicizing the ultimate effect. Ironi-cally, therefore, it is Branagh's ostensibly un-Oedipal and resolutely un-Medieval adaptation which is the most truly Gothic of these three films.

The second chapter, "Putting the Gothic In: *Clarissa, Sense and Sensi-bility, Mansfield Park,* and *The Time Machine,*" discusses four texts which were all originally written to demonstrate the value and importance of a rationalist perspective and the dangers and shallowness of an overempha-sis on emotion and on the darker corners of the mind. A key characteristic of the Gothic is the extent to which it focuses on the workings of the sub-conscious; however, Richardson wrote *Clarissa* because he was so stung by the critical response to his first novel, *Pamela,* which essentially ar-gued that the text betrayed truths which its author had never intended it to (specifically, that Pamela was not a virtuous innocent at all, but a de-signing minx). In *Clarissa,* therefore, he set out to create a novel whose actions and characters could not be read "against the grain" as *Pamela*'s had been. Jane Austen, who was so fond of Richardson that she cele-brated the date on which the heroine of his novel *Sir Charles Grandison* was married, was deeply wary of the unbridled emotion so valorized in the Gothic novel and satirized it both in her juvenilia and in *Northanger Abbey.* Finally, H. G. Wells wrote *The Time Machine* as a demonstration of a scientific idea, Darwin's theory of evolution by means of natural selec-tion. In the four adaptations discussed here, however, rationality gives place to pathology, and the materialist analyses advanced by the original books are replaced by psychoanalytical ones.

The third chapter, "Taking the Gothic Out: *'Tis Pity She's a Whore, Frankenstein, The Woman in White,* and *Lady Audley's Secret,*" argues that these texts, though Gothic when they were originally written, were comprehensively removed from the realm of the Gothic in being transferred onto the screen. *'Tis Pity She's a Whore,* like *Hamlet,* focuses on incest and murder, and Ford's detached attitude and refusal to supply any kind of explanation for the behavior of Giovanni and Annabella leave his audience with an overwhelming impression of the impenetrable mysteries of the human psyche. Giuseppe Patroni Griffi's film, on the other hand, offers rather a quasisociological exploration of the workings of family life in introverted, hierarchical, religiously oriented communities. Mary Shelley structured *Frankenstein* in such a way as to draw insistent attention to the disturbing parallels between Victor Frankenstein and the Monster who is his ostensible opposite, but Kenneth Branagh's film adaptation, for all the proclamation of fidelity to the novel in its title *Mary Shelley's Frankenstein,* keeps Victor and the Monster firmly apart and offers not Gothic dreams and doublings but scientific rationalism. Similarly, Mary Elizabeth Braddon's *Lady Audley's Secret* tells a complex and compelling story in which the secret of the title, so far from being revealed, acquires instead ever more layers of signification and resonance: is Lady Audley, as she claims, truly mad, or is she merely bad, or is her madness socially constructed, with the deepest and darkest level of the novel's meaning being that its heroine's crime is really to be a woman and, still worse, a mother? Donald Hounam's adaptation, on the other hand, cuts through all the suggestive ambiguities of the novel to provide a simple and clear-cut answer to that question which is rooted in social rather than psychoanalytic analysis. Finally, Wilkie Collins's novel *The Woman in White* asks some deeply troubling questions about the stability of the human psyche and the relationship between appearance and reality, but once again the TV adaptation is less interested in exploring the inner logic of its characters' experiences than in using them as a tool to expose the hypocrisies of Victorian culture (with Mrs. Thatcher's notorious advocacy of Victorian values giving a sharply political contemporary edge to the probing of Victorian inadequacies both here and in *Lady Audley's Secret*).

The fourth chapter, "Fragmenting the Gothic: *Jane Eyre* and *Dracula,*" discusses three adaptations, two of *Jane Eyre* and one of *Dracula,* and argues that the strategies deployed in these retellings, while often

Gothicizing in themselves, work to sharply contrasting effect in different cases, introducing the Gothic where it had not been before and banishing it from where it originally was. In Franco Zeffirelli's film of *Jane Eyre,* awareness of the ways in which the text may be made to speak to modern concerns produces an elegant piece of social commentary, but plays down the extremes of Jane's individuality; in Robert Young's 1997 ITV version, conversely, the danger of Jane's surroundings is played down but the dangers lurking within her own mind are significantly played up. Finally, Francis Ford Coppola's *Bram Stoker's Dracula* removes the Gothic element from the character of Dracula but finds it, instead, in fin-de-siècle London.

The fifth and last chapter, "Gothic and the Family: *The Mummy Returns, Harry Potter and the Philosopher's Stone,* and *The Lord of the Rings: The Fellowship of the Ring,*" looks at three films which were aimed primarily or largely at family audiences and argues that although elements of the Gothic are strongly present in all three films, they work in rather unexpected ways. These films feature mummies, ghosts, trolls, wizards, goblins, vampires, revenants, and a range of other monsters; but all of these together generate merely a pleasurable *frisson.* What these films find really frightening is, in fact, families. It is perhaps appropriate that only in the heart of the family, in the form of family-oriented viewing, can the dark, anarchic energies of the Gothic still be seen fully pulsing.

SCREENING THE GOTHIC

Chapter One | $\mathcal{G}$OTHIC REVENANTS
A Tale of Three Hamlets

$\mathcal{H}$*amlet,* with its ghost, its castle, its incest, its doublings, and its repressions, is so obviously a Gothic text that it is purely the fact of chronology that keeps it out of the Gothic canon: "[C]an *Hamlet* legitimately be described as 'Gothic'? The answer is a qualified 'yes.' "[1] Film adaptations of *Hamlet,* in contrast, are not subject to this constraint and are thus at liberty to locate themselves centrally in the terrain of the Gothic. Moreover, all the film adaptations I discuss are haunted by that sense of repetition and recurrences which, as I argue in my penultimate chapter, is central to a fully Gothic adaptation. Even the first film of *Hamlet* was already a repetition of the play, and every subsequent film is a further repetition of the films which have already gone before it, in an unstoppably cumulative process.

The fact that all films of *Hamlet* could potentially be Gothic, however, does not mean that they all are. In fact, I argue that the three most recent film versions, by Franco Zeffirelli, Kenneth Branagh, and Michael Almereyda, precisely encapsulate in miniature the thesis of this book. On screen, to court the Gothic explicitly is to banish it; to introduce its trappings is to foreclose on its spirit. Thus, I shall try to show that the most overtly Gothicized of these films, Franco Zeffirelli's, is also the least so in effect. Kenneth Branagh's light, bright, and sparkling nineteenth-century court, on the other hand, proves to be haunted and traversed by doubles. Finally, Michael Almereyda's spankingly up-to-date, technologically savvy retelling seems to be set in a world structured solely by science and rationality, but proves self-consciously to incorporate some of the key aspects of the Gothic.

Mad Max as a Sane Hamlet: Zeffirelli's Prince for the Nineties

I recently rediscovered an essay which I had written on *Hamlet* when I was seventeen and which had won my school's annual prize for the best essay on Shakespeare. As I reread it, I was very forcibly struck by the fact that, as a very serious and distinctly holier-than-thou teenager, I had not only identified with Hamlet but had unquestioningly and wholeheartedly assumed that his perspective on things was *right*. Being now considerably older and, if not wiser, indisputably more fallible, I am now more amenable to the idea of a Hamlet with a problem, whose view of events was a markedly subjective one and whose reaction was, in some respects at least, excessive. Franco Zeffirelli, however, seems to share the far simpler certainties of my adolescent self. As Robert Hapgood points out, "In choosing Mel Gibson he hoped to have found 'the Hamlet for the nineties' . . . Zeffirelli has never tired of recounting the moment of decision when he saw a parallel between Hamlet's abortive meditation on suicide in the 'to be or not to be' soliloquy and the scene in *Lethal Weapon* when Gibson as Martin Riggs cannot bring himself to pull the trigger that would end his life."[2] For Zeffirelli, then, appeal to a contemporary, and implicitly a youthful, audience was the vital consideration, and what he offered his audience is primarily the Hamlet that my teenage self used to see, the one who was simply saner and more sensible than all the weak fools around him; and since his target market was teenagers and students, this was probably an astute choice. What the average member of such an audience is offered is the possibility of identification, and indeed what is perhaps most striking about Zeffirelli's film, given the magnitude of Mel Gibson's reputation as a sex symbol,[3] is the extent to which we are invited to look not *at* him, but *with* him.

The effect of the film is thus a paradoxical one. Visually, it strongly underlines its affinities with the historical territory of the Gothic, the dark and distant medieval past. The opening of the narrative is heavily marked by signs which situate its events in this period: the architecture, the round-headed crosses, the costumes, and Glenn Close's wildly extravagant plaits all speak of a world very distant from our own, as does the later detail of showing Helena Bonham-Carter's Ophelia painstakingly stitching the Bayeux tapestry. Most notably, a hood and beard shade and obscure the normally familiar features of Mel Gibson, and although the hood soon disappears, the beard stays for the duration of the film. The impression created is that of a man in disguise, a shadowy figure whose hood speaks strongly of the sinister monks so frequently found in Gothic novels.

Although he is thus visually estranged, however, Gibson is nevertheless presented as a clear point of identification for us because we are consistently invited to share his perspective. Whereas many modern directors of *Hamlet* update the story, seeking to give it a context which is either explicitly contemporary or which is perceived as having the potential to be allegorically construed as such, Zeffirelli, while leaving the external chronological setting of the play pointedly untouched, has comprehensively rearranged its internal chronology, resequencing events with the twin results of clarifying and simplifying the unfolding order of the narrative and allowing the audience to learn of new developments at the same time as Hamlet does, thus insistently aligning their perspective and response with his.

This structural assimilation of the audience's viewpoint with Hamlet's own lends an added force to the film's careful instantiation of an official, public version of events and a private, secretive take on them. This is another device which, while bearing a superficial similarity to a characteristic Gothic strategy, actually militates against the creation of a Gothic effect, for while the Gothic would typically work to suggest a dark mirroring effect in the two versions, this has much more in common with the classic conspiracy or cover-up scenario so beloved of American moviemaking. Zeffirelli's film, unlike the play, begins with a moment which is clearly designated as public, as soldiers gather ceremonially outside the castle, and the element of ritual and formality persists even as the scene switches to the greater privacy of the actual interment, with only Hamlet, Gertrude, and Claudius present; but the formal and prescribed nature of the occasion is rudely disrupted as the distraught gaze of Gertrude, who is sobbing helplessly over the coffin of her dead husband, battens onto that of the strong, silent Claudius—a glance which we see Hamlet see and which we will doubtless remember as his suspicions begin to develop. A similar contrast between the public and the private underlies both the covert hand gesture with which Ian Holm's Polonius orchestrates the rising of Claudius's court and Gertrude's swift glance over her shoulder to check whether she has been observed kissing the returning Claudius.

We share Hamlet's perspective again when, just as he sees his mother gaze appealingly at Claudius, he hears Polonius warn Ophelia against himself. (Slyly, Zeffirelli has underlined the rawly contemporary nature of the appeal of Gibson's Hamlet by surrounding him with great Hamlets of the past—Holm, Bates, Scofield—who are here cast as villainous or, at best, ambiguous characters; when Holm's Polonius properly stresses "character" on its second syllable, what we register is not accuracy but pedantry, and Scofield's Old Hamlet is so emotionally distant that Gibson is said to have imagined Hamlet's meeting with the ghost to have been the first occasion on which father and son had actually talked.) Since we know that Hamlet has overheard Ophelia thus being poisoned against him, we are likely to interpret his subsequent attitude to her not as paranoia or as misogyny resulting from an unresolved Oedipal complex, but as simple and justified caution. Even more importantly, the film's complete omission of the first scene of the play means that we, the viewers, are as surprised as Hamlet to hear from Horatio about the appearance of the ghost. Whole books may have been written on the precise nuances of the meanings *Hamlet* once held for audiences who were acutely aware of the significance of Wittenberg and the Diet of Worms and who could register the shock entailed in having the (implicitly Catholic) ghost of a father in Purgatory appear to his Protestant son; Zeffirelli does not even attempt to deal with such theological complexities, but what he does offer instead, particularly to a first-time audience, is a vivid apprehension of the probable emotional impact of Hamlet's experience. Equally, when Hamlet is on his way to his first meeting with the apparition, he and we both look together from a high vantage point down at the feast below. This use of an elevated viewpoint not only underscores the lofty nature of Hamlet's dismissal of Danish drinking customs, it is also part of a sustained pattern in the film of positioning Hamlet aloft, as when he looks down at Polonius from battlements and bookshelves, in a posture that is strongly suggestive of not only literal but also moral superiority, thus making our own alignment with him implicitly welcome and indeed flattering.

It is presumably partly as a consequence of this empathetic positioning that, in Zeffirelli's film, we are never seriously invited to consider that Hamlet might really be mad. We do not, in fact, see or hear any suggestion of madness before his encounter with Ophelia, and, importantly, we observe this for ourselves rather than hearing of it through her and are thus able to observe that, from an early stage in the meeting, Hamlet appears to become aware of Polonius's concealed presence and can, therefore, be construed as acting in a deliberately misleading and stagy way. (Similarly, in Hamlet's next encounter with her, we are well aware that he observes the telltale shadow of a watcher before he embarks on his tirade about honesty.)

What is definitively not tainted by this awareness of being watched, however, is Gibson's delivery of "To be or not to be." Zeffirelli has rigorously separated this from the Ophelia scene, having Gibson walk downstairs towards the royal tombs of Denmark before delivering the first line so that on "To die, to sleep" he can actually lean on a tomb and close his eyes. This concrete reminder of the reality and indeed inevitability of death works to suggest that there is a core of rational, albeit troubled, decision making at the core of Gibson's Hamlet, while the cut from "lose the name of action" to a shot of him spurring his horse along the beach indicates that his instinct is purposeful, dynamic activity rather than passivity. The emphasis on Hamlet as a man of action rather than a troubled dreamer is complete when his admission to Rosencrantz and Guildenstern that "I have bad dreams" is subtly changed to "I have had bad dreams" and when he extracts their confession by kicking the stool away. Moreover, the fact that we have seen very little of Claudius means that, if we do not already know the story, we hardly know more of him or can be surer of his guilt than Hamlet.

Hamlet thus becomes the outsider who smells corruption but has the system stacked against him, and the fact that he and we are discovering the truth of events virtually simultaneously further works to align our perspective with his. The extent to which we are disposed to look *with* him rather than *at* him is strongly underlined when, on the line "What a piece of work is a man," Gibson simply looks at his hands, rather than the camera picking out any of the more unique or celebrated parts of his physique. This desexualizing could even be said to continue into the scene in Gertrude's closet, for though the simulated copulation is certainly titillating, it is offered in context as an acting out of his imagination of her with Claudius, "making love over the nasty sty," rather than as an expression of his own feelings for her. They do kiss, but this is initiated by Gertrude rather than Hamlet and seems visibly intended as her sole way of silencing her son rather than as an erotic gesture, and it certainly does not effectively distract his attention. Once again, Hamlet is thus normalized, as when we too see the ghost appear in the room and thus realize that he is not merely imagining it; and though it may seem odd that he speaks to the apparition and thus appears to be talking to himself, the moment is cleverly juxtaposed with Gertrude's "Alas, he's mad," which really is addressed to nobody at all.

Other changes also work to reinforce the emphasis on Hamlet's perspective as the dominant, normative viewpoint. In the play, Hamlet's murder of Polonius and subsequent dispatch to England allow a rest for the actor playing the prince, giving him a pause before the demanding fight in the grave and the final duel. The nature of filmmaking obviously means that this rest is unnecessary here, and it also makes little sense to have the film's most bankable star disappear for too long. Consequently, this later section of the film sees the deletion not only of Fortinbras but also of the letter to Horatio, allowing the audience to see directly what happens to Hamlet and his companions. Since we experience events at the same time that Hamlet does himself, once again our perspectives are aligned with his. The same technique means that we see Ophelia drown rather than merely hearing of it. This inevitably entails cutting some of Gertrude's speech describing the event, but Zeffirelli goes further than this and also cuts her contempt for the Danes, her defiance of Laertes, and her attempt to protect Claudius. The result is to produce a Gertrude who is totally passive and devoid of will and to engineer the strongest possible contrast between her behavior and that of Hamlet, who arrives back in Denmark before we have been warned that he will and who is thus presented as having comprehensively seized the initiative. Moreover, during his en-counter with the gravedigger, he does not muse about death in general, which an audience attuned to action might construe as wasting time. As Robert Hapgood points out, "Virile, dynamic, violent, wild, Gibson's Hamlet is not a more than usually thoughtful man. Zeffirelli in fact goes to elaborate pains to provide external occasions for his reflections, even in soliloquy."[4] Gibson's Hamlet consequently wants to know only about the deaths of those with whom he has personally been acquainted, Yorick and Ophelia.

The closing sequences of the film recapitulate all the motifs so far used to present and characterize Hamlet. Standing in a gallery, he seems both physically and morally raised above Osric and does not waste time quib-bling with him. When he is stricken by the premonition, he walks over to the window and stares out at the setting sun, something not of any par-ticular personal significance to him but rather a generalized emblem of mortality to which anyone in the audience can presumably relate. He con-tinues to reach for the common touch as he clowns about with his heavy sword (and simply resorts to his feet when things get really ugly), though it is notable that there is no undignified use of the word *fat* from Gertrude. Finally, when he dies, he falls flat on his back on the floor, and the camera slowly pans away. The moment is a doubly suggestive one. The hint of an ascent heavenwards allows a note of comfort — Gibson's Hamlet may be dead, but he is presented to us as the kind of hero whose death is not devoid of meaning or of the promise of redemption. At the same time, the suggestion of spirituality and the literal retreat from the body underline the extent to which the film has tried to avoid highlighting Hamlet's body, even though it *is* Mel Gibson's, preferring (perhaps because it was de-signed to appeal to young men as well as young women)[5] to stress the ways in which we can relate to him rather than the degree to which we might wish to ogle him. For Zeffirelli's Hamlet has no complexes, no dark Other revealing the shadow within; instead he is, simply and unproblematically, the Self.

"Denmark's a Prison": Branagh's *Hamlet* and the Paradoxes of Intimacy

Kenneth Branagh's film is visually very different from Zeffirelli's. In its opening shot, a gate with the name "Hamlet" written on it slides away to show us a guard profiled against a grille. The effect is one of entering the frame, of penetrating to ever greater degrees of intimacy, and it inaugurates a pattern of closing and opening of doors which persists throughout the film. Branagh is fond of this door motif and, I think, uses it with considerable success elsewhere in his *oeuvre,* as at the opening of his *Henry V,* when the two clergymen indicate the conspiratorial nature of their conversation by shutting the door (and including us inside with them) before the memorable shot where Branagh's Henry first appears, framed and silhouetted in a doorway and looking for all the world "like some medieval version of Darth Vader."[6] The door motif's reuse here appears to suggest that *Hamlet* is going to offer the same sort of experience as Branagh's previous Shakespeare films.

I am going to argue, though, that it doesn't do so. The primary reason for this is, I think, that Branagh's conception of this play has its roots in the theater and never breaks free of the concept of stage space; the principal effect is that Branagh's Hamlet becomes fissured and fragmented— Gothicized, indeed—in a way that Zeffirelli's never is. Thus, Philippa Sheppard argues:

> The consensus, especially among British reviewers, was that his *Hamlet* was grossly overblown. Yet I contend that Branagh is not a hamfisted director, but, rather, one with naturally Gothic sensibilities. These allow him to respond to Gothic elements in Shakespeare's tragedy, such as the setting, the Ghost, and the themes of death, decay, and madness, and make him admirably suited to the job of conveying this Gothicism to his audience.[7]

Branagh himself had been a famous stage Hamlet in the 1988 Renaissance Theatre Company production and in Adrian Noble's 1992 RSC version; moreover, when interviewed about his direction of the play on screen, his first remark was that *Hamlet* was the first play he had ever seen in the theater, when he was fifteen,[8] and he has reused here the actor he saw in the rôle, Derek Jacobi, as Claudius. He has also peopled the set with two other kinds of actors. The first category is those who are famous for acting on screen, though not generally in Shakespearean rôles, such as Julie Christie, Kate Winslet, Charlton Heston, and Jack Lemmon. In the second category, there are several actors in the cast who were noted stage Hamlets of the past, including Michael Maloney (Laertes), Sir John Gielgud (Priam), and of course Jacobi (Claudius). What Branagh *hasn't* included is anyone who is famous from an association with a previous film version of *Hamlet* (with the single and complicated exception of Maloney, who played Hamlet in the inset scenes of Branagh's own *In the Bleak Midwinter*—released in the United States as *A Midwinter's Tale*). Nor does he allude much to any of these, or indeed a great deal to other films (at least recent ones) at all. In *Henry V* he had signaled from the outset an allegiance to film as a medium, but in retrospect this signaling looks more like a witty reprise of Olivier's famous opening than a genuine acknowledgement of film as an art form in its own right, not just a medium for the popularization of Shakespeare. Moreover, this element of difference from Olivier serves as a reminder that in *Henry V* Branagh's closest comparator/competitor was dead and any acknowledgement of his existence is habitually constituted through contrast and difference. In *Hamlet,* by contrast, the proliferation of greats of screen and stage, and particularly of previous, alternative Hamlets, means that the predominant effect is one of doublings and of uncanny similarities. This leads, I shall suggest, to the other main problem of the film: that it does not have a secure visual, and hence emotional, focus.

In Branagh's *Hamlet,* the intimacy promised by the opening door fails to materialize. Moreover, I think one of the primary factors causing the absence of interiority in the film is, paradoxically, its use of interiors. This arises in the first place because of the sheer scale of Blenheim Palace, which was chosen as the film's Elsinore, and even when a set is being used, size seems to have been the primary consideration since the first thing the movie's official website tells you about the set is that it was "the largest single set in the United Kingdom."[9] (Courtney Lehmann and Lisa S. Starks argue that Branagh is anxious for so big a set because his desire to avoid Oedipal overtones drives him rigorously to eschew the "womb-like set designs featured in other, explicitly psychoanalytic *Hamlet* films.")[10] The problem is compounded by the fact that the door motif functions somewhat differently here from in *Henry V*, and indeed Philippa Sheppard identifies Branagh's use of doors as, along with his emphasis on the cold, one of the two principal Gothicizing elements of his film.[11] At the beginning of the earlier film, Branagh's clear signaling that this is a film studio, a constructed space, imposes a minimalist and functionalist aesthetic allowing only for what directly contributes to plot and mood: there are doors only where doors are needed. Elsinore, however, abounds in doors. We think we see a hall of mirrors, but at least some of them turn out to be doors; we think that, as in the Zeffirelli film, Hamlet is walking round a library, but he suddenly swings back a bookcase and reveals that it conceals an entrance. He enters by one door to talk to Horatio but opens another to admit Osric. Most noticeably, at the end of the nunnery scene, Ophelia slumps across a partially opened door.

The effect is twofold. In the first place, we are aware that whatever we are shown, something else may be concealed just beyond our field of vision. This is of course a technique used to great effect in horror films, but *Hamlet* is not a horror film; here the nagging suspicion that there is something you can't see is distracting rather than tension-building. (*Distracting* was a word used by a number of reviewers of the film.)[12] In the second place, the plethora of doors underlines the extent to which the spatial logic of the set has itself driven the interpretation rather than *vice versa*. A particularly distracting presence is the small wooden model of a theater to which Hamlet turns during the "Oh what a rogue and peasant slave" soliloquy, and almost equally intrusive is the use of the chapel for Polonius's speech of advice to Laertes. With apparent perversity, this scene begins outside, with Laertes dressed to go and in a hurry to depart, and then without explanation switches inside, with the gentle ecclesiastical music serving to dissipate any sense of urgency; and yet Laertes still leaves as if he is now departing, so it is difficult to understand the point of the cut to the inside in any terms other than the desire to show the audience more of the set.

At first sight, my contention that the play withholds intimacy may seem a paradoxical one because Branagh's *Hamlet* undoubtedly gives us more of the play than we have ever seen before, apparently offering access on an unprecedentedly generous scale. In the first place, it insists on its status as an uncut text (leaving to one side for a moment the textual issues which make this an impossibility): all of Shakespeare's words, it assures us, are here. In the second, it even more insistently supplements those words with pictures: whenever a character is mentioned, we are shown him, and a whole range of previous performances of Shakespeare in general and *Hamlet* in particular are evoked, particularly by the presence of so many famous former Hamlets. Even Tom Stoppard gets a look-in when Claudius, like his alter ego in *Rosencrantz and Guildenstern Are Dead* (in which Simon Russell Beale, the second gravedigger, was concurrently acting at the National), clearly cannot tell Rosencrantz and Guildenstern apart and has to be corrected by Gertrude—further underlining the ways in which the stage is at least as potent a presence as the screen in the film.

Shakespeare's own method, however, is rarely to expand or explain and often to suggest, and Branagh should, I think, have taken his cue from his writer because inclusivity, so far from facilitating intimacy, actually precludes it. For one thing, the manic inclusiveness of the film means that it must, inevitably, be large scale. Other things also conspire to bring this about: as I have suggested above, the very choice of Blenheim Palace dictates it, as does the Don Giovanni–like motif of the statue, which is on a more than human scale. Thus, we get scenes like I.2, which is really more reminiscent of a Cecil B. De Mille epic than of a Shakespeare play and which has dictated features of the film itself, most notably the wide screen which means, in turn, that the film is best viewed in the cinema, as a collective experience, rather than at home as an individual one. (Nicholas Farrell, who plays Horatio, observes that emotions in the film are produced "to inspect in the safety of your—of your cinemas," clearly realizing that the expected "homes" is inappropriate here.)[13] In one way, encouraging people to see the film in a group rather than alone might seem to be true to the viewing conditions originally envisaged by Shakespeare, but then sitting or standing in the Globe in the afternoon light is very different from sitting in a darkened cinema. In the Globe, one is aware of the other members of the audience and of their reaction; the viewing conditions produced by the cinema provide an ostensibly collective experience but actually focus on the individual one.[14] In the case of *Hamlet* in particular, the ensuing result is less to confirm the offer of intimacy than to underline the extent to which it is withheld.

To some extent, this can be seen as the result of a technical problem: cinematographer Alex Thomson found it difficult to get into actors' eyes because the mirrors meant that all the lighting had to be high above the stage so as not to be seen in reflection, thus creating a harshly top lit effect that shadowed eyes.[15] I think it is also, however, in large part due to Branagh himself, and perhaps it would be only fair to observe at this point that the reason I don't like Branagh's direction in this film is that I do like his acting. His stage Hamlet at the RSC got such rave reviews that anyone, like me, who missed it is always liable to feel as though they haven't really lived, and though I know it was naïve to suppose that watching the film was going to fill that gap, I expect I did nevertheless suppose so. (Perhaps Branagh too was aware of the possibility of that expectation; it might be one reason why the film keeps gesturing back to the stage.)

Rather than using the film to bring his Hamlet to the masses, though, Branagh seems, instead, perversely intent on hiding; perhaps it is no coincidence that in what I think is easily his most accomplished and joyous piece of directing, *In the Bleak Midwinter,* he does not appear at all. When Olivier both starred and directed in *Hamlet,* he hogged the camera; Branagh, on the contrary, avoids it. Instead, he is prepared to show us almost anything and anyone else. This pattern is established from the very outset of the film when verbal references to Fortinbras and Old Norway are backed up by vignettes poised, I think, uneasily between flashback and fantasy,[16] and it reaches its apogee in the speech of the First Player, when we seem briefly threatened with a rerun of the entire Trojan War. One of the most puzzling instances of it occurs when, on Ophelia's "I do not know, my lord, what I should think,"[17] we cut to a sex scene between Hamlet and Ophelia, and we do not know what we should think either. Is this Ophelia's memory of events—in which case she is here lying to her father and, Carol Chillington Rutter argues, thus "makes a credulous ninny of her brother who buries her as a virgin . . . [and] ceases to represent any value alternative to Gertrude's"[18]—or is it her fantasy? (Later, Fortinbras certainly is lying when he says "For me, with sorrow I embrace my fortune" [V.ii.393] after smashing his way into the palace.) Equally, what is happening when the words *"Doubt thou the stars are fire"* (II.ii.115) seem to come spontaneously alive to show us a closely similar scene of intimacy between Hamlet and Ophelia or when the newspaper which Horatio reads comes alive as Fortinbras? Most strikingly of all, Hamlet's vision of a dagger entering Claudius's ear may be clearly labeled as his fantasy, but we may be less alert to the fact that his subsequent vision of the death of his father is equally anchored in imagination rather than fact. Our uncertainty on this score seems to echo the ways in which the proliferation of past Hamlets leaves us wondering who is really the hero here (the first sequence after the intermission, for instance, clearly represents Claudius's perspective on events).

There is an interesting contrast here with both of Branagh's earlier self-directions, *Henry V* and *Much Ado About Nothing,* and also with his subsequent one, *Love's Labour's Lost.* The first time we see him in *Henry V,* Branagh advances in silhouette from the doorway in which he has initially been seen framed. Anticipation is clearly being built up as we see the close-ups of the nobles' heads bowing. Then Branagh sits down and slumps. Having been made to wait to see him, we know that our first clear sight of him will be significant, and arguably we learn as much from that initial shot as from anything else in the film about his conception of the play and character. In *Much Ado About Nothing*, too, the camera picks out and dwells on the face of each of the four riders to allow us to get an initial sense of them. In *Love's Labour's Lost* — where, for my money, everything which went wrong in *Hamlet* goes right — Branagh has recovered the ease in front of the camera which seems to have forsaken him in *Hamlet*. It is certainly true that there is generous footage of other characters, with Adrian Lester, clearly the best dancer of the four men, allowed what is in effect a solo sequence to showcase his talents, Alessandro Nivola's King of Navarre seen in military training, and a vignette of the heroic death of Boyet. However, throughout the revelation of the other three lords' love, Branagh cuts repeatedly to his own amused expression, and though he pares most of the language of the play to the bone, he not only retains the "Have at you then, affection's men-at-arms!" speech for his own char-acter,[19] but turns it into a bravura display of how Shakespearean verse should be spoken, with the camera clinging to him throughout.

Our first sight of Branagh in *Hamlet* is strikingly different. We see him first in the shadows, which might seem to recall the technique of *Henry V,* but there the similarity ends because, for reasons at which I simply cannot guess, the first close shot of Branagh's Hamlet is of his feet (see figure 1) (conceivably to draw attention to the chequered pattern of the floor and thus evoke associations with the strategies of chess, or perhaps as a pro-lepsis of the fact that when Osric brings the foils, we first see his feet and then subsequently cut to the running feet of Fortinbras's advancing sol-diers). Though the camera does then travel up to show his face, it seems almost to do so for purposes of identification rather than of revelation, because it immediately moves away again.

This inaugurates a sustained pattern of mutual avoidance between Branagh and his camera. Of course, the sheer size of the set makes it diffi-cult for this film ever to be about play of features and requires scenes to be blocked and shaped like a stage production rather than to adhere to the more usual aesthetic of film, but, even so, the effect is more pronounced with Branagh than with any of the other characters. At our first introduc-tion to Gertrude and Claudius, for instance, the camera is trained steadily on them, though it is clearly noticeable that we are looking *up* at them rather than on the same level. I do actually wonder whether this is part of the trouble — that Branagh is perhaps so in awe of this galaxy of stars

The hero's first appearance in *Hamlet,* dir. Kenneth Branagh (Castle Rock Entertainment, 1996).

that he has assembled and, in some cases, coaxed out of retirement and of the weight of associations that they bring. As Joe Baltake opined:

> The film's casting isn't so much a distraction, but it does call attention to the movie's one strange flaw. For all the perfectionism and dedication that Branagh has brought to the project, all the attention to detail and all the sweat and anguish to get it just right, for all his desire to appease his potential audience and expose them to Shakespeare, something vital got lost along the way: the personal touch . . . Branagh was so much in control that he overlooked himself.

Time Magazine, too, praised much of the acting, but felt that "If there's a lapse, it's in the central performance."[20] For Baltake, the reason for this was that "in bringing 'Lawrence of Arabia' dimensions to the play, Branagh dwarfed his own point of view."[21] Certainly Branagh does indeed seem to have been striving for an epic effect, not least by including Julie Christie, who had starred in David Lean's *Doctor Zhivago* (1965), and choosing as his cinematographer Alex Thomson, who had also worked with David Lean. But it is not a wholehearted generic affiliation because Branagh also wants to offer us the subjective camera more associated with *film noir* than with epic when he shows us those fantasy/flashback scenes and things which simply don't happen, like the dagger entering Claudius's ear. Indeed, the multiple genre markers seem to me to be another manifestation of the film's doomed attempt to offer the plenitude of the "whole play."

Whatever the reason, he won't look at us. Branagh himself has said that he believes the opposite of Olivier's dictum that the camera must retreat as soliloquies develop because film cannot take that degree of emotion and that in each soliloquy his aim is to move further and further inside the mind of the actor.[22] His own practice, however, comes closer to Olivier's theory than his own, at least when it comes to himself. Indeed, Lawrence Guntner remarks that "Having learned from Olivier, he does not interrupt long soliloquies but begins with a close-up and moves up and away with the crane to emphasize Hamlet's isolation,"[23] though this description applies in fact only to "How all occasions do inform against me." Throughout his opening exchange with Gertrude and Claudius, he looks either at Julie Christie or to one side away from Derek Jacobi or, usually when his dead father is mentioned, upwards to the heavens. Even when the doors are shut and he is left alone for the first soliloquy, with us closed in with him, he bows his head to look at the floor and is seen only in profile. Here too, as in *Henry V,* he slumps—but he slumps not into one throne but between two. This looks for all the world like a visual emblem of a man caught literally between two stools, but unfortunately this idea is one that could be applied as much to Branagh's own condition as to Hamlet's. Throughout this first soliloquy, there are no close-ups: we always see the whole upper half of his body, sometimes from behind, and never looking at the camera. In short, he is acting as if he were on stage and as if the ballroom were a set, except that if he really were on stage, he would probably look at the audience during his soliloquy (and he could do that even on film; the technique is used to great effect in the opening soliloquy of Richard Loncraine's *Richard III,* when Ian McKellen looks directly into the camera on "And therefore, since I cannot prove a lover").[24] Initially, this illusion of a stage performance at which we are the only audience and have the privileged viewpoint of the moving camera might again seem to promise intimacy, but that is comprehensively denied when on "Must I remember" (I.ii.143) Branagh actually puts his hands in front of his face as if to underline the extent to which he is in fact shutting us out. And the pattern of withholding continues: when he receives the momentous news that the ghost of his father has been seen, it is too dark and his face too much in shadow for his expression to be deciphered, and when he is left alone to digest the implications of what the ghost has told him, he throws himself face down on the earth, still in the dark, and again in profile.

To some extent, this is an inevitable product of the nature of the rôle.

The character of Hamlet is one who is famous above all for soliloquies, and for the greater part of the time, he lacks an interlocutor. In *Much Ado About Nothing*, Benedick looks primarily at Beatrice, and the nature of the dialogue between them naturally lends itself to a repeated use of a shot/reverse-shot technique; Branagh isn't looking at us there either, but we do know where he *is* looking. Hamlet, by contrast, can talk frankly only to Horatio. Even here, however, Branagh seems to shrink from the camera, for rather than using the shot/reverse-shot technique for the Hamlet/Horatio conversations, his preferred mode is to show one or both facing each other in profile, as in the "My lord, I think I saw him yesternight" (I.ii.189) exchange. This use of profile shots notably continues even after Hamlet, Horatio, Marcellus, and Barnardo have retreated into a smaller room for greater privacy and have closed the door behind them, underlining the extent to which doors are not in fact associated with increased intimacy. Even when the filming of the ensuing conversation does switch briefly to shot/countershot, it is notable that Hamlet and Horatio look at least as much at either Barnardo or Marcellus as at each other.[25] Conversely, when the shot/reverse-shot technique *is* used in the film, it is often in contexts in which Hamlet is in fact deliberately and explicitly concealing something, as in his initial encounter with Rosencrantz and Guildenstern when he is instantly suspicious of their motives for visiting him, in his conversation with the gravedigger when he is concealing his identity, or in his questioning of Ophelia during the nunnery scene—and on "Let the doors be shut on him" (III.i.133) the extent to which they are being shut on us too is sharply underlined as he closes his eyes. He does look directly at Laertes in the grave, but he also disables the authenticity of the moment by saying explicitly that he is ranting. Even when he does look directly at us on "No mo marriage" (II.i.149), the sight of Ophelia's face pressed against the glass beside him, distorting its flesh, reminds us of the screen which intervenes between us rather than serving to reach out across it.

There are one or two occasions when the film does not seem afraid of the shot/reverse-shot technique. One is during the play-within-the-play, when it is, I think, used to brilliant effect to collapse distance into loomingness and public into private as the repeated cutting between the faces and viewpoints of Hamlet, Claudius, and Gertrude makes their sightlines the paramount feature of the scene despite the crowd. This is in fact squarely in line with Branagh's own comments about how this "felt like a very strong scene to treat cinematically and we went in determined to cover it with endless numbers of angles. In editing, we could construct it and we've probably spent more time on that scene than any other in the picture."[26] His very use of "we," though, underlines the extent to which he is reluctant to present himself as the center of attention; it is, it seems, because he can showcase the others that he shows himself here.

The same is true for the other scene in which the shot/reverse-shot technique is used to great effect, the conspiracy of Laertes and Claudius. It is true that the technique is also used to structure the final conversation between Hamlet and Horatio, which is, for me, one of the strongest bits of the film. Even the risky use of Robin Williams as Osric cannot detract from Hamlet's clarity and stature here; there is an originality and firmness of vision signaled by everything from the small details — for once Branagh's Hamlet is distinctively rather than conventionally dressed — to the larger aspects, such as the fact that he is, for once, not afraid to look calmly and steadily at the camera, stand still while he is talking to it, and allow it to close in on him, especially in the "special providence" speech (V.ii.150). This is a speech which seems to be very important to Branagh: he quotes from it repeatedly when interviewed about the making of the film, shot it twice, once at the outset of the project and once towards the close, and devotes to it the longest gloss of any in his commentary on the shooting script (though the jokey and self-deprecatory tone of this seems to confirm his uncomfortableness with taking his own performance seriously).[27] Of course the notable contrast with his earlier demeanor which this scene clearly establishes may in itself be meant to make the point that Hamlet has matured, but I think that not letting us see anything of his journey until he reached the end of it was too great a price to pay. And the new-found intimacy is not sustained; no sooner has he begun to apologize to Laertes than the camera cuts away from him to the advance of Fortinbras, a widening of perspective which, together with the use of Robin Williams, seems to align the film more with the aesthetic of comedy — arguably, in fact, Branagh's forte — rather than that of tragedy.

These few instances of how effectively the shot/reverse-shot technique could have been used may well serve merely to underline its absence for the rest of the time and to highlight Branagh's general reluctance to engage with his camera. Ironically, the most sustained acts of avoidance seem to me to come in what is often considered the heart of this play, the "To be or not to be" soliloquy. Branagh has admitted that he found this daunting, claiming that he put in the opening shot to give himself time to decide "whether we dare do it in the mirror" and talking about his own indecision mirroring Hamlet's.[28] Though the self-deprecation is in many ways endearing, it also becomes apparent that it is not necessarily the quality best suited to a man directing himself in *Hamlet*. This is of course a strange and in many ways atypical soliloquy; its lack of any personal pronouns makes it seem more like a general commentary than a particular reflection on the condition of Hamlet himself, and it has been argued that Hamlet must know from the outset that he is being listened to and that this is therefore in no sense a revelation of his true thoughts.[29] Nevertheless, it is the most famous speech in the play, and everyone knows it, so it would be simply perverse not to acknowledge that status in any way. This speech certainly does receive special treatment in Branagh's film since perhaps the film's most spectacular setting, in immediate proximity to the mirrors which line the main set, is reserved for it. Though the speech itself is thus privileged and emphasized, however, Hamlet's relation to it is curiously fragmented and downplayed, and this is pointedly *not* because we are invited to believe that it is not in fact a genuine soliloquy: in a generally rather ambiguous scene, one of the few things that is actually crystal clear is that it is not until the word *nunnery* that Hamlet hears a noise and deduces that he is being spied on. And yet the whole effect of the scene is, nevertheless, one of restricting access to a purely surface level rather than genuine revelation of any sort of interiority. It is almost as though it is *we* who are the spies and whose access to truth must be frustrated.

This effect is made all the more obvious because the "To be or not to be" soliloquy is directly preceded by a striking moment of genuine intimacy and revelation, as Claudius muses on the discrepancy between his deed and his "most painted word" (III.i.53), with the camera closing in to dwell on his expression. Claudius and Polonius then retreat behind one of the mirrored doors, and the immediate cut to Hamlet makes, I think, for some initial ambiguity about who can see whom and who knows that who is there, which further problematizes the scene. When Hamlet does start to speak, his face is reflected to both him and us in one of the mirrors, underlining the degree to which this scene focuses on external appearance rather than internal revelation. Most strikingly, when Hamlet utters the word *bodkin* (III.i.76) and pulls out a dagger, the camera immediately zooms in for a close-up at last—but it is Jacobi's face, not Branagh's, which we see. Courtney Lehmann and Lisa Starks have argued that Branagh's stated desire to avoid Oedipal overtones in Hamlet's relationship with Gertrude only thinly masks a fixation on Derek Jacobi's Claudius which, they claim, makes this "the most oedipal filmed *Hamlet* of all time."[30] Certainly the strikingly similar haircuts and coloring of Branagh's Hamlet and Jacobi's Claudius have already suggested a close parallel between the two well before the advent of this literal mirroring motif.[31]

Again, though, this becomes an image of the failure of communication rather than the achievement of it. In particular, the insistent use of the mirror throughout the scene seems to me to evoke a previous Branagh film, the critically ill-fated *Mary Shelley's Frankenstein* (whose mingling of its fire and ice motifs also seems to be recalled when fire bursts up from the earth during the aftermath of the ghost scene). In Shelley's novel, there is famously a mirroring effect linking the ostensible hero to the ostensible villain.[32] In the "To be or not to be" scene of Branagh's *Hamlet,* we see only the reflected Hamlet, not the looking one (an effect that would have been technically impossible to achieve). Audiences acquainted with the Gothic logic of *Frankenstein,* therefore, may surely wonder who it is who is actually looking in the mirror, especially since the documentary *Hamlet—to cut or not to cut?* clearly shows a Branagh-double who looks as if he might well be required for use in this scene. (The shooting script confirms his existence, though not what he was used for.) Audiences may also wonder to what extent Hamlet's own status as the hero is compromised by his use of a motif which suggests doubling and split personalities. This is particularly so when Hamlet cries "no mo marriage" (III.i.149) and the camera cuts to Jacobi's expression so fast that it seems as if they must indeed be seeing each other, though a moment later it is clear that they are not. For a brief instant, the film has at last gestured at some of what film as a medium can do, in the rapid and suggestive juxtaposition of images, but it has to turn its back on that possibility because it is still committed to and bound by the more literal logic of stage space. Finally, when Ophelia is left momentarily alone, she slumps across a doorway. The floor beyond her is lit, but we cannot see into the room—a fitting emblem for the way in which the scene as a whole has teased us with the promise of something that is ultimately withheld.

Similar techniques apply in the film's treatment of the other soliloquies, and indeed it is a rich irony that only a speech which is *not* a soliloquy, "Angels and ministers of grace defend us" (I.iv.38), is performed in a way that is genuinely suggestive of access to the mind, as interior monologue until "Whither wilt thou lead me?" (II.i.1) (indeed there seems to be a hangover here from the radio performance which originally triggered Branagh's decision to perform a full-text *Hamlet*). Here the visions of Hamlet's dead father are for once unequivocally identifiable as representing his memories. However, this serves only to underline the far more ambiguous status of the scene which follows because the vignettes which appear during the ghost's speech work very differently. We first see Hamlet's father asleep while Claudius steals up on him: certainly this represents his memory of *what* happened, but the fact that he was asleep means that this cannot be his memory of *how* it happened. Even more insidiously, he cannot possibly be remembering the scenes of courtship between Claudius and Gertrude which follow: as Iago reminds Othello, the adultery of his wife is a thing which a husband is unlikely to be able to witness.[33] The fact that the ghost here assures us with such certainty of something he cannot know does of course have a spin-off benefit in that it makes Hamlet's reluctance to proceed on the ghost's word alone absolutely understandable. However, this does damage as well because in a film that shows us a great deal and seems to regard showing as an inevitable adjunct to telling, it makes us reluctant to believe what we are shown, especially when we note how many of these "flashbacks" are of people telling us about things of which they do not have personal knowledge. This is certainly the case with the Trojan war vignette, Hamlet's description of what is happening at Claudius's "rouse" (I.iv.8), and the ambassadors' account of the scene between Old Norway and Fortinbras, which appears to be a *tête-à-tête* and at which they could not, therefore, have been present.

A particularly persistent technique during the filming of the soliloquies and indeed of Hamlet's speeches in general is the movement of either Branagh himself or his camera. (He is even moving when he says "I am dead" [V.ii.338].) For instance, Branagh circles nervously when starting the Pyrrhus speech, while Charlton Heston's First Player, in noticeable contrast, stands stock still as the camera homes in on him. Heston also makes direct eye contact with a number of members of his on-screen audience until the cut to his mind's-eye view of Gielgud. During the play-within-the play, too, Heston's Player King remains absolutely static, indeed seated, while the camera lingers on him. Similarly, Derek Jacobi is shot in static, full-frontal view throughout his soliloquy about the state of his soul, with the camera advancing ever more closely towards him as it had on Heston, and the same technique is used for "Do it, England" (IV.iii.68). Fortinbras is similarly treated to a close-up as he advances out of the mist to order his men, with brilliantly underplayed menace, to "Go softly on" (IV.iv.7), as is Gertrude in her "To my sick soul" speech (IV.v.17). Even Robin Williams's Osric gets a close-up; when the cry of "Treason!" goes up, the film cuts to Williams's face before registering the injury he has sustained. When Hamlet begins "Oh what a rogue and peasant slave" (IV.iv.32), though, he starts with his face pressed partly to the wall and then moves around, with the camera not only following him but also being irresistibly drawn to the various unusual and striking objects in the room, particularly the model wooden building which he opens and looks into but which we are not, at first, allowed to see. Indeed, one of the most marked effects of Branagh's interest in his setting is that each soliloquy has its own location, which inevitably threatens to deflect interest from the speeches themselves: as Mark Thornton Burnett observes, "[T]hese locational moments complicate the implications of the play's rhetoric."[34]

The effect is most particularly evident in the highly stylized handling of "How all occasions do inform against me" (IV.iv.32ff). Throughout this speech, Branagh stands still while the camera steadily and determinedly retreats from him, with the scene eventually panning out into the vastest panorama yet, while an increasingly insistent musical score battles ever more successfully for our attention with his receding voice. The effect has been unkindly, though not inappositely, compared to the "As God is my witness, I'll never go hungry again" scene in *Gone With the Wind*.[35] It is a fitting image for the film as a whole: we see more than ever before of the world of *Hamlet* the play, the most fully realized and elaborate version of Elsinore that money could buy—and yet the result is that we see less than ever before of Hamlet the prince. By attempting to offer the whole, Branagh effectively refuses to disclose what he considers important, and thus the film, by showing us everything about Hamlet's world, shows us nothing about his mind. For Branagh, Denmark is a prison because he knows every corner of it. It is fully, concretely realized in his mind, and he desperately wants to show it to us too—but turning his camera so resolutely outwards becomes all too visibly a symptom of the fact that when Branagh's Hamlet looks in the mirror, it is Jacobi who looks back. Branagh himself remains locked inside, and his dream of a non-Oedipal Hamlet becomes a Gothic nightmare of a psyche constituted only by the dark and troubling glimpses of itself which it catches in the mirror of the Other. It may be Gibson who wears the hood and the medieval clothing, but it is Branagh who is most comprehensively trapped within the logic of the Gothic.

The Ghost in the Pepsi Machine: Technologies of Duplication in Michael Almereyda's *Hamlet*

Michael Almereyda's *Hamlet* is clearly indebted as much to Baz Luhrmann's landmark *William Shakespeare's Romeo + Juliet* as to any previous film of *Hamlet*. In Luhrmann's film, the twin poles of innocence and experience are represented by water and technology, and the trap-

Hero and heroine first catch sight of each other in *William Shakespeare's Romeo + Juliet,* dir. Baz Luhrmann (Twentieth-Century Fox, 1996).

pings of modern, cosmopolitan, stressed city life are in evidence as never before in filmed Shakespeare. Zeffirelli's sumptuous recreation made us acutely aware of the urban setting of the play,[36] but that had presented to us an environment rich in all the beauties and civic amenities of the Italian Renaissance. Lurhmann's film powerfully reinforces our sense of the pervasiveness of the urban environment and the manic nature of urban living: helicopters whirr, guns blaze, prostitutes ply their trade, and the characters use phones and cars and find their every move recorded on TV. Indeed, the film both opens and closes on the resonant image of a blank TV screen, which, neatly framed within our own screen, insistently reminds us of our own complicity and implication in this sophisticated world. This sense of the powerful, shaping force of culture, as opposed to that of nature symbolized by the green world, is in stark contrast with the fact that both Romeo and Juliet are first seen near water.[37] Although Benvolio says that Romeo was last observed "underneath a grove of sycamores," what is shown is the sea. Juliet too is first seen by an underwater camera as her face is thrust into a full basin; moreover, even before we see her, the association has already been established because the first time we hear her name is when Lady Capulet shrieks it while standing in front of a fountain The initial encounters of the lovers are also fundamentally structured by water. While fireworks light up the air and a cross-dressed Mercutio does a spectacular staircase performance of "Young hearts run free," Romeo turns and douses his head in water. Then, through a tank full of ornamental fish, he sees the eye of Juliet, who is looking in from the other side. Edging along the tank, they gaze and smile at each other, and we see both them and their reflections.

The water thus bonds them, but it also splits and separates them, looming between them like a miniature Hellespont. Even the "balcony scene" is not actually played on a balcony, but in a swimming pool. (The knowledge that later, in *Titanic,* water will kill DiCaprio's character gives the scene an added layer of extradiegetic irony.)

In Almereyda's *Hamlet,* both the water motif and the interest in technology of Luhrmann's film are echoed. (The obsession with technology also recalls Michael Hoffman's *A Midsummer Night's Dream.*) As in *Romeo + Juliet,* water is much in evidence: Claudius swims in the pool in which Ophelia later drowns, Ophelia is seen waiting for Hamlet by a fountain, and there is a scene in a launderette. Technology is also omnipresent in Almereyda's film: we see disks, a laptop, a fax machine, a palmtop, a camcorder, a security camera, a bug, a phone, videos, and photos. This, it seems, is a world structured wholly by reason and science, not by dark, irrational fears.

The technology on which Almereyda's film concentrates, however, is not randomly chosen but has a specific purpose. It relates to, above all, the film's insistent creation of a sense of doubling and replication. This is a world in which, although part of the film is set in a gallery, nothing is an original: "To be" already exists on video before Hamlet speaks it and is foreshadowed in the monk's reference to the concept of "To interbe," which does indeed describe the film's sense of a world in which everything is already conditioned by something else and uncannily replicates itself. Kyle MacLachlan's Claudius, already trailing his *Twin Peaks* persona, rips up *USA Today;* the "arras" is a mirrored wardrobe door and the mirror cracks; the flowers are photos; and Hamlet's injunction to Horatio "To tell my story" becomes merely the cue for further replication and duplication. Similarly, there are moments of specific doubling and mirroring, as when Hamlet's face is split in the mirror on "Except my life" and when it is tellingly juxtaposed with that of James Dean.

The proliferation of doubling is a classic genre marker of the Gothic,

Ethan Hawke's troubled hero in *Hamlet,* dir. Michael Almereyda (Miramax/Buena Vista Entertainment, 2000).

and the Gothic mode is also evoked when the ghost is first seen out-side a lighted window, just as Frankenstein sees his monster on the Ork-neys. The fascination with technology also echoes another quintessen-tially Gothic novel, *Dracula,* and the suggestion seems to be that the ghost is the ultimate trick-or-treater, since a child in a Halloween costume is seen entering the building. Most fundamentally, though, the entire perspec-tive of the film is structured by height, recalling both the sinister cityscapes of the Gotham City of the Gothic *Batman* and the soaring architecture of Gothic cathedrals. Towards the beginning of the film, as Hamlet exits from the press conference at which his father's death is announced, his en-tire conversation with Claudius and his mother is shot from a dramatically low viewpoint, reinforcing the skyscrapers looming behind; the line "the apparition comes" is accompanied by a starkly foreshortened view of the ghost from the security camera above him, and in an almost direct inver-sion of the same effect, on "I stay too long" Laertes looks up through glass and sees Polonius from below. Polonius is also seen from on high, from the angle of the security camera, in the "Still harping on my daughter" speech, while after "Get thee to a nunnery" we see Hamlet checking out videos from the angle of a camera which appears to be located below and behind the counter. Similarly, in the bedchamber scene the camera first looks up at Gertrude and Polonius, then down at Gertrude and Hamlet, and then sharply upwards in the "For England?" exchange between Hamlet and Claudius; in the Guggenheim, cameras veer up and down; and before "Now must your conscience," the camera cranes up at Gertrude and Claudius. The effect both underscores the sense of a pervasive hierarchy in which some people are literally as well as metaphorically under others and underlines the Gothic geography of the city.

Within this Gothic landscape moves Ethan Hawke's tortured prince. Here there is no particular sense of intimacy or engagement with the audience. The first view of Hawke's Hamlet shows him in black and white, looking at the camera and speaking the lines "I have of late, but wherefore I know not, lost all my mirth," and the fact that these lines are, in the play, spoken to Rosencrantz and Guildenstern serves immediately to estrange any viewer who is familiar with *Hamlet,* making them feel like a spy and a voyeur rather than a confidant. (Those familiar with the play are repeatedly challenged in this way by spiky, unexpected cutting, such as that of the famous line "And borrowing dulls the edge of husbandry" or of "the oppressor's wrong" from the "To be or not to be" speech.) Most characteristically, we watch Hawke watching, such as during the first soliloquy when we see him watching old home videos on TV, the camera focusing sometimes on them and sometimes on him, with his thoughts becoming concrete on "Oh, he would hang on her" and later when we see him watching the videos of Ophelia and of the monk. Our attention is also strongly drawn to the image of Hamlet himself. Unlike Gibson's Hamlet, whom we look with rather than at, or Branagh's, of whom we see so little, Hawke's Hamlet cuts an iconic figure whose presence is crucial to the framing and composition of all the key scenes, not least because of the strongly estranging effect of the dark glasses he occasionally dons and of his woolly hat. This is a Hamlet who invites us to look at him, and what we see when we do so is that he belongs to our own world but also, in one of the strategies most strongly characteristic of the Gothic, simultaneously suggests that our own world is the one we know least of all.

In the introduction, I suggest that the classic genre markers of the Gothic, as I define it in this book, are the occurrence of doubling and an emphasis on the idea that events originate, or primarily resonate, in the mind of the individual rather than in society (something often expressed by stressing facial expression or idiosyncratic visual symbolism). Any translation of *Hamlet* from stage to screen could be expected to give prominence to both these elements since the play already offers copious quantities of doubles and is famous for containing one of the most sustained and intense portraits of an individual psychology ever written. However, of the three films I have discussed, only Branagh's actually fulfills my criteria. For all the ostensible emphasis on individuals offered by Branagh's insistence on casting big names in small parts, the film actually offers split and doubled versions of its hero in both psychological and physical terms. Equally, its emphasis on the psychological rather than the social is securely established by the surprising number of scenes which cannot actually have happened and which must therefore be located purely in the mind of the individual, of which the vignette in which a dagger pierces Claudius's ear is merely the most famous example.

Zeffirelli's and Almereyda's films, by contrast, are both rooted in specific historical circumstances. Whereas Branagh's film gestures loosely but nonspecifically at some sort of nineteenth-century court, Zeffirelli's Gothic setting produces a paradoxically un-Gothic effect by allowing us to ascribe the troubles of the characters, and of Hamlet in particular, to the constraints imposed by their context rather than to individual psychology. Similarly, Almereyda's troubled prince is all too clearly a product of the urban jungle he inhabits: again the setting may be Gothicized in the sense that Gotham City is Gothic, but again this works to present the character himself as essentially normal, a point of stability who might perhaps have succeeded in rejuvenating and reinvigorating his world and whose death is therefore like that of a scapegoat. (It is notable that both Zeffirelli's and Almereyda's films end with the impression that all evil has been purged, while in Branagh's film, Rufus Sewell's distinctly sinister Fortinbras suggests that things will, if possible, soon be even worse.) In these three films, we see, then, that the Gothic is indeed double, in that its soul and its body cannot coexist. To evoke the material trappings of the Gothic banishes its spirit; to deny them, to saturate one's court in light and space, as Branagh has done, allows that spirit to flourish.

If each age remakes *Hamlet* in its own image and if the Gothic is a particularly sensitive barometer of culturally pervasive trends and fears, what do these three *Hamlet* films tell us about the fears and fault lines of the cultural moment that produced them? Notably, for all the apparently classic Gothic elements of castles, battlements, madwomen, and ghosts, the areas which actually spark Gothic energies in a contemporary *Hamlet* on screen are the cityscape and the family, particularly the issue of identity within the family, as Branagh's Hamlet stares into the mirror and sees Jacobi's Claudius looking back. As we shall see once again in chapter 5, it seems that it is within what is most familiar that fear is now to be found.

| *Chapter Two* | # *P*UTTING THE GOTHIC IN
| | Clarissa, Sense and Sensibility, Mansfield Park, *and* The Time Machine

*I*n this chapter, I discuss a number of novels which were originally born out of varying degrees of conscious opposition to the Gothic movement but which have nevertheless been transformed into Gothic texts during the course of adaptation for the screen. Samuel Richardson wrote *Clarissa* in direct response to critics who had claimed that the heroine of his first novel, *Pamela,* was not all she appeared to be; his intention was to portray the whole of a psyche in transparent terms, but the adapters of *Clarissa* have entirely subverted this by focusing not on Clarissa's consciousness but on what they see as her unconscious—in short, by reading *Clarissa* as Richardson's detractors read *Pamela.* Similarly, Jane Austen satirized the Gothic in *Northanger Abbey,* but on the big screen two of her other novels, *Sense and Sensibility* and *Mansfield Park,* have been given distinctly Gothicizing treatments. Finally, H. G. Wells wrote *The Time Machine* under the direct influence of Darwinian theory, which he had imbibed from "Darwin's bulldog," T. H. Huxley, and in accordance with Darwinian theory Wells stressed the extent to which chance rather than fate influences human affairs. His great-grandson's adaptation, however, replaces chance with fate, materialist analysis with psychoanalysis, and randomness with a scheme, in the shape of Gothicizing polarization and doubleness. Paradoxically, these texts, which at the time of publication epitomized values of reason and enlightenment, thus become on screen the home of doubles, dreams, and troubled psyches.

Clarissa

The prospect of transferring *Clarissa* from page to screen is in many ways a daunting one. The most obvious difficulty is, of course, its enormous length: the Penguin edition uses the shortest available version of the text (published in 1747–1748) and still comes in at 1,494 large-format pages, yet all this was boiled down to just three hours of television. It is no wonder that details, and indeed entire episodes, had to be omitted; what might seem much more surprising is that anything should be added. Nevertheless, it is so, and although what is added occupies only a short amount of time on the screen, it effects a sharp switch in emphasis from the original book which makes it no longer a product of the Age of Reason, but a distinctively Gothic romance of twisted psyches, hidden desires, and doomed love.

Remarkably, the adapters, Janet Barron and David Nokes, do manage to retain almost all the major incidents of the plot. As in the novel, Clarissa's family first encourage Lovelace (initially the wooer of her sister Bella) and then turn against him after his quarrel and duel with her brother James, and events thereafter follow in essence the Richardsonian pattern. Even when she is forbidden to write, Clarissa (Saskia Wickham) is nevertheless able to conduct a clandestine correspondence with both Lovelace (Sean Bean) and Anna Howe (Hermione Norris), is tricked into running away with Lovelace, and is taken first to the country and then to the house of the supposed Mrs. Sinclair on Dover Street. There Lovelace stages a false fire as an excuse to get into Clarissa's bedroom, but is persuaded by her pleas not to rape her; she escapes the next day to Hampstead but is traced there by Lovelace and returned by the means of the false Lady Betty and Miss Montague to Mrs Sinclair's, where she is raped. Escaping again, she is thrown into prison for money allegedly owed to Mrs. Sinclair, rescued by Lovelace's friend Belford (Sean Pertwee), and taken to a simple lodging with kindly people where she orders her coffin and then dies, having first effected the conversion of Belford, who, in the one major departure from the plot of the novel, kills Lovelace in a duel. The series closes with Clarissa's body being returned to her grieving parents, with Anna Howe's wedding to Mr. Hickman, and, rather surprisingly, with a final brief reprise of the major events of the story, showing Lovelace and Clarissa together in a series of intimate moments and ending with a shot of them escaping together into the night.

The very fact that a novel of such length can be compressed comprehensibly into so short a time without forfeiting any significant section of the plot could of course be taken as a rather telling indictment of the work, and certainly the first thing the adapters have sacrificed is that minute circumstantiality of the book which famously led Dr. Johnson to remark that anyone who read Richardson for the story would find their impatience so fretted that they would hang themselves. The detailed elaboration of motive and event which both Clarissa and Lovelace offer to Anna Howe and to Belford has been omitted and proves in fact to take up so large a part of the original work that the only other alterations necessary to curtail the adaptation to three hours are some slight rearrangements in the characters: Clarissa's two uncles are amalgamated into one, her aunt, uncle, and cousin Harvey are omitted, and the two Miss Montagues made into one, while various minor characters, such as her old nurse Mrs. Norton and Lovelace and Belford's friends Belton, Tourville, and Mowbray, are excluded. The only significant character to be omitted is Clarissa's cousin Colonel Morden, who occupies a very prominent position in the book in that from an early stage of the proceedings, we are repeatedly informed that his expected arrival from Florence is the one thing on which Clarissa pins all her hopes of saving herself both from the prospect of a forced marriage to Solmes and, later, from Lovelace. The constant buildup to Colonel Morden's arrival aptly prepares the audience for his eventual role as an avenging angel when he and Lovelace duel in Italy and the latter is killed.

The omission of Colonel Morden may of course seem to be completely justified by the need for compression and to be amply compensated for by the transfer of the rôle of avenger to Belford. Nevertheless, I argue that Colonel Morden is an important character and that leaving him out proves to have considerable repercussions. It also stands, I argue, as an apt image of what this adaptation for television has done to the book in general: it has flattened out complexities in the characters' psychology. It has not, however, done this uniformly: as I demonstrate below, it has effectively gendered the psyche, presenting the male characters as acting in accordance with a series of conscious plans designed to secure them what they want, but showing the women — Clarissa in particular, but also her friend Anna Howe — as actuated by psychological urges of which they have little or no comprehension and thus trapped as perpetual victims of their own misunderstood and repressed desires. Men, on the other hand, are simplified. The exclusion of Colonel Morden not only robs the story of an interesting figure in his own right, whose rôle as absent judge relates him suggestively to psychoanalytic concepts such as Lacan's law of the father and the phallus, but it also forces the adapters to use Belford as the agent of vengeance instead. This seriously simplifies the complex psychology of the Belford presented in the novel, who, alone among the characters, is able to see into the minds of both Lovelace and Clarissa and thus to occupy, increasingly, a role effectively analogous to that of narrator.

This loss is, of course, inherently compensated for in the very nature of the medium of television since the camera itself serves a similar function to that of Belford in the novel, providing a normative point of view, a safe point of identification for the audience and one which, like them, is fundamentally unaffected by the events it witnesses and survives the experiences which prove fatal to some of the characters. But such a change of narrative perspective, although it may offer some elements of continuity between the experience of reading the book and the experience of watching it, also effects some very profound consequences. For one thing, the chronological flow must be handled very differently: the narrative is linear and continuous in the television version, whereas in the novel it moves forward at varying paces, with the very nature of the letter form itself further ensuring that everything is told in retrospect, at significantly varying distances from the time of the actual events described. The adaptation in fact works very hard to keep the centrality of the epistolary form constantly in the minds of the viewers, with frequent references to the writing, sending, and receipt of letters. It would also be fair to argue that Richardson's own avowed technique of "writing to the moment"—having his characters write of events, as much as is practicable, as they are actually being experienced—also serves as an attempt to negate some of the constraints of the epistolary form and to render it transparent, drawing attention to the events being recounted rather than to the way in which they are told, so in this respect at least the two differing media of text and television are actually working towards each other.

This apparent transparency both of narrative and of television screen is, however, not without cost. As is clearly suggested in this version by the camera's loving obsession with Clarissa's face, neck, and bosom, the gazing position offered by television has been inherently gendered male, forcing female characters into the position of objects of the possessing look.[1] Perhaps the most obvious example of this is the treatment of the actual rape itself—the central event of the novel, the one single event for which it is most famous, and also the element which determined the title of perhaps the most celebrated study of the work, Terry Eagleton's *The Rape of Clarissa*, as well as being, one would cynically suspect, the feature which made the book marketable as a television series in the first place.

The rape scene in the television version is graphic—there could be no possible doubt about what is taking place—and could very easily be found distressing. But it pales into insignificance beside the suspense and horror generated by the way the rape is described in the novel, where, after so many long, agonising pages of buildup and uncertainty, we are simply told with casual brutality, "And now, Belford, I can go no farther. The

affair is over. Clarissa lives."[2] Unlike the television audience, the reader
knows at this stage merely *what* has happened, not how or why: whether
Clarissa has actually succumbed; whether, and if so how, she was tricked
or forced; and, most important of all, what has happened to her since.
Having been for so long the intimates of her mind, we are suddenly cut off
from it at the crucial moment; we are kept in a state of agonized suspense
before we are allowed access to it, and even when we do finally see into it
again we are little better off because we discover that she has temporarily
lost her senses and scribbles nothing but incoherence and madness. It is
many, many pages before we finally receive a lucid account of her experiences. And in this, perhaps, lies the most crucial difference between the
novel and the television adaptation: that of focus.

In the television adaptation, the focus is very clearly and unambigu-
ously on Clarissa herself. The few scenes in which she is not present are
there solely for the purpose of elucidating the situation—making plain
the nature of the plots against her, explaining why she is unable to apply
to Anna Howe for refuge, and so forth. The series, unlike the book, ends
almost immediately after her death, with only the most cursory mopping
up of the fates of the other characters, as opposed to Richardson's detailed
explanations of what became of them all. Much media attention was paid
to Saskia Wickham, the actress playing Clarissa, concentrating especially
on the two facts that this was her first major part and that her screen father,
Mr. Harlowe, was also her real-life father, the actor Jeffry Wickham (a doubling which one might perhaps relate to the "figure of the 'other father'—
the obscene, uncanny, shadowy double of the Name of the Father" identified by Slavoj Žižek);[3] a follow-up article in the *Observer*'s "A Room of
One's Own" series even revealed that the gravestone used for Clarissa
in the series had pride of place in the actress's living room. Most important of all in terms of shaping the perspective of the viewers, the camera
hangs lovingly on her, tracing every pant of her suitably heaving bosom,
shadowing her expression and reactions, and focusing particularly on her
experience of the rape scene, thus confirming its crucial centrality as the
series' main focus and selling point.

In the novel itself, however, the reader's attention is often rather differently directed. In marked contrast to Richardson's first novel, *Pamela*, in
which the vast majority of the letters are all from Pamela herself and critics
often complain that the other characters are consequently underdevel-
oped, *Clarissa*, like the later *Sir Charles Grandison*, features a wide variety
of correspondents. Whereas Pamela writes almost exclusively to her parents, Clarissa communicates at various stages not only with Anna Howe

but also with her parents, her two uncles, her brother, her sister, her aunt, Mrs. Norton, Colonel Morden, and Lovelace himself; and in addition to her own letters, there is copious correspondence between Lovelace and Belford, plus a considerable number of incidental letters between various minor characters. It is indeed very striking for the first-time reader of the novel to discover that, for a large and crucial section of the tale, Clarissa's voice is not in fact dominant at all: most of the major events which fundamentally affect her destiny are relayed to us first through the medium of Lovelace's letters to Belford and then, by a neat reversal, through Belford's letters to Lovelace. Obviously at least part of this is for purely technical reasons: Clarissa cannot describe her own death, nor the reactions of the various other characters after it, both of which are left to the pens of Belford and of Clarissa's cousin Colonel Morden. Occasionally, however, the choice of principal voice seems to be prompted by other considerations, whether aesthetic or psychological. Eighteenth-century notions of modesty would forbid Clarissa to be too precise about the actual circumstances of the rape, so we rely for the majority of our information about it on the account which Lovelace gives to Belford; indeed, these letters to Belford are later circulated amongst Clarissa's closest friends as a vindication of her conduct in the affair, in place of the minutely detailed account which she herself promises Anna Howe but is in fact never able to deliver. More important, however, Richardson (perhaps prompted by the furore which had sprung up over the interpretation of his earlier heroine Pamela, meant as an instance of virtue but widely interpreted as a scheming minx) seems perhaps to have had some kind of instinct that, in the case of Clarissa, it was safer to portray her from a distance. Trapped as he was in a process whereby the more he tried to clarify the motives of his characters, the more he found himself generating potential ambiguities, he may well have felt that letters from Clarissa herself were, as those from Pamela had proved to be, hostages to fortune.

Equally, however, Richardson himself may have felt, as so many of his readers have done since, the pull of the extraordinary psychology of Lovelace. In *Pamela,* the heroine's would-be seducer and eventual husband, Mr. B. (cruelly but memorably caricatured by Fielding as Mr. Booby) is merely a bumbling incompetent, in whom the reader can generally feel little or no interest. Lovelace, however, is not only the rapist of Clarissa: he is also a fascinating character in his own right, a truly masterly creation which shows that Richardson succeeds where Milton and many others before him had failed, in creating a genuinely evil personality which is also genuinely repulsive. His fantastic egocentricity, his massive capacities for self-deception, his desperate yet utterly unacknowledged needs all make him a gripping psychological case study as his ceaseless flow of letters brings him frighteningly alive for us. If ever a man failed to know himself or was ripe for therapy, it is Lovelace. And yet this exploration of his character is precisely what the television adaptation fails to undertake. It has indeed been obviously influenced by many of the findings and practices of classical Freudian psychoanalysis, most notably the insistence on the importance of sexuality and symbols: it is remarkable, for instance, to what extent this most verbal of works has been translated to the screen largely in terms of telling images such as the silent, rather brutal kiss in the garden between Arabella and Lovelace, the gravestone before which Anna Howe lays her wedding bouquet (interestingly emblematic of her own ambivalence about marriage), and the repeated fencing bouts which structure and eventually terminate the relationship between Belford and Lovelace, depicting forcibly if rather crudely the antagonism so delicately developed in the text. For the most part, however, the adaptation concentrates its attention on the psychology of Clarissa and leaves that of Lovelace well alone.

One clear instance of this is the adaptation's treatment of Clarissa's dream. She experiences this early in the story, when she is still undecided about how far to negotiate with Lovelace about his offers of protection from his family. In the novel, she describes it thus to Anna Howe:

> Methought my brother, my uncle Antony, and Mr Solmes had formed a plot to destroy Mr Lovelace; who discovering it turned all his rage against me, believing I had a hand in it. I thought he made them all fly into foreign parts upon it; and afterwards seizing upon me, carried me into a churchyard; and there, notwithstanding all my prayers and tears, and protestations of innocence, stabbed me to the heart, and then tumbled me into a deep grave ready dug, among two or three half-dissolved carcasses; throwing in the dirt and earth upon me with his hands, and trampling it down with his feet. (pp. 342–343)

Obviously the length of this sequence makes it unsuitable for straightforward transference to the screen, yet the adaptations made to it are interesting because they do not simply shorten it: ignoring its complexities and seizing simply upon the most obviously visual and most psychologically telling element of it, they overtly sexualize the scene, in such a way that it is read not as containing a comment on any inherent menace in Lovelace, but as suggesting a profound ambivalence in Clarissa's response to him.

No mention is made in the television series of Clarissa's family fleeing; they are indeed present, but it seems that they are there mainly as silent witnesses to the scene, for although Lovelace briefly threatens James Harlowe, the burden of the action falls between him and Clarissa. She enters the room dressed in white, like a bride, and passes through a series of filmy white curtains which are surely representative of the hymen. She then finds herself in a bedchamber, face to face with Lovelace, who, averting his sword from James Harlowe, levels it first at her throat and then, in a gesture of overtly phallic symbolism, at her left breast, which he pierces. With red blood vividly staining her white dress, she appears to fall dead at his feet, only for the scene to cut to her dreaming in her bed, emitting small grunts ambiguously poised between signifiers of nightmare and signifiers of orgasm. The significance of the scene is clinched by an immediate cut to a jubilant Lovelace, thrusting a letter under Belford's nose and exclaiming, "Mine, Jack!"

Clearly, we are to read this as an indication of Clarissa's subconscious desire and fear and consequently to see her as a fitting subject for the decoding of the psyche. Throughout the early part of the novel, she returns repeatedly to her fear that if she crosses Lovelace, he will take his revenge not on her directly but on her family; he has already crossed swords once with her brother and has clearly demonstrated that he could, if he had so chosen, easily have disarmed and killed him. This element is also present in her dream. On the screen, however, it is almost wholly suppressed: Lovelace's aggression is turned directly on her, inviting us to read his rapier not as a literal weapon but as a clearly phallic symbol and furthermore, since we no longer have our attention so insistently drawn to the objective existence of violent propensities in Lovelace, to interpret her reaction to him as, in effect, pathological, a product of excessive fear on her part rather than of genuine menace on his. (This reading of the scene might have been promoted for some viewers by Sean Bean's disclosure in the UK TV guide *The Radio Times* that he himself had once taken a sword to the apartment of a girlfriend whom he suspected of infidelity.) The effect is completed by another subtle but significant change from book to screen: in the text, one of the primary reasons why Clarissa's family is eager for her marriage to the repugnant Solmes seems to be their hope that (in contrast to the overfertile Lovelace) he will never give her children (pp. 81, 347–348), while in the adaptation her cruel sister overtly tells her that Mr. Solmes has prepared a nursery in his house, a remark which is immediately followed by a cut to a shot of Solmes inanely rocking and cooing to an empty cradle, though, interestingly, it is unclear whether this is a scene that is objectively taking place or one that is in fact being imagined by Clarissa in response to her sister's remark. Although there is textual warrant for Solmes's preparation of a nursery (pp. 347–348), the bizarre image reinforces its significance and again directs our attention to the unexplored depths of both Solmes's psyche (mercifully left relatively untouched in the novel) and, more important, Clarissa's, who, it is here suggested, has feelings of unease about the prospect of motherhood.

That Clarissa does entertain feelings of a sexual nature for Lovelace is, of course, abundantly clear in the book. Anna Howe tells her so quite frankly, and her own equivocations about "conditional likings" and constant references to his handsome appearance are further hints. But she is not the only one whose motivations are not all they seem: although the adapters have chosen to make so much of *her* dream, they have completely omitted the equally significant one of Lovelace, which gives at least as clear an insight into the workings of his unconscious mind as Clarissa's dream offers into hers. Lovelace, as Terry Eagleton points out,[4] dreams of mother figures — good and bad ones — and Lovelace's world is indeed haunted by mothers. Both Clarissa and his own relatives attribute his defective character to early spoiling by his mother (pp. 46, 606), while Lovelace himself claims that he has vowed revenge on the sex for an early disappointment by one of its members (p. 247). Interestingly, he refers determinedly to the false Mrs. Sinclair as "the mother" and to the other whores as her "daughters," and in the novel much stress is laid on the repulsiveness of the "mother's" appearance, which alone is able to terrify Clarissa — a point definitely not made in the adaptation, in which Cathryn Harrison's young and pretty Mrs. Sinclair is markedly neither motherly nor physically repugnant. One of Lovelace's most persistent fantasies, too, is to make Clarissa a mother: he is constantly clinging to the hope that the rape may have left her, like so many of his previous victims, pregnant, which will enable him to see "a twin Lovelace at each charming breast, drawing from it his first sustenance; the pious task continued for one month, and no more!" (p. 706). Lovelace seems indeed to have an obsession with mothers, echoing that of *Pamela*'s Mr. B., who shows no interest in Pamela until his mother dies, when he obsessively showers her with clothes of the old lady which he wishes to see her wear and forbids breastfeeding not just after one month but at all. However, the television adaptation's emphasis on Mr. Solmes and his nursery, while retaining the concern with motherhood, displaces it from Lovelace to Clarissa, who thus becomes the sole fully psychologized character of the series, surrounded by grotesques — the ludicrous Solmes, the vicious Lovelace, and her incipiently incestuous brother and sister. The effect is undoubtedly an interesting one, but it is also one markedly different from that created by the novel, in which so many other characters and their motives are also developed and laid before the reader.

For all his lack of Freudian training, then, Richardson's exploration of personality and motivation is ultimately richer and more probing than that offered by this exclusive concentration on Clarissa alone. What the adaptation offers is not just a version but fundamentally a simplification of the book, and a significantly gendered one at that: Clarissa, it is suggested, is profoundly riven by unrealized fears about sex and motherhood; Anna Howe's state of mind is emblematized by the bridal bouquet which she lays on the grave — a scene without textual warrant since we are explicitly told that Clarissa is buried in the family vault not in the churchyard, but one which does offer a very potent image of the association of sex and death. The men, meanwhile, are dramatically simplified: Lovelace is a rake; James Harlowe wants property; Colonel Morden, the avenger who is himself no innocent, does not appear at all; and Belford, in many ways one of the most sensitive and complex characters of the novel, becomes merely a straightforward chap in whom decency ultimately triumphs. The twin strategies of rewriting and of deploying the gendered gaze of the camera have served inextricably to associate psychoanalysis solely with the realm of the feminine, far from the rational, commonsense world of men.

Sense and Sensibility and the Double Heroine

Ang Lee's film version of *Sense and Sensibility,* with a screenplay by Emma Thompson, has been much acclaimed as one of the most sophisticated and intelligent adaptations of Austen. This is all the more impressive since it faced a problem not experienced by *Pride and Prejudice* or by any of the three versions of *Emma* (in which I include *Clueless*): instead of a single, memorable heroine, its interest is split between two female leads whom the title, moreover, invites us to perceive less in terms of character or intrinsic interest than as flattened abstractions. Here I trace some of the ways in which the film deals with the division of focus produced by the two heroines and also how it negotiates the issues of representing, and choosing between, sense and sensibility. Above all, I suggest that the ways in which it does this work against Jane Austen's ongoing schema of equating one person with one dominant characteristic, proposing instead a Gothicized, riven psychology at the heart of even the most rational-seeming human.

All of Jane Austen's novels are dependent for at least some of their effects on the use of contrasting pairs of young women: Catherine Morland and Isabella Thorpe (*Northanger Abbey*), Elinor and Marianne Dashwood (*Sense and Sensibility*), Elizabeth and Jane Bennet (*Pride and Prejudice*), Fanny Price and Mary Crawford (*Mansfield Park*), Emma Woodhouse and Jane Fairfax (*Emma*), and, to a lesser extent and in rather different ways, Anne Elliot and the two pairings of sisters and sisters-in-law — Elizabeth Elliot and Mary Musgrove, and Louisa and Henrietta Musgrove (*Persuasion*) — with whom she is juxtaposed. In *Sense and Sensibility,* Austen's first published novel, the device is used with particular insistence and force. Sisters are everywhere in this text: not only are the abstract qualities of the title given bodily shape in the forms of Elinor and Marianne Dashwood, but prominence is also given to Mrs. Palmer and Lady Middleton, Mrs. Jennings' two very different daughters, and to Lucy and Anne Steele, who are also strikingly unlike each other in many ways, with Lucy being pretty and having pretensions to gentility, and Anne being plain and unabashedly vulgar. Even Colonel Brandon has a sister, as we learn when, on the receipt of the letter announcing what has become of his ward Eliza, Mrs. Jennings asks him, "Was it from Avignon? I hope it is not to say that your sister is worse."[5]

In addition to literal sisters, Austen's novels also abound in female characters who are linked in other ways. In many cases, the traits of the secondary heroine of one novel seem to be developed into the main character of the next.[6] This process is most visible in those novels which were not extensively revised and which are in a clear chronological sequence: the impatience with the debility of Anne de Bourgh in *Pride and Prejudice* is atoned for by the choice of a sickly heroine for *Mansfield Park;* the demonization of Mary Crawford in the latter novel is revised by the privileged exuberance of Emma Woodhouse. Finally, the delicacy and elegance of Jane Fairfax, so little valued in *Emma,* resurface in Anne Elliot (*Persuasion*), who is, like Jane, associated with the sea. Jane meets Frank Churchill at Weymouth and is rescued from drowning by Mr. Dixon, and Anne is present at a seaside accident when Louisa falls from the Cobb. This, in turn, may alert us to the ways in which the sea often functions as a site of danger and passion in Austen, as when Georgiana Darcy meets Wickham again at the seaside. In the film of *Sense and Sensibility,* the potential danger of the natural is both strongly marked in itself and also used to mark a difference between the two sisters: Barton Cottage is near a bay, and the natural world in general is painted as threatening in the film by the lowering and lurid skies we often see, while whenever Marianne ventures outdoors, she has to be carried back (Elinor, in the film, goes outside only when Edward is there to pull up her shawl when it slips).

Differences between the two sisters are, then, clearly established and seem to be in line with the kind of systematic differentiation between the types of heroine visible throughout Jane Austen's canon. In the case of *Sense and Sensibility,* the problematic chronology of Austen's early novels makes it impossible to say with any certainty whether priority of conception should go to this work, in its earliest state as *Elinor and Marianne,* or to *First Impressions,* the genesis of *Pride and Prejudice* (or even to *Susan,* the original version of *Northanger Abbey*). It is, however, easily possible to discern a suggestive parallelism between the Bennet and the Dashwood sisters, and here too the logic follows that of the later novels, for if sensible Elinor is favored over passionate Marianne, the wit and vivacity of Elizabeth, and her insistence on marrying for love rather than prudence, are never quelled.

If Marianne in some ways resembles Elizabeth Bennet, we are also openly invited to consider her in relation to another Elizabeth. Having recounted the history of his ward, Eliza, Colonel Brandon reverts to the subject of Marianne:

> after such dishonourable usage, who can tell what were his designs on her? Whatever they may have been, however, she may now, and hereafter doubtless will, turn with gratitude towards her own condition, when she compares it with that of my poor Eliza . . . Surely this comparison will have its use with her. (p.219)

Whatever use the comparison may be to Marianne, the reader surely is invited to bear it in mind, and perhaps we might also profitably notice that there is another character in the novel, Lady Middleton's little daughter Annamaria, whose name comes so close to Marianne's that we may well perceive still another pairing here. Indeed pairings and parallels are of the essence of the book, but it is important to note that they are not Gothicized doublings, but rather parallels which are, as Colonel Brandon's remark reminds us, explicitly constructed on a basis of "compare and contrast." It is crucial to the effect of the book that dissimilarity be as clearly and strongly perceptible as similarity.

In Ang Lee's film version of the novel, however, many of these structural pairings have been lost. For one thing, Emma Thompson's script places far greater emphasis on the youngest Dashwood sister, Margaret, than the novel does: Kristin Flieger Samuelian observes, "Transformed by Thompson from a plot device to an integral character, Margaret serves both to voice reasonable dissent and to exhort unpalatable truths from the mouths of her more restrained and practical elders."[7] The Margaret of Lee's film is radically unsocialized, something which is underlined by changing her from thirteen years old in the novel to eleven in the film so that she seems less of an incipient woman and more of a child. She swordfights with Edward, must have Elinor explain to her that "houses go from father to son, dearest, not from father to daughter," has the very unfeminine appurtenances of a tree house and an atlas, and wants to head an expedition to China. This is in marked contrast to the Margaret of the novel, in which we read, " 'I wish,' said Margaret, striking out a novel thought, 'that somebody would give us all a large fortune apiece!' " (p. 117). Austen's irony here devastatingly reveals the pitifully second-hand nature of what passes for novelty in Margaret's mind. In the film, however, Margaret offers a genuinely alternative and indeed revolutionary perspective — indeed, so much so that Kristin Flieger Samuelian suggests that by including lines such as Edward's "Perhaps Margaret is right . . . Piracy is our only option," Emma Thompson has herself pirated the novel by suggesting that patriarchy can be effectively challenged, in ways that Austen herself does not conceive.[8]

Lee's film charts Margaret's development as well as that of her sisters: the rebellious girl who initially says of Mrs. Jennings, "I like her. She talks about things. We never talk about things," eventually matures into the embryonic young lady who, when Edward visits Barton Cottage after they have received the news of his supposed marriage to Lucy, embarks on a conversation about the weather (in the novel, it is Elinor who does this [p. 349]). Finally, Margaret is given a privileged position when, from her tree house, she spies on Edward's proposal — something which neither the other members of her family nor indeed the audience is privy to. All this gives an emphasis that is very different from that of the novel, in which Margaret is virtually dismissed: "Margaret, the other sister, was a good-humoured well-disposed girl; but as she had already imbibed a good deal of Marianne's romance, without having much of her sense, she did not, at thirteen, bid fair to equal her sisters at a more advanced period of life" (p. 42).

This added attention to Margaret works in conjunction with another marked feature of the film: its tendency, in the interests of narrative economy, to eliminate other sisters from the novel. Sir John Middleton is a widower, which means that neither Lady Middleton nor little Annamaria is present; there is no Anne Steele, and the name of the younger Eliza is, doubtless for reasons of clarity, changed to "Beth," making us less aware of the similarity of the destinies of mother and daughter to which Colonel Brandon calls attention in the novel. The narrative of the film thus downplays links between female characters—Fanny's voice, for instance, sets her apart by making her noticeably more cut-glass than her in-laws, an important distinction in a film which, unusually for a major Hollywood movie, has no American actors at all, depending instead on the interplay of differing English accents and their class connotations; and in the film Brandon draws no potential parallel between Marianne and Eliza, for Lady Allen has already told him that Willoughby's intentions towards Marianne were perfectly honorable. Dividing and separating the women, emphasising Margaret, and eliminating Lady Middleton and Anne Steele, Lee's film is thus no longer structured around pairs of sisters.

The novel's triad of pairs, made up of Dashwood sisters, Steele sisters, and Mrs. Jennings' daughters, is, however, important for its overall meaning, reflecting this text's fundamental interest in choices and contrasts. Even the landscape speaks of alternatives and oppositions: "The hills which surrounded the cottage terminated the valley in that direction; under another name, and in another course, it branched out again between two of the steepest of them" (p. 62). Equally, the two sisters vary not only in disposition but in avocations: "Marianne's pianoforte was unpacked and properly disposed of; and Elinor's drawings were affixed to the walls of their sitting room" (p. 62). The danger, of course, is always that such a structure of opposites will degenerate into crudeness, with characterization more suited to an allegory than a novel. Tony Tanner observes in his introduction that "the title and the use of the two sisters does seem to indicate a fairly primitive schematization" and that "[s]een in bare outline the plot displays a good deal of geometry" (p. 9). Moreover, if readers are invited simply to take sides, there is always the risk that they will choose the wrong one, as many readers of Sense and Sensibility have indeed been tempted to do, finding Elinor cold and Marianne vibrant, Colonel Brandon and Edward dull and Willoughby far more exciting. Even Tanner, who is sympathetic to the book, declares flatly that "Marianne does, in effect, die. Whatever the name of the automaton which submits to the plans of its relations and joins the social game, it is not the real Marianne, and in the devitalized symmetry of the conclusion something valuable has been lost" (p. 32).

Thompson's script and Lee's direction have clearly set themselves to counter both the elements of schematization in the treatment of the two sisters and the danger that we may come to see Marianne's story as a tragedy. One of the ways in which this is done is by forging a rather different set of links between the characters; Austen's grouping of the women may have been abandoned, but the use of grouping in itself has not been. Edward tells Elinor, "Our circumstances are therefore precisely the same," and when he reads "We perished, each alone," we are acutely aware of the way in which Marianne, Elinor, and he are all seeking companionship and a meeting of minds in this scene and of the obstacles which are working to prevent it. Edward is also developed in other ways. The Edward Ferrars of the novel "was not recommended to their good opinion by any peculiar graces of person or address. He was not handsome, and his manners required intimacy to make them pleasing. He was too diffident to do justice to himself; but when his natural shyness was overcome, his behaviour gave every indication of an open affectionate heart" (p. 49). Hugh Grant is diffident enough but is generally felt to be recommended by some distinctly "peculiar graces of person" and to be definitively "handsome." He is also more open than his counterpart in the novel: before the sisters leave Norland, he begins to tell Elinor the story of Lucy, but is interrupted. Finally, as well as stressing the parallels between himself and Elinor, Edward also forms a notable alliance with Margaret. Indeed, the first thing he says identifies his sympathy with her viewpoint; being told that she is shy of strangers at present, he replies, "N-naturally. I am sh-shy of strangers myself." Colonel Brandon also scores a hit with Margaret, intriguing her by telling her that the Indian air is full of spices. Interestingly, both men negotiate with Margaret primarily by giving her geographical information, literally helping her to find her way in the world and coaching her to the stage where, by means of her tree house and telescope, she is able to do so for herself. (It is notable that the McGrath film of *Emma* also proposes a stress on geography not found in the novel itself, opening with a globe embroidered with local features by Emma as Miss Taylor's wedding present, both reinforcing and simultaneously challenging the idea that Austen's novels are unduly local in their concerns and of little wider resonance.)

Brandon's character hardly needed this sympathetic touch, however, for the casting of Alan Rickman had already revolutionized our perception of the part. In the film, Willoughby calls him "the sort of man that everyone speaks well of, and no-one remembers to talk to," just as in the novel Willoughby calls Brandon "a very respectable man, who has every body's good word and nobody's notice" (p. 82); Alan Rickman, however, is an actor who generally has everybody's notice and, moreover, who made his name playing precisely the kind of dangerous, rakish role which in the novel is so closely associated not with Brandon, but with Willoughby.[9] Rickman first came to fame playing Valmont on stage in *Les Liaisons dangereuses* at The Other Place in 1985, and Lindsay Duncan, who played the Marquise, remarked after his first night in the part, "A lot of people left the theatre wanting to have sex, and most of them wanted to have it with Alan Rickman." An interviewer of Rickman further comments that, "In the 12 years since *Liaisons*, he has gained a reputation for playing the sardonic, sexy villain—almost creating his own sub-genre in this role,"[10] most famously, perhaps, as the wicked Sheriff of Nottingham in *Robin Hood: Prince of Thieves*, where he so upstaged Kevin Costner that Costner allegedly demanded that some of Rickman's scenes be cut from the film. Thus, just as Darcy in the 1995 BBC version of *Pride and Prejudice* seems to borrow from the iconography of the rake when, like Lovelace in the BBC's *Clarissa*, he is seen fencing, so Colonel Brandon here borrows glamour reflected from Rickman's other roles.

Our reliance on Rickman's image is significantly boosted by the fact that we see him before his character is named as Colonel Brandon, so we immediately make the identification. He enters silently, listening to Marianne's music and clearly moved by it. At this stage, his melancholy demeanor, our uncertainty about his past, the genre and setting of the film, and, above all, his costume may well induce us to read him predominantly as a reincarnation of a rather different character whom he made famous, Obadiah Slope in *The Barchester Chronicles*. Very rapidly, however, a quite different kind of character starts to emerge. Unlike Slope, Brandon is someone with whom we sympathize: it is impossible not to feel for him when he is completely ignored by Marianne as she eagerly awaits Willoughby, and it is equally impossible not to notice his rangy, louche attractiveness. (We may also pick up on the potential promise of Mrs. Dashwood's comment that he and Marianne have gathered enough reeds for a Moses basket.) Samuelian comments that he "exhibits a tension-creating sexual energy that his counterpart in the novel . . . lacks."[11] He is also allowed far more dynamism in the film: when Marianne is caught in the rain at Cleveland, Brandon goes to retrieve her and carries her back, directly echoing Willoughby, though he seems more drained by the effort—Marianne comments that Willoughby had "lifted me as if I weighed no more than a dried leaf," but nevertheless Emma Thompson's screenplay observes that "It is like seeing Willoughby's ghost."[12]

Brandon carries Marianne in *Sense and Sensibility,* dir. Ang Lee (Columbia/
Tristar, 1995).

Similarly, whereas the book has Brandon being found by Elinor in the
drawing room and needing a prompt to make the offer to go for her mother
(p. 306), the Brandon of the film waits outside the door of Marianne's
room, in shirtsleeves and with loosened necktie, saying "Give me an occu-
pation, Miss Dashwood, or I shall run mad." On his return, he disregards
propriety even further by actually coming into Marianne's sick room.
Samuelian suggests:

> What Thompson has done, in the characterization of both Brandon
> and Edward, is to endow them with a substantial portion of the life and
> attractiveness Austen originally located in Willoughby. In keeping with
> this effort to redistribute the attractiveness of the male characters, she
> eliminates Elinor's emotionally charged scene with Willoughby during
> Marianne's illness.[13]

The emotion generated in Elinor here is transferred in the film to her
scenes with Edward, but elsewhere Brandon is the clear beneficiary of
what has been stripped from Willoughby. Brandon reads Marianne poetry

on the lawn, and the rapprochement between them is evident well before we have any hint that Elinor's and Edward's story will come to a happy conclusion. Marianne calls him back into her sickroom to thank him, and there is no hint that she needs to be maneuvered into the relationship by her mother and Elinor—we merely see her growing dependence on Brandon and her receipt of the gift of a piano from him (clearly borrowing from Frank Churchill's gift to Jane Fairfax in *Emma*) and then cut to the double wedding of the two sisters, with Brandon (resplendent in the red coat of his army uniform) and Marianne emerging first and entering a carriage at the center of the picture, while Edward and Elinor disappear from the shot. The attention thus drawn to Brandon is increased still further when he scatters coins from a purse held directly level with his crotch (an emphasis underlined by the fact that John Dashwood's hand is also covering his crotch); this obvious ejaculation imagery, coupled with the presence of a rural fertility garland, makes the wedding seem very much to be Brandon's triumph and achievement—an effect added to by the fact that we see Willoughby on a horse at the end watching the wedding and are surely more inclined to see this as an emblem of what Brandon has gained, by triumphing over his rival, than of what Marianne has lost. This seems, essentially, like the conclusion to a story in which Brandon, rather than Marianne, has been a central character. If he entered as Obadiah Slope, he goes out as the hero, positioned virtually at the center of the emotional landscape of the film.

If it is primarily Colonel Brandon's story, however, is it still Marianne's? To some extent, of course, it never was: as the secondary heroine, Marianne is always subordinate to Elinor, and although her trials and tribulations often function as mainsprings of the plot, her own perspective is a severely limited one since she is quite ignorant of a number of important factors to which we as readers are privy. In negotiating the split focus of interest produced by the two heroines and their stories, therefore, Lee's film faces a difficult task, especially since the differences between them are so radically informed by the schematization which lies at the heart of the novel and which is made plain in its title. One way in which the film resolves this is by developing the figure of Margaret, who becomes of interest not only for her own sake but for the extent to which she serves to modify and mediate between the potentially polarized positions of her sisters. When Elinor learns that Edward will not be visiting them at Barton, her distress is clear in the unwonted brusqueness of her refusal to discuss his possible reasons; as she thus comes close to the emotional territory more habitually inhabited by Marianne, Marianne in turn nearly becomes Elinor as, to spare the latter's feelings, she frog-marches Margaret off for a walk.[14] The direct result of this excursion is her fall and the subsequent meeting with Willoughby, and again this brings out some unexpectedly Elinorish elements in her character: when she exclaims "What care I for colds, when there is such a man?", Elinor replies "You will care, very much, when your nose swells up," and Marianne is instantly and entirely won over to this perspective. But while she hastens to change, Elinor is seen in a far less practical mood, brooding over a handkerchief marked with Edward's initials—an act far more appropriate to *Emma*'s sentimental Harriet Smith than the sensible Elinor Dashwood. The sisters' characters are further modified when Marianne draws Willoughby's silhouette, an accomplishment which credits her with powers of observation that she exhibits neither in the novel nor anywhere else in the film. (Equally, while the Elinor of the novel definitively *cannot* play the piano, the Elinor of the film perhaps merely *will* not.)

The film also modifies the dichotomy between sense and sensibility in other ways. In the novel, we may be tempted to agree with Marianne that Elinor is cold and too inclined to conceal things; in the film, however, we are invited positively to revel in her ability to mask her emotion when Lucy Steele hovers, vulturelike, anxious for any sign of pain. Equally, when Miss Gray sneers at the way Marianne looks at Willoughby, we would surely prefer Marianne to be more reserved so as not to give her spiteful rival the satisfaction which she craves. Indeed, one could argue that, contrary to the usual imperative of acting, the success of film depends precisely on Emma Thompson's Elinor *not* emoting, at least not until the two moments when the floodgates break—first, when she upbraids Marianne, and second, when she learns that Edward is free. There is a notable departure here from the novel, in which Elinor runs out of the room and bursts into tears and "Edward . . . saw her hurry away, and perhaps saw—or even heard, her emotion" (p. 350); he undoubtedly both sees and hears it in the film since Elinor bursts into tears in the parlor and all the other women beat a hasty retreat to leave her alone with Edward.

Finally, if looks play a part in our reaction to Colonel Brandon and to Edward, they do so as well in our responses to Elinor and to Marianne, although in a less immediately obvious way. John R. Greenfield has commented of the Douglas McGrath film of *Emma,* starring Gwyneth Paltrow, that Emma

is the only character who is privileged to reveal her thoughts, but at times the camera distances and isolates her, demeaning her importance. Much of the point of view of other characters resides in Emma: it is through her that we view Harriet's foolishness, Mr. Elton's presumptuousness, and Mrs. Elton's pushiness. But she is also the object of the various male gazes Kaplan outlines as nearly endemic to film.[15]

In *Sense and Sensibility,* however, these twin rôles function rather differently. Being the object or possessor of the gaze is still crucial, as we are reminded early in the film when Fanny Dashwood wishes Edward to displace Margaret from her bedroom because the view from it is so good and when Lucy Steele first makes her mark on Robert Ferrars when she shares with him the result of her clandestine observations of Marianne's correspondence with Willoughby. Marianne, however, ignorant of the meanings and ramifications of many of the events she witnesses, has only a marginalized viewpoint; she is, though, consistently constructed as a thing of beauty to be looked at, with the pretty pastel colors and flowing, beribboned shapes of her clothes clearly set off against Elinor's plainer, drabber garb. Not only is Kate Winslet's Marianne the object of Brandon's passionate gaze, she is also the "bankable" female star who is presented as the object of our own gaze, as her recent casting as the romantic heroine of *Titanic,* the most expensive movie ever made, abundantly demonstrates. Emma Thompson, less of a "looker" in the slang sense, is, however, far more the "looker" in this film, the one whose viewpoint we share (and who has literally controlled our responses by having written the script). If Winslet is the object of the camera's gaze, Thompson comes close to being its eye; when Colonel Brandon carries in Marianne, Elinor runs towards him and the camera even tracks with her, literally equating her perspective with its own.

This difference between the sisters is established from the outset. When we first see Marianne, she is playing the piano and looking downwards, focusing only on the instrument, rather than at the camera. Elinor speaks to her and then leaves, going to see, in turn, her mother, Margaret, and the servants, and the camera moves with her, sharing her perspective. At dinner, after Fanny and John have arrived, Marianne consistently looks down; in the next scene, alone with Elinor, she looks only at her or to one side. Soon afterwards, we hear her playing and see Elinor at the door crying; Edward perceives her, and as they walk away together, we see Marianne just look up, but fail to see them, as indeed she has failed to observe almost all the exchanges between Edward and Elinor and between Edward and Margaret. Even when Edward reads to her, Marianne looks down, and when she corrects his emphasis, she looks upwards as if in rapture; the fact that she never looks directly either at Edward or at us, the viewers, underlines the extent to which we look *with* Elinor and *at* Marianne. Though she does, in the two ensuing scenes, look at both Elinor and her mother, she still never looks either at or with the camera, in marked contrast to the following scene in which the two Mrs. Dashwoods, together but with clearly different emotions, watch Edward and Elinor walking. At Sir John's house, Marianne won't look round the table, and she does not see Colonel Brandon enter, though we observe Elinor looking at him looking at her; later, as Marianne waits for Willoughby, Elinor virtually has to force her to turn her head towards Sir John and the Colonel, who have been exchanging significant glances about Willoughby, and while Elinor and her mother pore over their accounts, Marianne has eyes only for Willoughby.

The effect is even more marked on the several occasions on which Marianne looks at something which the viewer of the film cannot even see. When Colonel Brandon invites the two sisters to Delaford, Marianne looks away to see if Willoughby is in sight, and we do not follow her gaze. When Lucy arrives, Marianne is again peering into the invisible distance, beyond a field of cows; while Lucy talks to Elinor, Marianne gazes out of the window at something we cannot see. Later, while Elinor lies in bed with her face a picture of misery, Marianne, unseen, talks to her but does not see her, and again we have no idea what she looks at. In London, she peers through the window to see if Willoughby is coming; once again, we literally cannot share her perspective, and when she leaves the room as soon as Colonel Brandon enters it, she cannot share ours. So strong is the dissociation of her focus from ours that at first she does not even see Willoughby when Elinor meets him at the ball, though she is craning her neck for him; when she does catch sight of him, we are further made aware of how much she is an object rather than a possessor of the gaze when all heads turn to stare at him as she runs towards him. Her impercipience continues; at breakfast on the morning after the ball, she looks only at the table and at the note which, during the course of the meal, she receives from Willoughby, and she even fails to register the malice of Lucy's "Perhaps, Miss Marianne, you think young men never honour their engagements, great or small," though we see Elinor dart a very reproachful glance at Lucy. It is indeed with justice that Elinor accuses her sister, "What do you know of anything but your own suffering?"

Eventually, however, Marianne does start to see. She realizes instantly that Elinor already knew of the engagement between Edward and Lucy, merely from looking at her sister's face when Mrs. Jennings makes the announcement. Indeed, as with other instances of the two sisters' characterizations, their initially distinctive patterns of gazing actually start to blur into each other. Though Marianne stares out of the window of the carriage on the way to Cleveland, looking neither at Mrs. Jennings' farewells nor at Mrs. Palmer, on the party's eventual arrival it is Elinor who gazes abstractedly out of the window, and when Marianne lies on her sickbed, Elinor again moves away from her to gaze out of the window at a view we cannot share. Moreover, it is made very clear to us that Marianne's fated walk was taken only in order to see Combe Magna, as even Mr. Palmer guesses, and just as this moment of realization marks a complete transformation in his character, from churl to model of consideration, so it does for Marianne also: now, she wants to see. Most strikingly of all, her delirium in the film is wordless. In the novel, Marianne continues to look at things which no one else does: this time she literally imagines that her mother is coming to her. In the film, she has no such hallucination, and this underlines her move to a normal perspective.

Ang Lee's film has thus very successfully steered its way through some of the potential pitfalls of adapting *Sense and Sensibility* for the screen. Lee finds a balance between the heroines which plays to the distinctive strength of each so that instead of feeling our attention to be dangerously divided between them, we are invited, effectively, to watch the one with the other, and it engages our emotional interest in both of their stories. It could even be said to have offered some significant improvements on the original novel by involving us more in the outcome of the Marianne/Brandon romance and by making us feel that their marriage is a positively desirable outcome rather than an acceptable compromise, as well as by developing Margaret, a character whose potential had been largely ignored by Austen herself. It must be noted, however, that all this has been achieved at a cost which readers of the novel may well think a high one: the modification — at some points virtually the obliteration — of the structuring distinction between sense and sensibility and the replacement of a structure of parallels with one of Gothicizing doublings and blurrings.

Mansfield Park

It is hard to imagine any novel which could seem less susceptible to a Gothicizing approach than *Mansfield Park,* which eschews extremes of emotion and focuses with almost painful exclusivity on the quiet integrity of the self. Nevertheless, Gothicization is exactly what Patricia Rozema's controversial adaptation has achieved. Numerous small but cumulatively significant changes have been made to the novel. One of the most notable of these is to the character of Tom Bertram. In Rozema's film, Tom is not a selfish boy but a knight manqué who scorns his father not out of thoughtlessness but on the grounds that "Even I have principles—sir." Even when drunk, Tom retains a social conscience, saying "Ay—Antigua—all the lovely people there paying for this party." This change in the characterization of Tom also, of course, affects the image created by Mary Crawford since her willingness to speculate on the possibility of Tom's death becomes even less palatable when Tom is a character for whom we feel some regard. Thus, although Fanny Price and Mary may initially seem alike, both clearly weighing love against more prudential considerations, by the close of the film they seem revealed as Gothically polarized halves, with Mary completely demonized and a newly proper Fanny presented completely on the side of innocence and virtue, lauded by Edmund for her "infallible" judgement.

The greatest change to *Mansfield Park* as Jane Austen envisaged and created it is in the character of Fanny, however. Fanny, in this adaptation, becomes eerily like her own polar opposite, Mary Crawford (and is also clearly drawn to her in a strong lesbian attraction). Nor is the resemblance between Fanny and Mary Crawford the only instance of doubling. Lindsay Duncan plays dual rôles as Fanny's mother, Mrs. Price, and Fanny's aunt, Lady Bertram. On one level, this is clearly designed to suggest that mere social circumstances produced the startling difference between the two sisters and recalls Austen's own very similar authorial comments to this effect. On another, however, it invites us to read Portsmouth as being as much the dark underside of Mansfield Park as Antigua is; indeed, since we never see Antigua except for the brief glimpses of it which we catch through Tom's sketch book, Portsmouth can be seen to stand in for Antigua in this respect, representing a darkest England which has, moreover, the additional effect of being fundamentally *heimlich,* inevitably in both senses of the word.

Fanny has, moreover, the liveliness and acerbity of Austen herself since she is presented as the creator of Jane Austen's own juvenilia. Fanny becomes Jane Austen in other ways, too, as when she agrees to marry Henry Crawford and then changes her mind overnight, just as Jane Austen agreed to marry the wealthy Harris Bigg-Wither and then told him the next morning that she found herself unequal to going through with it. The fact that one of the scenes supposedly set at Portsmouth clearly shows the Cobb, which is in Austen's favored Lyme Regis, reveals very obviously the extent to which the biographical has infected the fictional here. Above all, Fanny has acquired not only the approval of Jane Austen—as in the novel, where she is famously referred to as "my Fanny"—but the acerbity: the sharpness of Austen's comments in her private letters has given rise to D. W. Harding's famous charge that she was governed by a barely "regulated hatred,"[16] and Susie (Fanny's younger sister) justly observes that "Your tongue is sharper than a guillotine, Fanny."

Indeed, the most remarkable achievement of this adaptation as a whole could well be the way in which it liberates the repressed subconscious of Austen's novel. When Susie says, "Your tongue is sharper than a guillotine, Fanny," she does not only comment on Fanny's character but also alludes openly to what Austen's fiction almost invariably conceals, the revolution in France which took the life of, amongst so many others, the Comte de Feuillide, the first husband of Austen's cousin and subsequent sister-in-law, Eliza Hancock, who has often been seen as the model for Mary Crawford. Similarly, we actually see Henry and Maria making love, something which is merely discreetly hinted at in the novel, and the hint that Henry's and Mary's partners will condone wife-swapping raises the specter of what would effectively be double incest.

The darkly Gothicizing overtones which are thus created are underscored by the fact that even stronger than this adaptation's resemblance to Austen's own juvenilia is its resemblance to the writing of the woman who identified herself as the antithesis of Jane Austen, Charlotte Brontë. If, as I suggest in the next chapter, Robert Young's 1997 *Jane Eyre* uncannily recalls Roger Michell's 1995 *Persuasion*, then Rozema's *Mansfield Park* repays the compliment by repeatedly echoing Young's *Jane Eyre*. This is established from the outset by the insistent emphasis on the point of view of the young Fanny, especially when the camera pans up to Sir Thomas and Mrs. Norris, making them appear to loom over her (see figure 5), just as Mr. Brocklehurst seems like a black column to the young Jane Eyre. *Jane Eyre* is also clearly recalled by the coachman's reference to "black cargo," which not only is not found in the original book but would be quite unthinkable there. Similarly, Fanny grows up while reciting the juvenilia, just as Jane Eyre, in all three film adaptations, bows her head over Helen Burns's grave as a young girl and raises it again as a grown woman. Rozema's film cuts to Sir Thomas's coach approaching Mansfield Park while the theatricals are in progress just as Zeffirelli's film cuts to Mason's coach approaching Thornfield as Jane Eyre prepares for her wedding. Equally, Tom's sketch book, for which there is no precedent in the novel, proves to reveal his character and story much as Jane

Mansfield Park, dir. Patricia Rozema (BBC/Hal Films/Miramax, 1999).

Eyre's does to Mr. Rochester, while Fanny's final voiceover clearly recalls "Reader, I married him." Perhaps most interesting of all is the way in which Rozema's adaptation, again without any warrant from the original text, includes references to Joan of Arc at both beginning and end. Joan, a woman famous primarily for being burned at the stake, might well seem to provide a structural echo of the fate of Bertha Mason, just as the ruins of the West Wing, seen so prominently at the close, seem to echo Thornfield.

There are other Gothic trappings as well. Mansfield Park is first seen in darkness as a cadaverous series of openings; the West Wing is completely ruined from the outset; and when we first see Fanny's attic, all the furniture is sheeted and the wind is howling through it. Equally suggestive of the Gothic is the gruesome line which Fanny delivers to Susie (actually borrowed once again from Austen's own juvenilia): Eliza is "imprisoned and partially eaten by her two young sons." In similar vein is Fanny's declaration that "I'm a wild beast," as well as the way in which she gallops off in the rain because "I won't be sold off like one of your father's slaves, Edmund." Lady Bertram drinks and takes opium; Mary Crawford smokes; and even the weather is more reminiscent of the wild tempests of the Gothic than of the calm sunshine more generally characteristic of Austen adaptations, with pouring rain driving Fanny into the parsonage. The way in which Fanny's acceptance and rejection of Henry Crawford are linked by a sequence in which she dreams uneasily clearly invites us to consider the extent to which this is reality or her nightmare.

Rozema's film, then, reads *Mansfield Park* against the grain to give us a version of the story which is very different in its effects and emphases from Jane Austen's original. In the Jane Austen canon, *Mansfield Park* is in a sense the direct inversion of *Northanger Abbey*: they are the only two of her novels to be named after places rather than characters or concepts, but they make very different use of their settings. While *Northanger Abbey* allows us to think, at least at first, that environment is deterministic in that those who live in an abbey are bound to behave in certain ways, *Mansfield Park* challenges this proposition from the outset by showing us that the house is shaped and molded by the people who live in it, with the physical changes being introduced by Mr. Rushworth to his home at Sotherton clearly being intended as an analogue to the spiritual changes taking place or being threatened at Mansfield Park. This stress on the reality and importance of human agency is missing from Rozema's adaptation, however, not least because its Fanny is so far from being the maker of her own destiny that she can even nearly stumble into a marriage with Henry Crawford and its Sir Thomas is no stern-minded patriarch but a debauched and selfish hypocrite. In Rozema's adaptation, in short, *Mansfield Park* has become everything that we are initially encouraged to believe that *Northanger Abbey* will be, before Austen's Enlightenment rationalism dispels those Gothic fears.

The Time Machine

There is much to like in Simon Wells's film of his great-grandfather's book. In the first place, the central performances are very strong. Guy Pearce, always an interesting actor, plays the hero, Alexander Hartdegen, and makes a sensitive, credible scientist, tortured by the memory of his lost love, Emma, but nevertheless sufficiently alert to the world around him to pull himself out of his grief and start acting decisively to save the world; he is even able to hold his own against Jeremy Irons camping it up so deliciously that a lesser actor would be blown off the screen. Emma herself (Sienna Guillory) is suitably enchanting, and Samantha Mumba is adequate as Hartdegen's second love (though it is perhaps fortunate that her main quality is reticence and she thus doesn't have anything too substantial to say). Phyllida Law is magnificent as Mrs. Watchit, the housekeeper.

There are also some good ideas. The "Stone language," for instance, is both an inventive touch and a useful counterpart for the crucial but ambivalent rôle played by classical culture in the novel, whose roots in the classical past are deep. Almost the first thing that the Time Traveller sees in this far-away future is something that speaks clearly of the past: a white sphinx.[17] This surely recalls Oedipus, who had to solve the riddle of the Sphinx.[18] (The suggestion of a Greek context will be slyly picked up on again soon afterwards when the Time Traveller describes the first Eloi he sees as wearing "sandals or buskins" [p. 20].) The Sphinx's famous question was, "What goes on four legs in the morning, two legs at noon, and three in the evening?", and the answer is "man," who crawls as a baby, walks erect in his prime, and leans on a stick in old age. Not only will the Time Traveller also have to solve a riddle about human identity, but the Sphinx's riddle becomes, in the context of the novel, a powerful parable about human development, advance, and then eventual decay—it becomes, in fact, a potted history of evolution and degeneration, as Wells's fin-de-siècle perspective sees them, while the Time Traveller's Oedipal identity is further underlined by his lameness (p. 52) and by his persistent and much-emphasized blindness about the real nature of what he sees (not the least instance of which is that he wants to break into the sphinx instead of solving its riddle). In our own unclassical age, it is difficult to find a parallel for this set of ideas, so the idea of making English itself the lost language is really ingenious.

However, there is also a crucial disappointment in the film. H. G. Wells's book asked some very disturbing questions about the nature and future of man; all Simon Wells's film does is provide some very pat answers. For one thing, the film appears to believe what the book so centrally and resonantly questioned, that there *is* such a thing as human nature. The only area where the book's many ambiguities about humanity surface even residually is in the question of gender, with the long hair of both Kalen (whom I took at first for a girl, not least because of the long wig which Omero Mumba wears for the rôle; his stunt double was, in fact, a girl) and Hartdegen initially seeming to blur the distinctions between masculinity and femininity in a way which recalls the book's own fears on this subject, as when the Time Traveller worries, "What if in this interval the race had lost its manliness" (p.19), in which the issue of speciation seems to be definitively inflected by gender. We are often reminded of the extent to which the Time Traveller's interpretation of the future is informed by expectations molded in the past: as he himself so suggestively says, "the expectation took the colour of my fears" (p. 53). In this connection, it is clearly notable that he comes from a period when the rise of the New Woman (of whose existence we are vividly reminded by the reference to Grant Allen, author of the notorious *The Woman Who Did* [p. 40]) was posing a sharp challenge to traditional notions of a marked differentiation between masculine and feminine; in the same year that Wells's novel was published, *Punch* lamented, "A new fear my bosom vexes; / Tomorrow there may be no sexes!"[19] At first, therefore, the Time Traveller interprets the Eloi's apparent lack of gender differences as resulting from a logical continuation of this trend, and even though that idea eventually fades from view, the question of gender continues to puzzle him, and he is never even really certain that Weena is a woman. In the film, however, the replication of this uncertainty is only superficial: Alexander Hartdegen may be eccentric, but when it comes down to it, he can still get the girl and fight the bad guy.

This is only one of the film's startling deviations from the book's representations of the species on which it focuses. Jeremy Irons's Morlock is not a Morlock at all, but recognizably a man, albeit an albino one; indeed Simon Wells notes in the first feature accompanying the DVD that "some people" think the Über-Morlock *is* "Alexander, still alive after all these years." The film did in fact initially contain the line "I am your future," spoken by the Über-Morlock to Alexander; this was removed in the final cut, but, as the producer points out on the second feature, it is still easy to see Alexander's laboratory as closely foreshadowing the industrialized Morlock world, creating a doubling effect. Another major difference between book and film is that in the book, class is obviously an issue: for H. G. Wells it seems that the primary differentiator of humanity is not race, or nationality, or even gender, but class. Inheriting from his mother's time at Uppark a horror of the upper classes' relegation of their inferiors to the realm of the subterranean (introduction, p. xxxix), he has his Time Traveller openly refer to the possibility of a Communist future (p. 7), remember to wonder who does the work (p. 37), and speculate on the Morlocks' situation in terms of the East End and workers on the underground (p. 44). The Time Traveller even stresses the residual humanity of the Morlocks when he speaks of them keeping the Eloi "as a man enjoys killing animals in sport" (p. 52), and we are clearly invited to compare his own hungering for meat with theirs, as well as noting that the direct result of the vegetarianism of the Eloi is that "horses, cattle, sheep, dogs, had followed the Ichthyosaurus into extinction" (p. 24). This thing of darkness Wells does, indeed, acknowledge as his own.

In the film, however, class as an issue is submerged, and there is certainly no longer a question of acknowledging any uncomfortable similarities. The Morlocks have subdivided into different castes, and Irons is a controlling, telepathic representative of the master race—I use the term advisedly because he is billed as the Über-Morlock, which clearly flags race rather than class as the dominant area of concern. The Eloi too are fully human—Simon Wells notes in the accompanying feature that he felt it was important to "have Eloi that were worth saving"—and indeed Mara, unlike Weena, behaves for all intents and purposes exactly like a second Emma. This lack of any essential change in the makeup and nature of humanity is startlingly emblematized in the sequence towards the end of the film when the old and the new map directly onto each other, with Philby and Mrs. Watchit occupying one part of the screen and Hartdegen, Kalen, and Mara the other.

Of course, the fact that Mara is so reminiscent of Emma may be partly attributable to the film's race agenda, so clearly hinted by at by the term *Über-Morlock*. This emphasis is notably absent from the book, which stresses the whiteness of both the Eloi and the Morlocks, and indeed racial distinctions, evident though they were in H. G. Wells's London,[20] seem to have entirely died out in its future. Though Weena "dreaded the dark, dreaded shadows, dreaded black things" (p. 39), when the Time Traveller first sees the Morlock, he is careful to reverse our expectations by registering it as "some greyish animal" and "a solitary white, ape-like creature" (p. 40). The nonblackness of the Morlocks is even further insisted on when he describes them as "these whitened Lemurs, these new vermin that had replaced the old" (p. 46) and, in a sense, "whitened" is indeed what the Morlocks are since Wells is at such pains not to paint them as black and thus not to make race an issue — the Time Traveller explicitly tells us to "think how narrow the gap between a negro and a white man of our own times" is (p. 37). The film, however, takes this much further because there the gap is not just narrow but nonexistent, and race is not just a nonissue, but one which is loudly addressed by the casting of Samantha and Omero Mumba and Orlando Jones and the many hues of the Eloi's skins.

This desire to stress race instead of class is, then, one of the factors producing the distinct shift of overall emphasis. Mainly, though, the film's reluctance to take on board H. G. Wells's central point—that human nature is *not* stable but changes over time—seems to arise because Simon

Wells's film is not sure whether its allegiances are to psychoanalysis or to cultural materialism. More damaging still, it doesn't even seem to realize that there is tension here; indications of both perspectives are sprinkled through the film apparently at random. Jeremy Irons's words are repeated on surround sound as though he does indeed occupy our heads. The moon hovers too low in the sky, like a collective cultural nightmare, clearly taking us into the realm of the dark and dreams (the original concept of having a piece of the moon hitting a skyscraper was abandoned in the wake of 9/11, but the moon is still much emphasized: it was carefully added into the scenes around the pond, and when Emma says the word *moonstone,* she looks up at the moon significantly). Almost equally haunting is the idea of everyone having the same dream (which, appropriately enough for a film made by the Freudianly titled Dreamworks company, turns out to mean the opposite). This suggestion of the psychological is accentuated by a notable shift in literary allegiances. The original novel is clearly indebted to Rider Haggard's *She,* which tells a yarn about an adventurer in Africa finding a beautiful queen who offers him her love and who eventually dies by fire. *The Time Machine,* in which a traveller befriends a young woman who would like to jump into the fire, echoes Haggard at various points — the Time Traveller's rescue of Weena from drowning parallels Holly's rescue of Billali, and his desire to take Weena back with him recalls not only Ayesha's wish to visit England but also Good's attachment to Foulata in *King Solomon's Mines,* while the equipment the Time Traveller wishes he had brought — arms, medicine, tobacco, more matches — is very much part of the colonial adventurer's kit wielded by Haggard's heroes. The film, however, loses all these episodes and hence these allusions and flags up instead an allegiance to a very different source text, with Emma's moonstone engagement ring gesturing so obviously in the direction of Wilkie Collins and hence of the Gothic, an affiliation also indicated in the bats which Hartdegen finds when he first ventures underground.

However, there are equally clear signs of an interest in the material as well as the psychological. The collapse of the moon is explicitly attributed to greedy overexploitation of its resources, and even the robber who shoots Emma is presented as a genuine victim of necessity who kills only by accident. Materialist and psychoanalytic analysis, however, offer opposed and to some extent mutually exclusive explanatory models, with one seeing events as conditioned by time and the other tending towards the transhistorical. For a film about a time machine not to know with which of these two perspectives it wants to affiliate itself suggests a deep-seated confusion. Ultimately, then, the many good ideas of Simon Wells's film pull in different directions, so the film as a whole fails to cohere. Once again, the response of cinema to a rationalist narrative has been to inject the Gothic.

In these four films, then, the Gothic proves to be present where it might be least looked for. In *Clarissa* and *The Time Machine*, works originally either actively opposed or completely antithetical to the fundamental principles of psychoanalysis, the prominence which has been given to dreams repeatedly assures us that we are dealing with the dark and Gothic logic of the psyche rather than the rational principles of Richardson's unflagging attempts at authorial control or Wells's materialist perspective. In *Mansfield Park* and *Sense and Sensibility*, characters presented in the original novels as virtually emblematic of diametrically opposing principles are subjected in film to that other classic Gothicizing technique, doubling, so that they blur into each other instead of standing as opposing principles. Once more, texts originally enshrining Enlightenment values and materialist perspectives prove, on screen, surprisingly ready hosts to the haunted worlds of dreams and doubles. And once more, the ways in which they do so provide a telling index to the fears and beliefs of the cultural moment which created them—one which does not believe in feminine virtue of the kind of which Richardson and Austen both worked so hard to provide reasoned and credible exemplars, but does believe in female weakness, irrationality, and desire for sex, complemented, in the case of *The Time Machine* at least, by the innate heroism and propensity for action of even the most seemingly bookish of men.

| TAKING THE GOTHIC OUT

'Tis Pity She's a Whore, Mary Shelley's
Frankenstein, The Woman in White, *and*
Lady Audley's Secret

The first film I discuss in this chapter, Giuseppe
Patroni Griffi's *'Tis Pity She's a Whore* (1973), may
well seem an odd choice. Like *Hamlet,* *'Tis Pity She's a Whore* clearly pre-
dates the traditional chronological period of the Gothic. However, like
Hamlet, it also has strong affiliations with the genre, especially in its focus
on incest, its sinister Cardinal, and the gruesome scene where Giovanni
cuts out the heart of his pregnant sister Annabella. Even more significant,
Ford in general, and *'Tis Pity* in particular, was an important influence on
many Gothic writers (and also on Richardson: there are clear echoes of
'Tis Pity in *Clarissa,* with Anna Howe's mother being called Annabella
and a definite whiff of incest in the close relationship between Clarissa's
brother and sister). Most especially, Ford and his works seem to have
been of intense concern to Mary Shelley, who used Ford as a source for
her novel *The Fortunes of Perkin Warbeck* (1830), and this, as I discuss
below, is an influence which clearly seems to be picked up on in Kenneth
Branagh's *Mary Shelley's Frankenstein* (1994).

Ford's play, then, has affiliations with both the Gothic mode and the
Gothic tradition. Patroni Griffi's film of it, however, is significantly different from the original not only in language, as I discuss below, but also
in emphasis. Though Ford's play is of course much interested in individuals, it also goes to considerable pains to present an overall portrait of
Giovanni and Annabella's society, and although I argue in the previous
chapter that an emphasis on materialist analysis was not generally characteristic of the Gothic, an ability to hint at uncomfortable suggestions
of its own society undoubtedly is. In Ford's case, as in so much English
Renaissance drama, what is essentially suggested is that not just the main
characters but in fact the whole society they inhabit is riven with Gothic
dualisms and traversed by dark fissures within the apparent stability of the
self. Patroni Griffi's film, however, removes almost all of the social setting
indicated by Ford and concentrates, instead, exclusively on family, pre-

sumably because its principal function was, in the director's eyes, to act as a metaphor for an exploration of his own homosexuality and its effect on his place in society.[1] As a result, his film comes closer to a sociological critique of family politics than to Ford's darkly Gothic vision.

Frankenstein (1818), Wilkie Collins's *The Woman in White* (1860), and Mary Elizabeth Braddon's *Lady Audley's Secret* (1862), on the other hand, need no apology. These are three texts which might well be thought to encapsulate the Gothic *par excellence*. (Although *Lady Audley's Secret* is, as discussed below, more properly classed as sensation fiction, it contains an unusual number of Gothic elements for the genre and has clear affiliations with *Jane Eyre*.) Nevertheless, the three recent adaptations of these novels are all remarkable for their almost complete lack of Gothic features. Kenneth Branagh's *Mary Shelley's Frankenstein* supplies what Mary Shelley's actual *Frankenstein* pointedly does not, a scientific account of the genesis of the monster; *Lady Audley's Secret* becomes no secret at all, but a tract about postnatal depression, social inequalities, and the exploitation of women; and *The Woman in White* also offers social criticism rather than psychological exploration.

'Tis Pity She's a Whore

The first time I showed Giuseppe Patroni Griffi's film of *'Tis Pity She's a Whore* to my third-year students, I got a reaction which rather surprised me. From about twenty minutes in, the majority of the students were sobbing with silent mirth. When Giovanni asked Annabella, his sister, why she didn't stab him, the girl sitting next to me hissed, "Because you've got the knife, cretin"; when Soranzo rather unfortunately asked, "What game must I invent for you? . . . Is patience the answer?" many students were literally howling with laughter; and at the end of the film when a dog loped into the banqueting hall, deserted now except for the corpses, somebody exclaimed, "Oh my God, it's Scooby Doo, come to work out who did it!"

It is not hard to see why the film inspires mirth; in scenes such as that in which Giovanni, for no apparent reason, throws himself down a well, the film seems almost to invite it. It is also hard to keep a straight face when Fabio Testi's Soranzo tries to encourage Charlotte Rampling's Annabella to consummate their relationship by taking her to a field to watch horses copulating, when he tells her that her refusal doesn't matter although his body language so evidently reveals that it does, or when he tells Bonaventura to save his prayers "for worthier bastards." It is impossible, too, not to speculate rather irreverently on why Soranzo, in weather so cold that people's breath is visible, thinks it is a good idea to ride around bare-chested; and it is equally impossible not to notice that when Giovanni lifts up his white-jacketed arm to put it round his sister, he reveals a large rift in the armpit. For those who know the play, moreover, matters are not helped by the dialogue: the opening credits announce that the film is "Freely adapted from John Ford's tragedy," but the freedom actually arose, legend has it, essentially as the result of an initial decision to make the film in Italian, so a translation into Italian was commissioned. When, according to the story, it was decided to film in English after all, the Italian translation was promptly retranslated back into English without any further recourse to Ford's original. The saddest thing about this tale is that it is perfectly credible. Finally, the very presentation of Redemption Films' video version of the film undermines any attempt to take it seriously: the inside of the box lists the other titles in the series as *Vampires with a Whip*, *Venus in Furs*, *Requiem for a Vampire*, *Chill of the Vampire*, *The Naked Vampire*, and *Succubus*. As still further encouragement, the back of the case assures you that the play is notorious, that Oliver Tobias (Giovanni) appeared in *The Stud*, and that the camerawork was done by the man who photographed *Last Tango in Paris*.

Nevertheless, the film deserves serious attention, and not only because it affords an almost unique example of an attempt to market commercially a filmed adaptation of a non-Shakespearean Renaissance play. (Alex Cox's recent *The Revengers Tragedy*[2] and Derek Jarman's *Edward II* are the only other instances that come to mind.) Ironically, the key to the film's most serious interests lies precisely in its vulnerability to ridicule. My student's reference to Scooby Doo, however facetiously intended, spoke truer than perhaps she knew, for the stress throughout Patroni Griffi's adaptation is on the childlikeness of Giovanni and Annabella and the extent to which their actions—and indeed those of Bonaventura and Soranzo as well—are rooted in a not too distant childhood: when Giovanni gives Annabella his dagger with the instruction to "Strike home," we are indeed aware of the extent to which experiences are rooted in the home. Once more, then, the effect of adapting a Gothic text is essentially de-Gothicizing: here, it is not the psychological which configures humans but social and material pressures. It is true that the play allows for this to some extent—Hippolita objects to Annabella not only because she has replaced her in Soranzo's affections but because she is from the merchant class[3]—but the film insists far more strongly on it.

This emphasis is illustrated in many ways. Bonaventura is no father-figure to Giovanni, but his contemporary and peer. He, Giovanni, and Soranzo were all childhood friends, albeit clearly across a class barrier — Soranzo teases Bonaventura by calling him "Your eminence" and a "stableboy," just as Florio tells Putana to remember her place — and Soranzo at least wants to continue this relationship. He sends for Bonaventura to visit him and asks "Giovanni, surely you'd *like* me as a brother-in-law?" and when he marries Annabella, he says to Giovanni, "May we always feel as real brothers together." Similarly, Annabella's father reproaches her, "You act as if you've been weaned only three days ago," and the relationship between Annabella and Soranzo is repeatedly presented as different from that between Annabella and Giovanni because it is less gamelike: Annabella asks Soranzo, "Why do you call me by name, I'm no longer a child," and he tells her that "The time for playing is past" and that "It's about time you began behaving as a woman and not a child." When Giovanni jealously tells Annabella that Soranzo must be "one much cleverer in devising night-games than two innocent children as we were," he again measures the distance between the two relationships, as does the very different nature of the music, lyrical for the scenes between Giovanni and Annabella and more mannered and patterned for those between Annabella and Soranzo.

The most important consequence of this stress on play is that it drains the guilt from the incest, presenting it, in effect, as a regrettable but understandable perversion of treasured, innocent childhood games; even the close seems like a ritual, when Annabella bares her breasts and holds Giovanni's hand as he strikes, recapitulating their earlier pledging of their love, their hands joining over the dagger as he lays it down. In a significant development of a hint arguably but not certainly present in Ford's play, Annabella literally does not recognize her own brother at the beginning of the film. In the play, this may be explained by the fact that she is looking down on him from above, but in the film she gets a clear, head-on view of him and nevertheless asks, "Who is that boy?" Her attendant replies, "Your brother, Giovanni, back from his studies in Bologna," and Giovanni echoes the sentiment when he says to Bonaventura, "My sister? I don't know her. What I know now is a woman. Have you seen her? A goddess before whom I must kneel." If Annabella and Giovanni have not seen each other for so long that she literally does not recognize him and he regards her as something exotic and strange, the stage is set for what has come to be known to modern science as genetic sexual attraction: people who are closely related to each other but are unaware of the fact may well experience a strong sexual attraction. To understand the affair of Giovanni and Annabella in this light is to make it a tragic fluke rather than any kind of systematic exploration of incest in general, and of course any element of shock is further dissipated by the fact that the audience knows full well that Oliver Tobias and Charlotte Rampling are not brother and sister, nor do they even look alike.

If this Giovanni and Annabella come together primarily as strangers, however, their relationship is structured by their shared family past. They pledge their love not only by their mother's grave, but actually at it; moreover, the grave is adorned with lifesize statues of their younger selves, made out of a pure white substance which clearly symbolizes purity and innocence. Later, when Annabella has married Soranzo and left, Giovanni finds comfort in addressing this younger version of himself, whom he calls "little Giovanni"; immediately afterwards, he wishes that Annabella would remain "My sister and no-one else's." Though he twice tells her "Don't call me brother. Call me love," in a tone of increasing irritation, their relationship does in fact remain fundamentally underpinned by the brother-sister bond, not least in the fact that Giovanni bosses her about like a brother. Just as the three young men are all visibly renegotiating their relationship as they pass into adulthood, so too are Giovanni and Annabella.

If the dynamic of the personal is thus so strongly marked, what about that of the social? It is often suggested in critical readings of Ford's play that we are inclined to excuse the two lovers because we see how corrupt the world around them is. A parallel can be drawn here with *Romeo and Juliet*, to which the play is clearly indebted: Putana and the Friar echo the Nurse and Friar Lawrence, and Bergetto's mistaken death is structurally similar to that of Mercutio. Romeo and Juliet can be seen as innocents in a guilty world, and film adaptations of the play have often been keen to stress this: both Zeffirelli's and Baz Luhrmann's versions, as well as *West Side Story*, cast young, beautiful actors as the central couple and consistently point up their difference from the age or the decadence of those around them.

The original version of *'Tis Pity* can certainly be seen as operating very much within this paradigm of innocent lovers in a guilty world. Putana, Annabella's "tut'ress," thinks nothing of condoning her charge's incestuous affair as long as it does not become public knowledge; Florio plays fast and loose with her suitors; Grimaldi murders Bergetto and is protected by the unabashed nepotism of the Cardinal; Soranzo is himself an adulterer, and his cast-off mistress, Hippolita, is not only an adulteress but a would-be murderess. Adaptations of the play, however, have traditionally omitted most if not all of these characters. The version shown on BBC in the 1970s cut the Bergetto subplot, and Angela Carter's short story, retelling the story in the style of the film director John Ford,[4] pares the characters down to the bare minimum to heighten the introverted, claustrophobic feel of a couple who, in a small and isolated society, become a world in themselves. Patroni Griffi's film similarly strips away all those characters who create a sense of a wider society or community. There is no Bergetto, no Philotis, no Poggio, no Hippolita, no Richardetto, no Grimaldi, no Cardinal, no Donado, no Watch, and no citizens; even Putana is presented primarily as the mistress of the household rather than as Annabella's own particular companion, and Vasquez, who is not named, is reduced to a vaguely sinister presence, whose menace derives principally from his resemblance to Boris Karloff and who delivers Soranzo's invitation and kills Putana. There are, however, two areas in which the social background sketched in the original play is developed rather than deleted in the adaptation. The wedding and the final banquet are attended by numerous members of Giovanni's and Annabella's family, including their maternal grandmother — Soranzo instructs the Vasquez-figure, "Let not one member of her family survive" — and indeed Florio hands Soranzo a knife with which to stab Giovanni once the incest has been revealed. Similarly, Bonaventura, instead of being a solitary religious figure, is a monk and a member of a monastery. Omitting names, he recounts the lovers' predicament to his superior, who pronounces both the advice that Annabella should marry Soranzo and the Cardinal's final verdict — unchanged, except in grammatical "emendation," from the original play — "Who would not say 'Tis a pity she's a whore?"

Although both these additions bolster our sense of the size and power of both the family and the church, they do nothing to fill in the picture of society as a whole; indeed, if anything, they seem to suggest that there is no influence exerted on the characters by anyone not connected to them by relationship or residence. Moreover, the adaptation has gone still further in cutting the narrative adrift from the social — and hence political — moorings deftly but firmly suggested by Ford. Ford set his play in Parma, a city under the domination of the Habsburgs, who had institutionalized incestuous marriages between uncles and nieces as a means of consolidating and maintaining land and power within the family.[5] Patroni Griffi, however, blunts the force of this powerful if silent juxtaposition by transferring the setting to Mantua, the city to which Romeo had been banished (though, in fact, we learn of the location in only a single throwaway reference). In a further move away from the Parma of the original, Soranzo, finding his new bride unresponsive to his sexual advances, decides to take her to Venice. Though this location is signified for us by little more than a sight of water, boats, and a landing quay, we are nevertheless invited to register it as significant by the fact that in this new environment Annabella, in a further departure from the original, fully capitulates and begins to find Soranzo an acceptable and indeed a welcome lover. In the original play, Soranzo is in fact associated with Venice; we see him alone in his study perusing Jacopo Sannazaro's encomium to Venice and comparing it unfavorably to the depth of his feelings for Annabella; to transfer the action there is thus not without textual warrant, but nevertheless it further dilutes any sense of a single city whose customs and atmosphere exercise a decisive control over the lovers. The play is even robbed of its temporal as well as its geographical location when, in yet another departure from the original, Soranzo swears that the pleading of the king himself would not induce him to spare Annabella. In the original play, it is the pleas of angels which Soranzo claims he would be able to disregard; the change to a king subtly but unmistakably positions the play in the brief historical window of a post-unification, pre-republic Italy. While this period of Italian history is by no means devoid of interest of its own, it is certainly a long way from the complex politics of the Renaissance city-states of which Ford, in several of his plays, showed himself to be, for an Englishman, unusually knowledgeable.

The single remaining reference which might seem to point us suggestively back towards the dominant concerns of seventeenth-century Italy is Annabella's line "Thus men have died in war." This seems to echo the troubled political situation sketched in the original, in which Grimaldi has, it seems, recently been able to distinguish himself in war, leading to Putana's reflection that a soldier is likely to make a bad husband since his potency will probably have been impaired by war. However, any sense that Annabella's remark may refer to actual, recent combats is likely to be undercut by the fact that it is apparently prompted by one of the film's least realistic, indeed surreal, images: a close-set forest of flagpoles from the tops of which flutter white sheets, which could, it seems, be anything from the washing to symbolic representations of the sheets exhibited after a wedding to prove the virginity of the bride. These flagpoles are, moreover, merely a few of the notably tall or straight objects in the film which, individually and certainly cumulatively, take on a clearly phallic significance. We certainly seem invited to read the many scenes of plunging, galloping, or copulating horses in such a way — our earliest introduction to Soranzo is Putana's assurance that "He's as randy as a stallion," and we first see him on horseback—and to notice the contrast between their freedom and the societal constraints placed on the humans, a point made with particular force when Annabella and Giovanni discuss their predicament in a formal rural seating structure which both contains and immobilizes them, in a manner reminiscent of the trap-chair in Ford's companion-piece *The Broken Heart,* while their horses are untrammeled behind them.

Indeed, phallic symbols are everywhere in this play. Appropriately enough for Italy, the roads are generally lined with pollarded poplars, emphasizing their length and straightness, an effect that becomes even more striking when Bonaventura, having finally renounced both Giovanni and the monastery, is seen walking away down a long, straight road between poplars. His decision to depart has been carefully contextualized for us, having its origins in his superior's decision that the pregnant Annabella should marry her suitor, at which, presumably mindful of his childhood friendship with Soranzo, he interjects, "But what about the suitor?" After his protests prove unavailing and he is told that the Church demands unquestioning obedience, he tells Giovanni, "I'm never going back to the monastery.... I'm going to beg for me and my brothers. I'll be more useful to the community that way." After this swingeing indictment of the role and efficacy of religion in the society depicted in the film, Bonaventura declares his intention to sever all ties with Giovanni, and the next time we see Bonaventura he does, indeed, refuse to acknowledge his erstwhile friend; he simply strides on down the road, taking no notice even when Giovanni throws dust in his eyes. This suggestively echoes the original play's numerous references to both involuntary and deliberate blindness, not to mention the title of another, more oblique modern film adaptation, Stephen Poliakoff's *Close My Eyes,* which is also paralleled in Soranzo's words to Bonaventura at the close, "Don't shut your eyes."

This striding through the open landscape also provides a telling contrast with the many images of enclosure and constraint elsewhere in the film, in which open skies and vistas are repeatedly played off against confinement and restraint. Although the Italy of Renaissance drama seems so often to be envisioned as a place primarily characterized by heat and passion, what Patroni Griffi's film presents is unequivocally love in a cold climate: outdoors, the characters' breath condenses, the trees are all bare of foliage—indeed the opening credits roll over scenes of the bare branches of wintry trees—and rooms invariably contain blazing fires, which seem to serve the dual purpose of connoting both passion and the need for warmth. But if outdoors is inhospitable, indoors is confining, for the film repeatedly emphasizes doors, barriers, and cages. The lovers play in a birdcage; the jealous Soranzo pursues Annabella through doors like a husband in a French farce. When Bonaventura tells Giovanni to take to his room, the camera follows him as he does so, and we see him watching the fire, which, appropriately enough given its emblematization of forbidden passion, burns in a fireplace shaped like the head of a lion; later, a fire blazes by the bed on which the lovers have just slept together for the first time. The repeated juxtaposition of fires and windows, the latter paned or barred, becomes a *leitmotif* of the film, accompanied by frequent and pointed use of candles: Giovanni has a table full of candles in his room, the lovers plight their faith in front of their mother's tomb and beside a mound of lit votive candles; Soranzo holds Annabella's arms behind a candleholder; and the fatal banquet at the close, although it takes place in daylight, shows a large white candle lit on a table in the middle of the rows of diners. This both contributes to the stress on the use of artificial lighting, which in turns heightens the sense of interiority and containment, and also serves to accentuate the length and straightness of the room. This transforms it into yet another of the film's long, straight paths, and we are surely invited to contrast Giovanni's manic march down the long, straight corridor, bearing aloft his sister's heart, with Bonaventura's quieter, more purposeful trek away from the monastery.

These scenes provide only some of the film's many striking visual contrasts; though it may have sacrificed much of the language of the original, it has compensated by using the visual potential of cinema to explore themes, juxtapositions, and oppositions (as well as using the swelling, romantic score to create and enhance mood). Bonaventura's bid for freedom, for instance, affords a marked contrast with Giovanni's voluntary confinement in the well and with his final walk to his death: when Giovanni is down the well he ignores the pleas of Bonaventura and when Bonaventura walks away he ignores those of Giovanni, but the difference is that Bonaventura has a path marked out before him, while Giovanni has literally nowhere to go. This fact is further emphasized by the bleak opening shot in which Giovanni stares blankly at the screen and says "There is no more to say," which, together with the long pause that follows, creates the feel of closure and ending rather than of a beginning. Mood and rôle shift are conveyed by the strong emphasis on costume and dressing—Giovanni carefully dons a white suit to court Annabella, and we are powerfully reminded of Oliver Tobias's previous incarnation in *The Stud* when the camera lovingly picks out the swaying of his buttocks as he walks towards his sister. That the white here may suggest his last moments of freedom from guilt is perhaps implied by the fact that as soon as the relationship has been consummated, he switches to a red cloak as he and Annabella romp around the bed, while she, by contrast, changes her earlier red dress for a white one; finally, the inscrutability of his motives in the scene in which he kills her is signaled by the fact that his face is concealed beneath a wide-brimmed hat. Moreover, the scene immediately following the consummation forms part of still another contrasting pair, for although we see the sibling lovers romping round the bed, we never see them engaged in actual sexual activity; indeed, the numerous references to game-playing and the emphasis on the extent to which Giovanni and Annabella's relationship is rooted in their childhood invite us to see the innocence in their sex-play as much as the guilt. By contrast, the eventual rapprochement between Soranzo and Annabella includes overtly erotic activity, providing the film with its sole (and rather tenuous) claim to feature in the same series as *Venus in Furs* and *Vampires with Whips*. Here, again, the film seems to capitalize on the resources of its medium to signal interpretative interventions: the striking unusualness of the camera angles in these love scenes — at one point our viewpoint rotates through 45 degrees — seems to suggest that it is the relationship between Annabella and Soranzo which is exotic and strange, while what characterizes the relationship between Giovanni and Annabella, initially at least, is precisely its normalcy and its grounding in the customary and familiar.

Soranzo is also associated with the film's most sustained and striking visual patterning, into which many of its images and contrasts fit: imprisonment. Giovanni's period in the well, the barred windows, and the general emphasis on interiority all obviously form part of this, as does the scene in which the lovers play in a birdcage and that in which their strained posture in a baroquely artificial seating structure is contrasted with the liberty of the horses running free behind them. When we first see Bonaventura, he is weaving some sort of enclosing contraption of ropes, and after Giovanni jumps down the well, we see Bonaventura carrying a caged bird to a huge dovecote; the wall behind Giovanni's bed has a pattern of stripes, and his window is gridded, while the window behind the bed on which he and Annabella consummate their love has a trellis pattern, and bars are even suggested by the vertical lines of the hair which falls over Annabella's face. The lovers' father first mentions marriage to Annabella as they stand by the gridded end of a cloister, and she waves the ring he gives her through the grid to taunt Giovanni. Giovanni watches through columns as Soranzo courts Annabella, and while they are being married, he paces up and down between columns. The marital bed in Venice has bars at its head, and Venice as a whole is suggested by columns and by the piles driven into the canals. After discovering his new wife's infidelity, Soranzo makes the metaphor of imprisonment literal as he pulls her arms back behind a stone candle-holder set into the floor (neatly alluding at the same time to the imagery of light and candles); later, although he has (unlike his counterpart in the original play) survived the final holocaust, Soranzo is seen with his neck in a collar — echoing the leather studded collar around Giovanni's neck when he kills Annabella — his back strapped to a board, and his torso in an extraordinary wicker cagelike object which may or may not be a form of splint or support, but which certainly suggests that, although he may be alive, he is hardly free. Finally, blood makes straight vertical stripes down Giovanni's chest, and his corpse is borne beneath rafters which make a further pattern of stripes. Though this film of skies and vistas ends with a red sky which may indeed seem to promise a new dawn, it also closes on an image of fire and of a silhouetted tower, suggesting, ultimately, that as long as humans continue to be consumed by the fires of passion, the openness and emptiness of the landscape cannot prevent them from making prisons of their own.

These prisons have, though, been clearly constructed as social rather than psychological. This is most strikingly suggested by a particularly significant departure from the play, which is to make Bonaventura not only the direct contemporary of Giovanni but also someone who is at least as trapped as his friend. Ford's friar is a self-sufficient and apparently independent figure who is able to cut his losses and walk away from Giovanni without either worldly penalty or lack of faith; Patroni Griffi's, by contrast, is left with no option but ostracism and beggary. What we have here, then, is less a troublingly Gothic view of an uncertainty at the heart of all society than a detailed examination of the workings of one particular society at one particular time — and it is quite clear that what causes the trouble in the world of the play is not any universal impulse, but a specific set of cultural practices.

Mary Shelley's Frankenstein

Kenneth Branagh's version of *Frankenstein* takes a rather different attitude to the past from the nervous sense of remoteness shown by so many eighteenth-century adaptations. For all its nineteenth-century trappings, it simply assumes that *Frankenstein* is obviously and effortlessly updateable to the twentieth century. In the opening sequence of *Mary Shelley's*

Frankenstein, to give it its full title, the voice of Mary Shelley speaks to us out of a blank screen, uttering a short section of the preface to *Frankenstein*, which recounts the genesis of the novel. The moment is brief, but it is also telling, for it stages a number of contests for authority.

The first of these concerns naming. The nomenclature of *Frankenstein* has always been problematic, for though Victor Frankenstein is the eponymous hero of the novel, popular usage has expropriated the name "Frankenstein" and bestowed it on the otherwise nameless monster. Indeed memory and popular culture have made very free with *Frankenstein* in general, adding on Igor and a bolt through the neck and taking away the Monster's ability to speak, and it is doubtless to distinguish its own practice in this respect from that of previous adaptations that this film calls itself *Mary Shelley's Frankenstein*. In the same moment that it gives Mary Shelley an authorial voice, however, it also implicitly disables the power and scope of that voice by keeping the screen blank. Shelley's power lay only in words, rather than in the visual possibilities of film, and thus, it is implicitly suggested, the film itself surpasses her (especially since Branagh, who has learned a thing or two about directing since he first started, makes use here of a number of neatly ironic visual juxtapositionings—Victor unpacks as Elizabeth packs, after his mother's death he screams "Bring her back" and we cut to Elizabeth performing the same actions that Caroline used to do, and soon sparks literally fly between Elizabeth and Victor). We are thus firmly reminded that, as with any adaptation, the film is indeed as much Branagh's *Frankenstein* as Mary Shelley's, especially since Branagh plays Frankenstein as well as directing. But the situation is also inflected by the fact that the voice of Mary Shelley is recognizably provided by Helena Bonham Carter, the film's Elizabeth, who will have some sharp critiques of Branagh's Victor to offer as events unfold.

A further complication arises from Branagh's turn to sources other than Shelley herself to supplement the events of the narrative. In particular, the tearing out of Elizabeth's heart and the repeated references to her and Victor as brother and sister unmistakably evoke *'Tis Pity She's a Whore*, especially since the death of "their" father is announced immediately after the removal of Elizabeth's heart. (Clerval's warning that Victor will imperil his soul also aligns him with Bonaventura in Ford's play.) This is by no means an inappropriate association for Mary Shelley since Ford was an acknowledged influence on her fourth novel, *The Fortunes of Perkin Warbeck*, as well as on the fiction of Lady Caroline Lamb, sometime mistress of Byron and therefore a figure of whom the Shelleys would have been well aware. (The heroines of Lamb's novels all have names taken from

Ford's plays.) Nevertheless, it does add yet another layer to the already vexed question of whose version of the narrative this is.

This is an issue which also surfaces elsewhere in the film. Branagh's valiant attempts to fund films have often been bedeviled by the necessity of using big-name Hollywood actors as box-office draws; there was, for instance, much negative response to the presence of Keanu Reeves as Don John and Michael Keaton as Dogberry in *Much Ado About Nothing* (though American actors who could actually act, such as Denzel Washington as the Prince and Robert Sean Leonard as Claudio, escaped censure). This time, there is a bad moment towards the beginning when Captain Walton (played by American actor Aidan Quinn), on his first sight of Frankenstein, demands "Who the hell are you?" No early nineteenth-century English gentleman could have asked such a question of a stranger. Shelley's original certainly didn't, and the fact that the question is in the script at all, and said in such tones, points firmly in the direction of the American cultural influence which is the indispensable concomitant of American film financing. This influence also makes itself felt in other ways. When a student called (of all things) Schiller, who never appears on any other occasion, bumps into Victor and Clerval in the streets of Ingolstadt, nineteenth-century students are suddenly and inexplicably confronted by that distinctively American twentieth-century phenomenon, the jock. The contrast is made all the sharper by the fact that we have just witnessed the positively eighteenth-century wig of Robert Hardy (comically, for a British audience, playing much the same rôle of the conservative and disapproving older practitioner that he did in the popular vet series *All Creatures Great and Small*). Clerval (played by Tom Hulce, eerily reprising his previous foray into the past as Mozart in *Amadeus*) is also much closer to the twentieth century than to the nineteenth-century image of a medical student, with his principal aims being to have lots of fun as a student and then make lots of money afterwards; moreover, he has an American accent. There is also the wildly improbable idea that Victor and Elizabeth's wedding ceremony, rather than following the standard format, is "personalized" with special vows about the revealing of the truth—not to mention the fact that *she* has proposed. Most comical of all, to a British or European viewer, is the scene in which we are asked to believe in a Swiss crowd forming a lynch mob. The Swiss, famous for efficiency and neutrality, are not really given to such behavior.

In this film, however, modernities of all sorts abound. Events and language are modeled not on what was likely to have occurred within the frameworks of the society in which they are set, but on practices which are assumed to be familiar to the viewer. Of course, it could well be objected that *Frankenstein* itself spectacularly fails to be bound by the rules and norms of its own society. However, that would not be entirely just, for as the preface's explicit reference to Erasmus Darwin and the text's implicit engagement with Godwinian theory make clear, *Frankenstein* is a novel rooted in the philosophical theories of its day; indeed it could never have been so menacing if it had not been something more than pure fantasy. Many of the casual modernities of the film version, though, serve to dislodge it from the nineteenth century without adding anything useful from the twentieth century. Victor's mother, with more verve than syntax, tells him that he is "the most wonderfullest boy in the whole world," which displays an insensitivity to the rhythms of nineteenth-century prose similar to Walton's brusque opening gambit and his ungrammatical question to the captain, "What do you suggest we do? Lay down and die?" When Caroline dies shortly afterwards (in cinema time), her gravestone (which is, ludicrously, not in a churchyard) bears the name "Caroline Beaufort Frankenstein," a coupling of maiden and married names which would have been unthinkable then (I am well aware of the complex history of Mary Shelley's own nomenclature, but no version of it resulted from such a practice as this). In similar vein, scenes of formal dancing such as one would not be surprised to find in a Jane Austen adaptation jostle uneasily with a hideously graphic scene of a blood-bespattered birth, and the appearance of Helena Bonham Carter hovers nervously between eighteenth-century grande dame and louche punk. (This juxtapositioning will be pointedly played with when Victor dances with the hideously reconstituted Elizabeth.) Victor imagines heart transplants, finds that acupuncture provides the key to reanimation, and describes his creation in thoroughly modern language as having "massive birth defects." Despite all the use of period detail and though the very title of *Mary Shelley's Frankenstein* ostensibly flags its authenticity, the film does not so much attempt to bring the past to us as fail to recognize that the past is the past at all.

Along with this goes a failure to respond to the original genre of the novel, Gothic. This film is not nightmare but science. We see far more of Victor's experiments than we do in the novel, and they clearly proceed along rational principles: when the disembodied hand grasps Clerval's, Victor presses the switch and says "Now this must work," and it duly does. Moreover, not only is there no independent confirmation that Krempe is right to dismiss Paracelsus, Albertus Magnus, and Agrippa as charlatans, but the Leonardo drawing in Waldeman's study and Waldeman's own insistence that what he does is based on Chinese medicine and acupuncture provide a perfectly legitimate pedigree for the kind of work he and Victor undertake (the fact that Waldeman is played by the comic actor John Cleese also precludes much suggestion of the sinister). When Victor compares what he's doing to vaccination and heart transplants and tries artificial resuscitation on Waldeman, what we see is not a Gothicized hero-villain but simply a medical practitioner ahead of his time. Even the Monster's behavior is more rational than in the novel: he kills William because the locket, which contains a picture of Victor rather than, as in the book, one of Caroline, identifies him as a member of the Frankenstein family; and although this is not spelled out, it seems that he leaves it with Justine to frame her, rather than because of any emotional impulse. Victor's behavior towards women is also noticeably different from that in the book. There, it might well seem that Victor's reluctance to make a female monster is as much pathological as rational and arises from the same concealed uneasiness that makes him at least as eager to flee from Elizabeth as to marry her. Here he *does* make a female monster, which completely disposes of any idea that he might not be able to do so. Moreover, the fact that the Monster makes an appointment to meet Victor on the Sea of Ice makes it clear that the appearance of the Monster there is not in any sense a product of Victor's imagination.

The fact that Victor is thus much less incriminated than in the novel (he had, for instance, no opportunity to prevent the death of Justine) further means that, although the Monster is more sympathetically treated than in any previous adaptation, there is essentially neither polarization nor uncanny doubling. In the novel, the crowd in Ireland which has previously seen the Monster subsequently mistakes Victor for him;[6] that could never happen in the film. Indeed, the stress throughout is on the continuity between the Monster and the other characters rather than on any differences: after Caroline's death, Victor's father howls just as the Monster has been doing, and it is also notable that although the Monster generally retains the rhythms and diction of the Augustan prose which characterizes him in the novel, this is jettisoned when he advises Elizabeth, "Don't bother to scream." Even he is thus ultimately conceived of as being able to switch effortlessly between the vocabulary and registers of today and those which prevailed one hundred and seventy years ago, for all the world as if there were no difference between the two.

In Branagh's film, then, one of the most celebrated Gothic novels of all time paradoxically ceases to be Gothic at all and becomes instead a rather trite parable about overwork and the potential dangers of science. It has, it seems, a great deal to tell us about our own time—but it has lost any sense of what it might have meant in its own. At the end of the film, Walton—in flat contradiction of everything which happens in the novel—first invites the Monster to accompany them and then, when asked where they are going, says "Home." On this word, the credits roll, so we have apparently reached a satisfactory conclusion. There is no sense at all of what the novel knows so well—that home, the location of the *heimlich*, can be one of the most dangerous places of all.

The Woman in White

In its time, *The Woman in White* encapsulated a significant number of the most urgent of contemporary concerns, including some which had a particular personal force for Wilkie Collins: the subjects on which it touched included identity, illegitimacy, respectability, and the question of married women's property, all mediated through a pervasive awareness of the ways in which art could represent society. (It is not for nothing that the narrator is an art master.) What is really remarkable about the 1997 BBC version is that, with just a few turns of the screw, it proves equally effective at reflecting so many of our own contemporary concerns back to us, echoing both the plot of Michael Crichton's *Disclosure* and the recent disinterment of the French actor Alain Delon for posthumous DNA testing to establish paternity. In the process, though, it loses contact with its Gothic roots.

The adaptation does of course have to take liberties with the original text to produce this emphasis on the contemporary, and it is clearly targeted primarily at those who are not likely to know the original text. The video case (which is, appropriately enough, in shades of gray) bears beneath the title the words "Not all villains wear black." This makes no sense to anyone who knows the book—it is Glyde and Fosco who are the undoubted villains, not either Anne or Laura, who compositely make up the woman in white—but it neatly preserves the suspense for anyone who does not. Moreover, it not only maintains the idea of color symbolism which, I argue in the next chapter, dominates other Gothic adaptations, but also hints at a more than usually subtle approach to questions of rôles and identity. Therefore, although *The Woman in White* is marketed as part of the safely familiar tradition of BBC costume drama, as indicated by

The opening shot of *The Woman in White,* dir. Tim Fywell (BBC, 1997).

the leaflet inside the video case with Metin Hüseyin's 1997 *Tom Jones* and Simon Langton's 1995 *Pride and Prejudice* on the cover, we had better be on our guard. It is particularly ironic that the brief opening advertisement features the whole current range of BBC drama videos, arranged as if on an invisible shelf, with *Tom Jones* prominently pulled out at the front, as if it offered the closest comparison. In fact, *The Woman in White* epitomizes virtually the opposite approach to *Tom Jones,* for whereas that capitalizes on the audience's knowledge of actors' previous appearances to offer a recognition-led, typecast-like shorthand approach to characterization, with Squire Western as the apotheosis of an already well-established Brian Blessed persona, Benjamin Whitrow reprising his ineffectual patriarch from *Pride and Prejudice,* and Lindsay Duncan playing Lady Bellaston much as she had the Marquise de Merteuil, the effect in *The Woman in White* is quite different, and one can never be sure who anyone is.

Identities are repeatedly blurred and confused. The adaptation opens on a white memorial angel and crisscrossed lines which might at first represent wire rather than the leafless branches which we soon afterwards see them to be. Then we see a woman. In the novel, Walter Hartright is the narrator; here, Marian, rather than the vapid Laura, is unequivocally presented as not only the heroine but the central character. Tara Fitzgerald, who plays Marian Fairlie, gets top billing and supplies the opening voiceover, which begins, "The bad dreams always come back again. . . . Normally, people who are dead stay dead."

Initially, this promises to set up the classic Gothic ambiguity of whether the events which we are about to witness are fully parts of external reality or the product of a disturbed psyche and also links to another ambiguity, in that we are unsure of the identity of this woman — whether she is herself the woman in white or whether that title perhaps belongs to the shiningly white angel being worked on in front of her by the monumental mason or to some other figure altogether. Moreover, our uncertainties are compounded by the soundtrack, which mixes weird, distinctively modern instrumentation with vocals more reminiscent of plainsong or religious music. The combined effect epitomizes the competing expectations of natural and supernatural explanations, accounts of events grounded in social critique or those grounded in the arguably eternal dualities of the psyche.

Issues of identity continue to puzzle us as we see the figure of Hartright (Andrew Lincoln) walking up a drive and watch him from behind. The use of a following camera is a classic technique of the horror genre, and when Anne Catherick (Susan Vidler) is suddenly seen wearing what looks remarkably like a shroud, our suspicions about the nature of events may well seem to be confirmed. We soon see that we cannot afford to be complacent, however, when the strange woman demands, "You don't suspect me of wrong, do you, sir? Why do you suspect me of wrong?" Very probably many viewers *do* suspect her of wrong since the words on the video case have virtually instructed them to do so; but her question makes us see that we have no substantive grounds for our suspicions. This will prove to be merely the first instance of a characteristic technique of this adaptation, which lures us temporarily to think ill of a number of characters in turn, though we are sometimes forced to revise our opinion. Everyone has a secret, and even the most respectable of characters runs the risk of suddenly appearing in quite a different light. The camera's following of Hartright is almost immediately echoed by its similar following of Margaret the maid, focusing initially on her buttocks in a way which not only invites us to ask who she is but also, by reminding us of the ways in which the camera's gaze is so often sexualized, insinuates a question mark over Hartright's gender identity as well as over his role.

In some ways, as in our initial introduction to her, many of these ambiguities are crystallized in the person of Anne Catherick herself, the eponymous woman in white; indeed she overtly offers herself up as a focus for other people's fantasies, asking Hartright, "Do you want to tell me, sir, what to do?" In the vicinity of Anne, identities prove troublingly liable to blend and merge, as when Laura Fairlie is first seen in white, apparently attired as a bride, prefiguring the eventual exchange of the two women.

Even more tantalizingly ambiguous than Anne Catherick, however, is Marian Halcombe. In this adaptation, her very identity is fundamentally uncertain, for she has been transmuted into Marian Fairlie, sharing with Laura a father instead of a mother. Moreover, her most centrally defining attribute has been taken away from her, for Tara Fitzgerald is not ugly. Arguably, she is prettier and more stylish-looking than Laura, and though here, as in the novel, Marian describes Laura as an angel and herself as the opposite, what is much more apparent here is how similar they are, which again blurs the polarities typical of the Gothic. Marian Halcombe, perhaps the most fascinating woman in nineteenth-century fiction, never looked like this. Nor did she act like this: like Clarissa in the 1991 BBC adaptation, this Marian has been sexualized in ways her original creator could never have dreamed of.

Our awareness of the complexities of the adaptation's representations of its characters is considerably heightened by its own self-consciousness about art and its representations of society. Mr. Fairlie's fey connoisseurship, with its emphasis on aesthetics and close examination, is presented through the classic shot-countershot technique of static conversation, but the camera circles round the two men rather than staying still, thus suggesting that even the apparently simple may prove to possess complexity. This conversation is also the prelude to Marian's remark, "My sister and I are so fond of Gothic novels that we sometimes act as if we were in one" (once again raising the question of the relationship between external events and internal perception), and Hartright's agreement that they have the perfect setting for it. Shortly afterwards, when the two sisters discuss Laura's marriage and the future and we see them only in silhouette, thus being unable to read their faces and experiencing them merely as dark, opaque outlines, we may well be tempted to agree that we are indeed in a Gothic novel. But Gothic novels have one major characteristic which this adaptation does not share: they are utterly unselfconscious about their status as Gothic. The adaptation's announcement that it is Gothic is therefore of itself sufficient to disable any claim it may have to belonging to that genre, much as a lucid dream cannot turn into a nightmare.

Questions of representational style are even more explicitly raised when Marian and Hartright gaze together at a Rossetti portrait of Elizabeth Siddal and discuss his disinterment of her until they are interrupted by the sound of Anne Catherick screaming outside. (One might note that the adaptation as a whole favors the rich palette of the pre-Raphaelites rather than the grays and whites which the case of the video version seems to prefigure.) The allusion to the pre-Raphaelites draws further attention both to the Gothic nature of the story's style and to the centrality of Anne's secret to its content; but, in one of the adaptation's typically abrupt switches of tone and focus, our attention immediately turns not to Anne's secret but to Hartright's, as, through Marian's pained eyes, we watch him and Laura fall in love. Moreover, having openly announced to Hartright that she has discovered his secret, Marian goes further and reveals that she has one of her own: in the classic language of the Gothic, she has an "uncanny" feeling about Glyde. Again, the effect of this is ostensibly Gothic but is in fact not so at all: *uncanny* (or, in the original, *unheimlich*) was the word which Freud later applied retrospectively to the Gothic rather than any mark of its understanding of its own condition, and its use thus bespeaks not only the genre marker but, once more, a belated self-consciousness which had no place in any of the original works of the genre.

A similarly de-Gothicizing effect is created by the fact that in this adaptation, it is not only the villains who are sinister. Indeed, secrets seem to proliferate everywhere. When Mr. Fairlie meets Mr. Gilmore, what we initially see seems to be a scene familiar to all the best traditions of BBC costume drama, in which two immensely distinguished classical actors (Ian Richardson and John Standing) engage in conversation. But, as in our previous experience of Mr. Fairlie in conversation with the camera circling him, something unusual is going on, for as he talks, he gently caresses the crotch of a painted male nude, while at the same time dismissing Hartright as "not a man." Are we, perhaps, offered here a clue to *his* secret?

We are certainly given to understand, almost immediately afterwards, that Hartright has a sexual secret. The maid is clearly frightened by her nocturnal encounters, and to anyone unfamiliar with the plot, it may well begin to look at this point as if Hartright is the villain. In many ways, it could be said that the characteristic project of the Victorian novel is to probe interiority, by mapping the inside of not only the bourgeois home but also the bourgeois consciousness; here, though, we are repeatedly denied privileged access to the interiors of minds, and we may, indeed, even be led to wonder whether there is anything inside them which is consistent and coherent enough to be properly knowable. Laura's mind can be so radically destabilized by a change in her external circumstances that further action against her proves unnecessary; the same circumstances effect a change not only in Marian's social standing but also in her entire moral outlook. Since the whole idea of personality thus seems to be under pressure, it is no wonder that characterization seems troublingly insecure. Sir Percival Glyde (James Wilby), for instance, seems virtually perfect until his astonishingly abrupt transformation into an ogre.

One possible source of certainty might perhaps be the church, the building around which significant sections of the novel revolve. However, it proves to offer little comfort. Marian says suggestively, "I cannot get the shape of the church," and for her wedding in it, Laura is so veiled as to appear almost shrouded, an image which offers a significant contrast to our introduction to her, playfully garbed as a bride. Moreover, marriage itself seems to be not a sanctified state, but one of horror, with Laura changed beyond recognition and apparently turned into a Stepford wife *avant la lettre*. Marriage, teleologically the goal and ideologically the heart of so many Victorian novels, is in Wilkie Collins's tale almost overwhelmed by negative connotations: it reduces Laura to an inmate in an asylum and Countess Fosco to a puppet; it is violated by the late Mr. Fairlie and disregarded by the current one; the fact that his parents were not married haunts Sir Percival Glyde, while Marian, almost uniquely among Victorian heroines (although Trollope's Lily Dale offers another example), finds herself forever estranged from this all-important institution because of her ugliness.

For the Marian of the adaptation, marriage proves to be the entry to a world of virtual nightmare as Laura changes almost beyond recognition. When Laura does finally speak to her, Marian immediately exclaims, "Laura, oh Laura, it was a bad dream. Why would you not talk?" In Marian's eyes, marriage has silenced Laura. It is like a bad dream, but perhaps we should not forget that dreams are still the product of the psyche and may, in however perverse a sense, somehow express its wishes. Thus, the apparent transformation in the character of Laura, who moves so abruptly from virtual symbiosis with her sister to snubbing her completely, comes to seem even more alarming: since Sir Percival does not seem to have initiated the transformation, we must conclude that its origin lies in Laura's own wishes and that these are therefore not so predictable as we might have supposed. Once again, the entire concept of personality is under threat, introducing a staple motif of Collins's *oeuvre*, in which *The Moonstone*, for instance, is entirely dependent on Franklin Blake's seeming to act completely out of character.

The idea of the unstable personality is even more clearly marked in the scenes which follow. First, Marian asks Sir Percival whether she has offended Laura in some way; then Laura asks Marian what she herself can have done to Sir Percival. Moreover, in the ensuing conversation, Laura speaks to her sister in terms which startlingly juxtapose tombs and vaginas, clearly suggesting that marriage has, disturbingly, given her access not only to the place of birth but also of death. However novel they may be in some respects, however, there are some ways in which Laura's experiences after marriage worryingly echo those before: when Sir Percival, with astonishing suddenness, turns nasty, the previously sinister-seeming Count Fosco abruptly takes over his role as the ostensible voice of sweet reason. Simon Callow, who as Fosco abundantly makes up in bravura and brilliance for what, compared with his original in the novel, he lacks in weight, thus further robs us of any psychological landmarks we may ever have thought we possessed.

Eventually, Fosco too openly reveals his malice and duplicity. The occasion on which he does so aligns him, Glyde, and the male servants who follow them against Anne Catherick, Marian, and Laura, and at this point we may well begin to wonder whether wickedness is gendered; Hartright, after all, has already seemed to fall, Mr. Fairlie is clearly suspect, and, most damningly of all, mild, gentle Laura has said to Marian, "I have no evidence against my husband except that he is cruel. What is that? So are half the men in England." But although the housekeeper has apparently fueled this idea by telling Marian that only men ever see Anne Catherick, Marian immediately disrupts any such schema by seeing Anne herself, and our sense of predominantly male wickedness is further challenged by the advent of Countess Fosco (Kika Markham), whose existence has not previously been suspected (Fosco having been introduced in his own right as Glyde's cousin), as well as by the declaration of malice from Margaret, which, moreover, retrospectively exonerates Hartright. Equally, we are also invited to view femininity itself in a radically dual perspective when we watch Marian and Laura strolling across the lawn, outwardly two perfect embodiments of the proper Victorian lady, inwardly plotting subversion and sedition against the master of the house. Fosco may persevere in a comfortable sexism with his expression of the belief that when a criminal is "a resolute and highly intelligent *man* he will get away with his crime," but we can hardly subscribe to such platitudinous certainties. Indeed, Fosco challenges by his actions his own expressed attitudes: until the sudden arrival of his wife, his behavior to Marian is so attentive that we might well assume him to be courting her, and he speaks of the bond between himself and women in general. Even Sir Percival behaves at this point in a way which suddenly challenges both our sense of his wickedness and the sharpness of gender definition: when he questions Laura about Hartright, she falters, "I do not understand," and Glyde replies, "Nor do I; I never have."

Things become even less clear-cut after the break in the narrative caused by Marian's unconsciousness, which, because of our dominating sense of hers as the controlling intelligence, seems if anything even more cataclysmic a rupture here than it does in the book. We see a series of shots, taken clearly at night and lit in the lurid blue which is, I argue in the next chapter, characteristic of TV and film adaptations of the Gothic, which seem to represent Marian's consciousness, in that Hartright is, otherwise inexplicably, present in one of them, but also to show us what, we later learn, Marian could not have seen—a woman, who seems to be Laura, falling or being thrown from a tower. From this blue, nightmare sequence, Marian wakes wearing red—the other preferred color of the Gothic on screen—and thinking that all she has seen is a dream, only to find that Gilmore thinks her mad and that her place in respectable society is fundamentally imperiled, which is neatly emblematized when, as she rummages in Fosco's room, the camera swings wildly, just as the public perception of her now does. When Fosco disturbs her and, like Glyde before him, turns vicious with devastating rapidity and has her thrown out into the street, it is a blue world into which she is plunged; once again, she has entered a world characteristic of the Gothic, and with Fosco's slurring of her character, she has virtually changed places with Anne Catherick. It is no wonder that when she finds Hartright, she responds to his warning "I am changed" with "I have changed too," thus fulfilling the prophecy of Fosco (and also eerily prefiguring the language habitually used for Lucy in Bram Stoker's *Dracula*).

The first sign of this change is dramatically apparent when, after Hartright's initial refusal to help her, Marian openly attempts to solicit in the pub. This inaugurates a sequence of events which would have been quite inconceivable to Wilkie Collins, though their general tenor is by no means incompatible with the logic of his original design. Marian tells Hartright that something may be achieved "if we work together, as equals." Being a woman, she cannot even travel alone, as both she and Margaret point out; moreover, her sense of women's vulnerability is such that she wants to start the investigative process by targeting the women. Soon, though, she moves on to a more intriguing strategy, which involves simultaneously inverting sexual politics and, in a sense, targeting men as though they were women: reversing the tactics earlier used on Hartright, she tells the doctor that she will accuse him of sexually assaulting her. At first, the doctor hardly seems to mind and indeed almost seems to admire her resource-fulness. But as he talks, the dangerous comparison with Anne Catherick comes into play again: he first informs Marian, "[W]hen she was twelve [Anne] came to see me because she was morally degraded," and then adds, "[W]ithout the protection of your class, you'd certainly be on the streets yourself." Once more, the social indignation here means that we have left the Gothic far behind.

In keeping with this emphasis, Marian is actually in serious danger of moral degradation not as a cause of her visit to the doctor, but as a re-sult of it, for it shakes the founding assumptions of her moral code to the core. Hartright attempts to comfort her by saying, "[Y]our father did no greater wrong than many men," but, given the fact that the adaptation has earlier seemed to flirt with a possible gendering of evil, this is hardly re-assuring. Moreover, Marian not only does not believe him, but does not believe that the taint is confined to her father: if he is in fact Anne's father, too, then she herself has been lying and burgling not because she has been driven to it by the outrages of Glyde and Fosco, but "because it's in my blood."

If Marian's disclosure-like threat taps into some distinctively twentieth-century concerns, the adaptation also shows that it has not forgotten its nineteenth-century roots. Laura, imprisoned at the top of a building and staring blankly at Marian and Hartright without apparently recognizing them, recalls not only her strange behavior after her honeymoon but also Bertha Mason in *Jane Eyre*, and *Jane Eyre*, or at least Zeffirelli's adap-tation of it, is also echoed again when Marian has a blue-tinted dream of her father lying in a red-lined coffin. The red lining is reminiscent of the classic iconography of Dracula, while Anne's washing of her face in the same dream is strongly suggestive of the behavioral patterns associated with rape victims. Anne's secret does indeed prove to be that, at the age of twelve, Glyde had made her his mistress; as in Robert Young's *Jane Eyre*, we are clearly asked to recognize that what we are dealing with is child abuse. Indeed, Marian actually uses the word *abused*.

This heady mixture of modern and Victorian horrors reaches its cli-max in the exhumation of the father, a scene which recalls both Rossetti's disinterment of Elizabeth Siddal and our own preoccupation with DNA testing, as demonstrated by the 1997 disinterment of the man suspected of being the serial killer Bible John. In this reduction of the dead to the in-sistently physical, the church offers no comfort either; it becomes merely the place where Glyde burns to death, though we see that Marian is only inadvertently responsible since she did not know that there was no other way out and opens the door for him when she discovers it (only for the backdraft to kill him). The adaptation ends on an apparently happy note, with Laura "almost restored to full health," but as we revert to the opening shot of the angel, we may well have many unanswered questions about the soul, and a deep ambiguity hangs over Marian's closing remark, "Let it be over." The only comfort is that since the adaptation has placed its sense of the origin of human evil in social circumstances rather than in the psyche, we can indeed hope that it is over.

Lady Audley's Secret

Although it is undoubtedly true that Mary Elizabeth Braddon's *Lady Audley's Secret* belongs, strictly speaking, to the genre of sensation fiction rather than Gothic, it is equally true that it has many of the classic trappings of the Gothic novel. It is set in an old house, where a hidden passage leads from the nursery to my lady's boudoir in a way obviously reminiscent of passages such as the one leading out of the cellars in Ann Radcliffe's *The Sicilian*. Much emphasis is placed on the medieval past and Catholic heritage of Audley Court, firmly associating it with the historical period most beloved of Gothic fiction, and at the end of the book, Lucy Audley is immured in a *maison de santé* which is explicitly compared to a convent. In many ways, *Lady Audley's Secret* strongly and obviously reprises a novel with clearly Gothic affiliations, *Jane Eyre*. As in *Jane Eyre*, a character has a dark secret, bigamy, which they have committed or attempted to commit — though the dark twist here is that it is not the wealthy head of the old mysterious mansion who has committed the crime, but the young, innocent-seeming governess herself. Also as in *Jane Eyre*, a desperate woman sets fire to a building in order to burn alive one of its residents — but again the culprit is the innocent-seeming governess, who, terrifyingly, seems to have collapsed within herself the previously separate rôles of both tormented, murderous madwoman and respectable heroine set to rise through marriage and who thus raises wide-ranging questions about the nature of madness and sanity and of self, other, and society. Here the madwoman is not even in the attic, but sitting smiling on the chaise longue, foreshadowing the terrifying duality which will later prove to lie at the heart of *Dr. Jekyll and Mr. Hyde*.

Donald Hounam's Warner Sisters adaptation of *Lady Audley's Secret*, however, is having none of this. Hounam (abetted, presumably after the fact, by casting director Marilyn Johnson) has made a number of very significant changes to the novel which have entirely altered its original emphases. In the first place, and perhaps most strikingly, Braddon's conception of Lucy Audley has been completely transformed by the casting of Neve MacIntosh, who is a brunette rather than the blonde which Lucy Audley is so repeatedly said to be in the book. She is also not childlike but a tall, imposing figure who is always clearly in control of the situation and does, indeed, ultimately emerge victorious when Alicia Audley (Juliette Caton), in an act of pity and of sisterly solidarity, connives at her release from the asylum and leaves her free to embark on a new career of adventuring—this time as a blonde after all, although this is clearly for purposes of disguise rather than as any kind of signifier of innocence or vulnerability.

Most of all, the Lucy of the adaptation is no villainess but a rational and indeed basically benevolent creature who finds herself trapped by unjust social circumstances. She does make a genuine attempt to resist Sir Michael's proposal at first, rendering quite unjust George Talboys' cruel comment, "So I'm not the only one who's made a success out of gold-digging," when he is told that Robert Audley's uncle has married a governess. She is consistently concerned about her maid Phoebe: she is horrified when she sees the marks on Phoebe's arm and begs her not to marry Luke; she promises Phoebe that "I was very fortunate: I rose in the world. And with my help you can too"; she warns Luke that "If I hear that you are mistreating Phoebe, I—" and eventually offers Phoebe her old job back to enable her to leave him; and almost her last act while still at liberty is to give Phoebe a bracelet and instruct her to sell it to provide herself with finances. She is also genuinely kind to Alicia, pinching her cheeks to make her pretty for Robert, apologizing when she has shouted at her for letting George and Robert enter her apartments—"Don't hold last night against me. I was desperately over-tired"—and saying at the end "Let her stay. She should know about the world outside these walls" and "I should have been kinder to you." Despite her claim that she could not love her baby, Lucy is even an attentive mother: she has dreams in which she is distressed at having to leave the child and promises him, "I won't let you live like this." And she thinks of others too: her sarcastic remark, "You never told me that Robert had a social conscience," proves to be the prelude to her own determination to provide local employment— "The men need the work since Lord Cumnor gave up his improvements," which bizarrely imports a line directly from the very different and much more realist *Wives and Daughters*. She also fares much better than Robert in their exchange after the fire:

"Mr. and Mrs. Barkamb?"
"Don't worry. I bought their silence."
"That's not what I meant."

Robert may attempt to sum up events with "Lady Audley's secret. A pretty collection of self-interest," but in fact it is clear that self-interest is not only not Lucy's primary crime, but is also understandable, as we see when Alicia is reduced to crying, "What about me?" Lucy's awareness of the inequities of the class system is also clearly shown in her acid remark to Robert, "Many crimes go unpunished. How do you think the Audley family came by its estates?" We can surely only sympathize with such a woman; after all, as she herself says, "No hunted animal accepts his fate," and even the attempted murder of George turns out to be merely an accident—he overbalances and falls into the well, and she even thinks of helping him before apparently concluding that it is too late. (The fact that we see this, of course, also removes the element of suspense which added to the Gothicness of the original book.) Above all, we are aware of how trapped she is: her constant refrain, to Alicia, to Robert, to Luke, is "Get out," but we know that she herself cannot get out because we so often see her trapped behind doors. It is not a coincidence that the last scene takes place at a railway platform where "Way Out" is written in big letters.

In striking contrast to this newly empowered, socially aware Lucy is Steven Mackintosh's Robert Audley. In the book, Robert is gradually roused from his habitual indolence to become the nemesis of Lucy, dealing justice before settling down to marry Clara Talboys. What effects this transformation in him is perhaps unclear, and many readers may feel that it is best attributed to a fondness for George Talboys which, they may well think, verges on the homoerotic. No such possibilities are present in the adaptation, however, because here it is clear that, as Lucy herself points out, Robert's primary motive is his overwhelming desire for her, which he cannot fully admit even to himself. He keeps Lucy fully abreast of his enquiries, apparently as a way of exerting pressure on her; he exhorts her, "If only you would trust me," and, even more improbably, "I'm trying to save you. You disappeared before, you could do it again," so the clear implication is that he would forgive the murder of George Talboys if only she would sleep with him. He is so little the master of his fate that he even proposes to Alicia. This downgrades the rôle of Robert from that of an avenging angel to a pitiful representative of a corrupt, repressed, and shortsighted system. It is a suitably feminist statement for an adaptation made for a company named Warner Sisters, but it entirely drains the adaptation of any possibility of an overarching spiritual order in which characteristically Gothic concepts such as vengeance, fate, and damnation remain vividly possible, as they do in the original novel.

The idea that such things are not possible is, of course, a distinctively modern viewpoint rather than a Victorian one, and this adaptation is indeed distinguished by its modernity rather than by any attempt to recreate the society of 1862. Apart from the fact that she wears long dresses, Neve Macintosh's Lucy Audley could well seem to have stepped straight out of a suburban house near you, complete with distinctively contemporary fears, concerns, and language. For example, Sir Michael frankly insinuates that he may be infertile, and Lady Audley speaks of her hope that she will soon conceive, despite the fact that these phrases and episodes could never have found their way into any Victorian novel, the first because it was a term which did not exist then and the second because representation of anything to do with any of the processes of maternity was utterly taboo, as is made quite clear in, amongst other places, *Wuthering Heights* when there is no syllable spoken of Catherine Earnshaw's pregnancy or labor.

Equally modern in its emphasis is the perspective taken on the question of Lucy Audley's madness. In the book, Lucy claims to believe that she suffers from hereditary insanity. Robert Audley duly consults a doctor, who does not believe that Lucy is mad but does think that she is dangerous and therefore agrees to have her confined in a *maison de santé* where she can do no further harm and where her circumstances need never become known. Lucy herself fully expects to be locked up, and indeed Mr. Talboys senior thinks that she has escaped very lightly, accusing Robert of "having smuggled this guilty woman out of the reach of justice."[7] The film, however, represents the decision to incarcerate Lucy as the ultimate crime of a thoroughly hypocritical society, committed by a man who resents her rejection of him and another who is scandalized by her audacity in presuming to wish to lead a happy, comfortable life. For Hounam, it would seem that even if Lucy had succeeded in murdering George, it would have been no more than he deserved since he not only willfully abandons her, but also gratuitously punches Captain Maldon in the stomach. He is also, in a striking departure from the original novel, so indifferent to her fate that he has already secured himself a new partner, something at which even Robert is shocked. But then we surely know what George is from the moment that we see him in a flashback buckling a swash, just like Sergeant Troy in *Far From the Madding Crowd*.

In Hounam's adaptation of Braddon's story, then, there is no dark possibility of any taint of hereditary madness, no secret which merely becomes more mysterious the more is revealed, nor indeed any sense of the shadow of time and of the pastness of the past. There is only hypocrisy and cant, which, we are given to understand, worked in much the same ways then as they do now. For Braddon, the Lucy Audley of the novel might be seen either as ruthless survivor in a Darwinian jungle or fiend whose appearance in her portrait clearly indicates apocalyptic overtones, and indeed the tension between these two possible viewpoints provides one of the most energizing forces of the novel; but for Hounam, she is a protofeminist heroine who not only succeeds in casting off the shackles of society on her own behalf but also persuades Alicia to do the same—indeed Alicia effectively morphs into Lucy as she runs away from Robert. It is in some ways a positive and inspiring message, but it is one that seriously distorts the original novel and utterly obliterates any sense of the processes of history.

These are films of four texts which either were openly marked as Gothic or had strongly Gothic affiliations. But in them interest in social causes displaces the dark interior motives which both the Gothic and psychoanalysis habitually find to be the mainsprings of human action. Above all, in all of them, evil is firmly located in society or in the family rather than in the self. Branagh's Frankenstein is no selfish, half-crazed egotist whom we might even suspect of being the Monster himself, but rather a rational and well-meaning scientist who goes slightly too far. In 'Tis Pity She's a Whore, incest is the result of a household presided over by a compromised and venal father and of an introverted, stratified society which has left few alternatives. In The Woman in White, elements of the original Gothic conception do undoubtedly remain in the interest shown in dreams and the psyche and in the unexpected blurrings of one character into another, but nevertheless it is ultimately the unfairness and constraints of society that condition events, and here too are suggestions of family strains in that Laura's withdrawal from intimacy with Marian seems to be entirely voluntary. In Lady Audley's Secret, similarly, the source of evil resides not in Lucy but in the world outside her, and we are presented, not with the rock-like solidarity of the Audley family in the book, but with a resentful and rebellious Alicia and a Sir Michael who is well aware of Robert's potential conflict of loyalties as his heir. In their original forms, these texts were powerful explorations of the mystery and perversity of the human psyche, but on film they have become social tracts and indictments of patriarchal family structures, with only the most nugatory vestiges of Gothicness still clinging to them. Science, incest, and patriarchy—these, it seems, are things we think we know more about and understand better than our benighted forefathers, but the more rigorously we try to analyze them, the more their rich suggestiveness entirely eludes us.

| $\mathcal{F}$RAGMENTING THE GOTHIC
Jane Eyre *and* Dracula

Charlotte Brontë's *Jane Eyre* (1847) and Bram Stoker's *Dracula* (1897) both clearly signaled a debt to the Gothic tradition. Equally, all three of the adaptations I discuss in this chapter (two of *Jane Eyre* and one of *Dracula*) also deploy Gothicizing techniques. But I argue that, in doing so, they do not reinforce the Gothic elements of the original texts but, rather, subvert them, for whereas the original novels present the Gothic as an externalized menace confined to specific physical locations, these films regard it rather as a product of the psychology of the characters — and, above all, of the heroines.

Zeffirelli's *Jane Eyre* (1995) and the ITV *Jane Eyre* (1997)

The local radio station recently rang our department to ask if we had an English lecturer who could talk about the classics. The secretary helpfully offered to transfer them to a colleague who works on the cultural influence of Sophocles and Euripides. "Oh no," came the horrified reply, "we mean proper classics. You know, like *Jane Eyre.*" Though considered distinctly *im*proper in its day, *Jane Eyre* has thus, apparently, achieved paradigmatic status as the classic classic, and this is perhaps not inappropriate. Though fulfilling perhaps the first requirement of a "classic" by being unimpeachably old, it retains both popularity and accessibility, being particularly amenable to new critical approaches such as psychoanalytically informed and feminist readings which have offered it new voices. While clearly claiming its own place in a tradition inaugurated by Richardson's *Pamela,* it has also proved to be a seminal text not only in the development of the romance genre but in the inspiration of independent works of fiction such as Jean Rhys's *Wide Sargasso Sea.*

Above all, though, *Jane Eyre* is recognizably identifiable as a Gothic text. It has become famous primarily for motifs which have passed straight into the collective consciousness and indeed have configured subsequent paradigms of literary study—the madwoman in the attic being the prime example of this—and which are clearly Gothic in their emphasis on the idea of the riven psyche and the dark, lustful Other which lurks in the hidden chambers of the soon-to-be-ruined mansion. Together with the fire, the hint of unwitting near-incest posed by Jane's meeting with the cousins whom she does not recognize (one of whom does indeed propose marriage to her), and the clear presence of the supernatural in the shape of the voice which summons her back to Mr. Rochester, these elements combine to make this novel one of the greatest inheritors of the Gothic tradition.

Though the novel itself is so securely equipped with both a genealogy and a progeny, however, the various film and television adaptations of it which I discuss have much less clear points of origin. One of the most remarkable features of the 1943 Robert Stevenson film, starring Orson Welles and Joan Fontaine, is that it not only offers itself as an adaptation of the text, it effectively replaces it, at times even going to the extreme of actual rewriting. The original trailer (now re-released with the video version) shows a hand running along a shelf of "classic" books that have been turned into films (*The Grapes of Wrath, Gone With the Wind, How Green Was My Valley, This Above All,* and *Rebecca*) and explicitly presents *Jane Eyre* as another such book. The opening of the film itself continues this emphasis: we see a book whose turning pages bear the cast list. Then we see the first page of the book and both hear and see the words of the first sentence: "My name is Jane Eyre.—I was born in 1820." That dash is so perfect, so much in the true nineteenth-century style of punctuation; and yet the words themselves, as any reader of the book instantly knows, are *not* the opening words of *Jane Eyre*. To present them so insistently as if they were is to effect a strange mystification and falsification of the adaptation's origins; for all its anxiety to market itself as *Jane Eyre,* the film seems almost to find the real *Jane Eyre* an embarrassment which must be replaced. Perhaps we need to connect this with one of the other major changes the film makes, which is that Jane does not even attempt to fend for herself after her flight from Thornfield, but instead seeks shelter from Bessie. The fact that it is a woman's hand which ranges along the bookshelf in the trailer clearly suggests that this is a "women's film"; perhaps those women who might see the film without having read the book—and are thus likely to belong to the less educated and less leisured section of society—are not to be exposed to dangerous ideas about women's potential for self-reliance and economic independence. (One might also notice how often the camera angles, particularly when shot/reverse-shot sequences are used, stress that Jane must look up to Mr. Rochester.)

Though the Stevenson film is thus curiously ambivalent about its indebtedness to the book, both Franco Zeffirelli's 1995 film and the 1997 ITV adaptation of the novel make no attempt to conceal their own homage to the first screen version. Minimizing the preliminary skirmishes which lead to Jane being banished to the Red Room, all three of these retellings focus strongly on that initial horror and proceed all to adopt the same general structure and narrative line. More specific debts are also clearly marked. In both the Stevenson and the Zeffirelli versions, it is Helen Burns's hair which is cut, and in both cases Jane publicly protests (though Zeffirelli typically infuses the moment with a vigor and sensuality absent in the earlier version, having both Helen and Jane provocatively toss their luxuriant locks). In the ITV version, the dancing china dolls which Mr. Rochester presents to Jane recall the puppets with which Adèle plays in the Stevenson film. But there are also significant differences. In the first place, the older film was perforce made in black and white, while in the more recent versions color is not only an enhancement but, as I hope to show, of considerable thematic importance. And in the second place, these nineties retellings have been structured and reconfigured by contemporary concerns no less pervasive than the "little woman" slant of the forties.

Awareness of other contexts is created partly by the pervasive habit of recycling actors in classic adaptations. Ciaran Hinds, who appeared in the 1995 BBC version of *Persuasion* as Captain Wentworth and later stole the show as Bois-Guilbert in its 1997 *Ivanhoe,* plays Mr. Rochester in the ITV *Jane Eyre,* improbably marrying the Harriet Smith (Samantha Morton) of the ITV *Emma* after she has stayed in a house where the housekeeper is Gemma Jones — Mrs. Dashwood in Ang Lee's *Sense and Sensibility* — and has been looked after by Elizabeth Garvie, the Elizabeth of the 1979 BBC version of *Pride and Prejudice,* who here plays Diana Rivers. In the case of the Zeffirelli film, the doubling is even more marked. There is a striking overlap between the cast of his film and that of Roger Michell's 1995 adaptation of Jane Austen's *Persuasion,* almost as though Zeffirelli, whose previous attempts at adapting classics such as *Romeo and Juliet* and *Hamlet* have not met with universal critical acclaim, was seeking to compensate for his own reduced credibility with these actors' accumulated aura of "classic" prestige. Amanda Root (Anne Elliot in *Persuasion*) resurfaces as kind but powerless Miss Temple; Fiona Shaw (Mrs. Croft in *Persuasion*) is now widowed, unloved, embittered Mrs. Reed, suffering from her late husband's fondness for Jane rather as Mrs. Croft perhaps compared her own childlessness with her husband's pleasure in playing with Mary Musgrove's children; and Samuel West (Mr. Elliot in *Persuasion*) has metamorphosed into St. John Rivers, whose character, though the part has been swingeingly cut and altered from that in the original novel (where St. John is actually given the honor of the closing lines) still retains some of the unctuousness which marked his Regency avatar.

Indeed an unkind commentator might, perhaps, suggest that the Zeffirelli film of *Jane Eyre* actually bears a closer resemblance to *Persuasion* than it does to *Jane Eyre*. As always with Zeffirelli, of whom Ace Pilkington has recently said that "no modern director has a better claim to the dangerous title of popularizer-in-chief,"[1] much has been cut or rearranged, and the overall effect is to remove from the story all of the suggestion and indeterminacy so fundamentally associated with the Gothic and replace them with the schematic or with details which serve to anchor the story firmly in the realm of the social rather than the psychoanalytic. Jane's relations with the Reeds, the Rivers, Helen Burns, and Miss Temple have been reduced to the merest of sketches. Characters have been cut altogether, such as Diana Rivers,[2] Bessie, and John and Mary, or are merely glimpsed without being named, like Eliza and Georgiana Reed. Most strikingly, time has been telescoped in a number of instances. Helen Burns dies almost as soon as she coughs, and the Jane who rises from mourning at Helen's grave is a decade older than when we saw her last.

Later, Jane flees from her abortive wedding straight into an apparently passing coach, and Mr. Rochester has barely started to pursue her on horseback when he is called back by some harvesters with the news that the hall is burning; with similar compression, however, he does not have long to wait, for Jane returns to him as soon as she is well, with no intervening period of teaching.

Most striking of all is the extent to which, as the continuity of casting with *Persuasion* presages, Charlotte Brontë has been morphed into the woman whom she herself identified as her absolute opposite, Jane Austen. Even the setting is rich in Austen connections: much of the action was filmed on location at Haddon Hall in Derbyshire, halfway between Chatsworth (often thought to be the real-life original of Pemberley in *Pride and Prejudice*) and Bakewell (where Austen herself may have stayed). The Peak District is, admittedly, an area generally rich in literary associations—Matlock, mentioned in Mary Shelley's *Frankenstein*, is close by, and Haddon Hall itself is said to have provided the inspiration for Bly in Henry James's *The Turn of the Screw*—and amongst these are some

The young Jane at Helen Burns's grave in *Jane Eyre*, dir. Franco Zeffirelli (Buena Vista, 1996).

which are closely linked with *Jane Eyre* (a novel which is indeed openly evoked by the governess's story in *The Turn of the Screw*). The book's village of Morton was based on Hathersage, close to Haddon, and Eyres are represented not only among the tombs in Hathersage church but also in the several Eyre Arms pubs in nearby villages. Thornfield Hall itself appears to have been based on North Lees Hall in Hathersage, so Haddon is, despite the Austenian associations of its environs, by no means an unsuitable location for a Charlotte Brontë film.

In fact, this is the way that Zeffirelli's film works as a whole: details or moments which initially seem odd prove, on further reflection, to have an underlying logic or to be part of an overall coherence—but a coherence driven by very different and far more practical and material considerations than the dark imperatives which drive the Gothic. The untried and half-French Charlotte Gainsbourg, for instance, may seem an improbable choice for the very English Jane until one hears the ease with which she can speak French to Adèle. The phenomenon of French women playing Brontë heroines—Gainsbourg's Jane Eyre having been preceded by Juliette Binoche's Cathy in Peter Kosminsky's *Wuthering*

Heights (1992) — also echoes the sisters' own Continental connections, particularly Charlotte's crucial experiences in Belgium, as well as usefully reminding British audiences of the extent to which foreign interest in the Brontës has helped shape whole areas of perception of Englishness — as was recently underlined by the widespread panic caused in Haworth by Japanese tourists' threat to boycott it because they feel they receive an insufficiently warm welcome. It is perhaps salutary to look at the Brontës through other eyes, while the entire phenomenon of a half-French leading actress directed by an Italian and playing against an American costar (William Hurt) serves as a further guarantee that *Jane Eyre* is indeed a "classic," able to cross cultural divides as well as the intervening years.

It is not Gainsbourg, however, who is marketed as the film's primary draw: top billing goes to Hurt's Mr. Rochester. Some interesting things have been done to Mr. Rochester in this adaptation, presenting a marked contrast with Orson Welles's fiercely overbearing romantic hero. Jane's first encounter with Mr. Rochester comes through a painting of him as a child. The image underlines the film's strong interest in representing childhood and its perspectives: trouble has, for instance, been taken

Jane is transformed into her adult self in the Zeffirelli film.

over the portrayal of the young Jane, played by the Oscar-winning Anna Paquin, and our strong sense of sympathy for her is echoed in the fact that we are less aware of the frivolousness of Adèle than of the fact that she, too, is young, vulnerable, and sometimes at a loss in an adult world. A society acutely, tragically aware of child abuse has produced a *Jane Eyre* in which the experiences of children loom large, and the fact that our first introduction to Mr. Rochester is as a child is of a piece with that.

This impression of vulnerability in Mr. Rochester is maintained. It is of course merely in line with the novel that the first time we (and Jane) actually encounter Mr. Rochester, he falls off his horse and requires Jane's help to move, but other emphases are more distinctively the film's own. All of Mr. Rochester's teasing of Jane is cut; from the outset, we are aware that it is actually Blanche Ingram (played by an imaginatively cast Elle Macpherson, the supermodel) who is being manipulated by him, as his repeated protestations of poverty are seen to irritate her at a far earlier stage than that at which the Jane of the book, and through her the reader, is made aware of the comparable design. Thus, we never have a sense of Mr. Rochester as powerful or in control of events; after the fire, nothing but shyness or lack of self-confidence seems to hold him back from kissing Jane, which appears to be the outcome towards which the shot is inevitably leading, and he also clearly suggests genuine uncertainty over whether Jane will return to him from the deathbed of Mrs. Reed.

Most strikingly of all, there is no explanation to Jane after the wedding has been called off and he has finally revealed the existence of an existing wife, Bertha, nor even any real attempt to detain Jane (though admittedly he hardly has time for one); all he says is "I love you. Say you love me." Though the adaptation omits, unsurprisingly in the light of the current strong prejudices against male cross-dressing, any trace of the episode in which Mr. Rochester disguises himself as a fortune-teller, he is just as effectively feminized by these words since the demand that one's partner should verbalize love is, in our culture, so solidly identified as a female one. Similarly, when Jane returns, Mr. Rochester takes her to be a dream and merely says, "Before you go, kiss me," further underlining his passivity. It is also notable that, amongst the relatively small proportion of dialogue allotted to Mr. Rochester, he assures Jane that he is not naturally vicious and tells Bertha that he would never hurt her. For all that he puts a bullet through the brain of his rival for Cécile's affections instead of merely through his arm (or lungs as the Stevenson version rather gruesomely has it), Mr. Rochester, it seems, has become a New Man, and this softening and smoothing over of the original's wildness and potential for violence is further echoed in the toning down of his injuries, with only his eyes hurt and not his hand as well. A man who suffers passionately and has had a string of exotic-sounding mistresses with foreign names may be a stirring and exciting character to meet between the pages of a nineteenth-century novel, but in a film which has already reminded us so powerfully of child abuse, such actions would hover too dangerously on the edges of domestic violence.

It is doubtless for similar reasons of political correctness that the treatment of Bertha Rochester differs significantly from that of the book. The question of race receives only the lightest of touches in the film — Bertha's brother, Mason, seen only briefly, is a very light-skinned black, but Bertha herself is distinguished primarily by her pallor — and there is no mention at all of Bertha's nymphomania, nor of Rochester's assertion that he would continue to love Jane in such circumstances but cannot love Bertha. There is thus nothing in the film to direct our sympathies away from Bertha, and when we first see her, she indeed looks more pitiable than anything else, cowering close to the fire as if she is cold. Though we are left with no doubt that she is violent, it is by no means so clear that she is malevolent; it would seem absurd to hold such a creature responsible for her actions.

The taming of Mr. Rochester and the softening of Bertha are also in line with the overall image pattern of the film. There is a sustained series of alternating images of redness and of blueness which is established from the outset. The opening shot is unusually austere and has no title music; then a voiceover says "My parents died when I was very young" (another bold jettisoning of one of the most famous opening lines in the history of prose fiction), and the credits roll over a backdrop of unrelieved red, accompanied by the swelling, romantic theme music. To those who know the book, it is apparent that this represents the episode in the Red Room, but it is not actually named as such in the film; instead, typical of the ways in which Zeffirelli's film eschews any sense of the psychoanalytic perspective in favor of a resolutely materialist one, the emphasis is less on any psychological implications or supernatural resonances of Jane's sufferings than, in keeping with the child-abuse perspective, the viciousness, unjustness, and physical violence with which she is treated by the children and Mrs. Reed alike. We also see that the Reed house, although large, is bleak and unadorned, while the film is totally faithful to the novel in its presentation of Mr. Brocklehurst (John Wood), who, being lit from behind, does indeed look like a black pillar and appears almost as sinister to the viewer as he does to Jane in the book.

Mr. Brocklehurst removes Jane from the house with the Red Room in it and takes her to a blue world. All the tones at Lowood are cold and muted, signifying both its literal chilliness and its emotional coldness, and this phenomenon is particularly marked on the night of Helen Burns's death, when snow falls outside and all the events are seen in a harsh, cold, blue light. As well as signaling the coldest and wintriest moment of Jane's life at Lowood, however, this intense blue also marks the moment when we realize that she will remain unconquered by it, thus suggesting that material circumstances are only that and can therefore be fought by material means. Earlier, Mr. Brocklehurst threatened Jane with hell; this harshly dominating blue is the antithesis of that and, coupled with the snow, can indeed be read as emblematizing not only cold but purity and cleansing too. Moreover, Helen's death also becomes, in the visual logic of the film, the catalyst for change and growth in Jane, for when she rises from her friend's grave, not only has the film's palette changed to brighter, fresher colors but Anna Paquin, the young Jane, has been replaced by Charlotte Gainsbourg, the older one. In the same shot, we see the first flowers of the film: for Jane, spring has come at last. This change is further emphasized by the kindness and cordiality with which Mrs. Fairfax (Joan Plowright) welcomes her to Thornfield and by the very great contrast which is quickly marked between the cruelties of her own childhood and the sympathy and care offered to Adèle.

Not everything at Thornfield is sweetness and light, however. Though there are rich colors, a lovely landscape, splendid architecture, and beautiful gardens, all photographed with characteristic Zeffirelli lushness, Grace Poole (Billie Whitelaw) is a truly terrifying figure, and her charge also broods ominously over these scenes. Though the film does not really try very hard to present the concept of the madwoman in the attic, no doubt rightly concluding that the majority of the audience will be well aware of the solution to the mystery from the outset (and perhaps hampered by the fact that the main block of Haddon has no attic storey), it does not let us forget that there is something lurking in Thornfield which may well spoil Jane's idyll. Jane, teaching Adèle to draw, reminds her, "The shadows are as important as the light," and immediately afterwards she herself walks with Mr. Rochester through the deep shadows of the gatehouse before they re-emerge into the light. But we are invited to read this episode not only in terms of the ominous "shadow" of Bertha: what worries Jane is Rochester's neglect of Adèle; she tells him, "You should not treat a child thus" (a marked shift from the perspective of the book, which presents Adèle as too self-obsessed to be sensitive to neglect by others). His response to this, figuring Adèle in terms of her flirtatious manner, provides the film's nearest approach to the book's open dismissal of Adèle as not an analogue but a contrast to Jane. To Mr. Rochester, Adèle is not a child, but a miniature adult towards whom he happens to have certain obligations, and this makes her, as far as he is concerned, a direct parallel to the other woman for whom he feels himself responsible, Bertha. For Rochester, therefore, the "shadows" are less the stuff of Gothic nightmares than questions of the practical discharge of long-term commitments; moreover, his conflation of Adèle and Bertha implicitly posits the idea of character as innate and unshakably settled from an early age rather than as something dualistic or in flux.

The prosaic and radically un-Gothic nature of Rochester's preoccupations in this scene resonate both with the general toning down of both his character and Bertha's and also with the image pattern's implicit insistence that the cold of blue is not merely a contrast to the passion of red but may also represent a value in itself and that the value which it connotes is that of civilized restraint as opposed to the wild impulses of the psyche. Blue light begins to dominate at Thornfield when Jane awakes immediately before Bertha's attempt to burn Mr. Rochester in his bed. When she and he have extinguished the fire by throwing water on it and the red of the flames has thus disappeared, the light reverts to a strong blue, though there is also red on Jane's hands from the thorns on the roses, which she had picked up so that she could throw the water from their vase on the fire. The obvious symbolism of all this underscores very clearly that restraint, as well as passion, may have its charms. Though Jane may be shivering with cold and though we may feel that all the signals in this scene call for it to end with a kiss, the chill blue light of purity holds its own strongly against the red of blood and fire. While the film's careful downplaying of Bertha's racial identity suggests that it may have been reluctant to explore any issues of blackness and whiteness, redness and blueness do quite as well, it seems, to demarcate an absolute opposition between Jane and Bertha.

The pattern of red-blue opposition is continued with the introduction of Blanche Ingram (who, perhaps in a further attempt to avoid any suggestion of the wholesale demonization of dark women, is presented as a blonde). The overall impression of the drawing room, with Blanche standing spectacularly at its heart, is of a glowing red; marginalized in a corner, Jane sits alone on a sofa, wearing blue. In the book, the first hint that Mr. Rochester's sight is returning comes when he asks whether Jane is wearing a blue dress, and although that question is omitted from Zeffirelli's film, blue is strongly marked as Jane's color. Alone on the stairs with Mr. Rochester, she is seen in a blue light which darkens virtually to black as she is called on to help care for Mason, a scene during which, in a neat analogue to Jane's inability to fully understand events, we see only by glimmerings. Later, when she and Mr. Rochester first embrace, the camera picks out the blue of her cuff, and although Mr. Rochester says after the interruption of the wedding that Jane is "at the mouth of Hell," we remain confident that she will not actually enter it when she flees Thornfield wearing blue. Moreover, the color serves also to complete the presentation of systematic contrasts between her and Bertha, whom we see immediately afterwards setting fire to Jane's wedding dress and then jumping into the stairwell as though she were indeed plunging into Hell. Jane wears blue again when she recovers, both when she hears Mr. Rochester calling her and again slightly later when she receives St. John Rivers' proposal, and she is in blue yet again when she returns to Thornfield (which, in line with the overall muting of the film, is merely charred, and thus still habitable, rather than burned to the ground). Having steered a safe course between the extremes of temperature and passion, Jane Eyre can be happy at last, and as she and Mr. Rochester stand together in the meadow by the river (echoing the Reeds and Rivers imagery of the original novel), the growth and springtime promised when Jane rose from Helen's grave have finally blossomed into summer.

If Zeffirelli's *Jane Eyre* has affiliations with *Persuasion,* the ITV version, directed by Robert Young, comes closer to *Northanger Abbey* in its constant suggestions that what the heroine encounters in the various ancient mansions she inhabits may be the product of her imagination. (The other point of overlap with the *Northanger Abbey* adaptation, and of difference from the Zeffirelli, is that this adaptation clearly flags its status as television rather than film with frequent blankings out where advertisements can neatly be inserted.) The ITV adaptation has one main interest, the psychological, and one dominant characteristic. heavy-handedness. Sadly, the two all too often occur in conjunction.

In many ways, the similarities between the Zeffirelli and the ITV versions are striking; they even have "Jane Eyre" written in virtually identical cursive script on the tape cases. Once again, we see Jane being dragged to the Red Room before the opening credits have finished rolling, and here, too, we have no idea what she has done to deserve it; once again, Mr. Brocklehurst is introduced immediately afterwards and is again lit from behind; the shift from a child Jane to a grown one comes, once again, immediately after Helen's death, with Samantha Morton looking up from a pencil drawing of Helen. Helen herself, however, is much less securely defined in this version than in Zeffirelli's; she appears only briefly, and her death registers less forcibly with the viewer since it has been preceded by the sight of a girl of not dissimilar appearance who is dead of typhus and lying in a coffin. Indeed, the whole nature of Lowood is less deftly characterized here: though Jane *tells* us in voiceover that it is a terrible place, what we actually *see* is first the kindly face of Miss Temple and then Jane talking earnestly with Helen. Even the standing-on-a-stool episode has less impact than in the Zeffirelli film since it is featured not as Jane's cruel and arbitrary introduction to Lowood but, as in the book, as a response to her dropping her slate and disrupting the introduction of Mr. Brocklehurst's wife and daughters. Mr. Brocklehurst's action is still not reasonable, but it comes closer to being so, and there is no hint here of the gratuitous cruelty of the shorn hair.

The voiceover which gives us Jane's reaction to Lowood is a persistent feature of this adaptation, even at moments of tension such as that when Mr. Rochester first hints of his feelings for her. Unfortunately, it is an oddly distracting device for two principal reasons. In the first place, Samantha Morton's pronunciation is horrific: her renditions of *meager* and *vulnerable* grate almost as much as her appalling French later or as the hopelessly gung-ho St. John's declaration, "I didn't wanna distract you." In the second place, the adaptation is all too apt to use the words to do the work which film more usually accords to images: although it does at times share something of the red-blue patterning of the Zeffirelli film, with the red of the first fire contrasting with the blue light playing over the sleeping Jane, it has no consistent visual effects (and no hinting at a possible race issue — Bertha is just a white woman with graying black ringlets). Even the use of the red-blue contrast is undercut by the emphasis on the diegetic lighting provided by the insistent use of candles, which, in accordance with the suggestion of dreams, directs our attention to the characters' own limited perspectives rather than to the overarching directorial one. Perhaps its best trick is to flirt with blurring our perspective with Jane's own, which is done to considerable effect on two notable occasions. When Bessie enters the Red Room, we see her first from under the bed, where Jane lies asleep. Much later, our first view of St. John again presents him as if we shared the viewpoint of Jane, who is lying on the bed, once more asleep.

What is particularly interesting about these shots is that both are taken from Jane's perspective, yet she is asleep each time. Technically, she ought to be unable to have a perspective at all since her eyes are closed and her senses are, literally, dormant; the effect is, therefore, to present what we see as effectively a product of Jane's unconscious mind, her dream state. The same thing is suggested on many other occasions; the first of which is when Jane is locked into the Red Room. Though the room is not even particularly red in this adaptation, it nevertheless has an extraordinary effect on Jane's psyche: we hear weird wailings and see a corpse in the bed, but we are insistently aware that these may be products of Jane's imagination rather than reality. (There is a marked difference here from the Stevenson film, in which we see a door rattling and are shown some scenes where Jane is not present, leaving us in no doubt of their external reality.) This is indeed a technique which we might expect to find in the Gothic, but it is very oddly applied, for while the novel presents Jane's surroundings as Gothic and her own mind as resolutely moral, sensible, and practical, here these emphases are directly inverted so that it is Jane herself who is pathologized.

We are not, however, asked to judge Jane as solely neurotic, for subsequent events make it plain that she does indeed live in a world where strange things may happen. Though the Reeds are externally a much more secure and comfortable family here than in Zeffirelli's version, with an elegant house and luxurious clothes, Mrs. Reed (here played by Deborah Findlay) verges so closely on being unbalanced and hysterical that even Mr. Brocklehurst visibly registers the oddity of her behavior. This offers a considerable contrast with the grim, angular psychology of Fiona Shaw's Mrs. Reed in the Zeffirelli version, and the difference is accentuated by the fact that we do not see Mrs. Reed again. Bessie (not present at all in Zeffirelli's film) arrives at Thornfield and asks Jane to return with her, but the shot of her departure is followed immediately by one of her return. The suggestion of the lack of control in Mrs. Reed's behavior is, moreover, echoed by the sinister demeanor of Mrs. Fairfax outside the locked door to the West Wing; whereas Joan Plowright in the Zeffirelli version looks like a model of solid respectability who finds the whole attic business exceedingly distasteful, Gemma Jones's Fairfax hovers behind Jane like some noiseless supernatural creature. The script does Jones no favors, however: though her performance wildly outclasses almost every other one in the adaptation, she has her hands tied behind her back when she has to tell Jane, after Mr. Rochester has introduced them to Bertha, that she had no idea that the patient was Mr. Rochester's wife—which makes one wonder why she has been wandering around red-eyed for the last twenty minutes.

This is one of many instances where the film hammers home matters on which it would have done better to keep silent, as when the vicar helpfully informs us that Mr. Rochester's plan to marry Jane while Bertha was still alive would constitute bigamy and when Diana tells St. John not to bully Jane and he remarks with earth-shattering redundancy, "I know Diana thinks I'm a bit of a bully sometimes." Other moments similarly lay on their effects with a trowel: when Jane echoes to St. John a remark made by Mr. Rochester, she adds "I suddenly remembered something"; there is an inserted meeting with Blanche Ingram, whose reaction to the news of the wedding is clearly designed to clarify her character as a mercenary snob for anyone slow-witted enough not to have discovered as much before; shots of the wedding are repeatedly interspersed with the classic cliché of an urgently galloping horse; and after Mason's interruption, the wedding ring falls to the floor and, with blindingly obvious symbolism, stays there, neglected. All this makes one realize that Zeffirelli's far greater reticence was wise, for less really can be more.

The character who suffers the most from this lack of subtlety is undoubtedly Ciaran Hinds's Mr. Rochester. Like William Hurt, Hinds gets top billing and is thus obviously considered to be the adaptation's major attraction, and yet it hardly seems to know what to do with him. The case of the video version refers to him as "Mr. Rochester (CIARAN HINDS — *Ivanhoe, Cold Lazarus, Persuasion*), an impenetrable man with a mysterious past and harsh manner." This is a definition which comprehensively undoes itself, for the Mr. Rochester thus introduced to us is, in one sense, not a man with a mysterious past at all, but one whose history we are explicitly invited to track in terms of the most relevant and notable achievements on his CV. This lack of clarity is symptomatic of the presentation of Mr. Rochester throughout the adaptation. Our initial introduction to him figures him, like so much else in the adaptation, as essentially the product of Jane Eyre's imagination: she has just been saying that Thornfield is too tranquil when we suddenly see her standing beside a waterfall in a storm, with Mr. Rochester thundering towards her on his horse. The accident, too, is much more dramatic than in the Zeffirelli version, with echoes of Willoughby's first introduction to Marianne in Ang Lee's *Sense and Sensibility*.

These strong hints of Mr. Rochester as a romantic, elemental character are, however, not altogether endorsed when he begins to speak. In the first place, he is ungallantly furious, and in the second, he disorientates us with his misleading request to Jane to "Give my regards to Mr. Rochester." This comes much closer to the puckish Mr. Rochester of the novel than to the emotional correctness of William Hurt, and indeed the variations between the two heroes form one of the most significant areas of difference between the two adaptations; but though ITV's version of Mr. Rochester may come closer to that of the text, it is less successful in other respects. Ciaran Hinds may have made a very handsome Captain Wentworth in *Persuasion,* but here the addition of sideburns and the injudicious use of dye make him resemble nothing so much as Dick Dastardly, with matters reaching their nadir when he ill-advisedly dons a nightshirt.

Rochester's appearance, of course, need not necessarily matter since it is hardly an asset of his character in the book. Much more serious is the question of what he says. Here, too, he is too toned down to disguise himself as a gypsy, but he nevertheless retains much of his acerbity, accusing Jane of having sent a letter even to his dog Pilot (though it is, typically, made agonizingly plain that this is meant to be funny). Unfortunately, though, he tends to be funny even when he is not meant to be; this is the more or less inevitable consequence of dialogue like "Marry me, Jane?" "Me?" "Yes." "Why?" (There is an intertextual echo here with Roger Michell's *Persuasion,* in which Hinds's Captain Wentworth announces to Sir Walter Elliot that he wants to marry his daughter and is at once asked "Why?": once more, the effect is to stress Hinds's affiliations with things other than the Gothic.) We are hardly likely to think any better of him when he proudly presents Jane with a perfectly hideous pair of musical Dresden dolls and pleads, "Tell me that you love me. Go on. I want to hear you say it," before they too dance to the music made by the dolls. The symbolism is, as usual in this adaptation, abundantly obvious, but it has more to do with Ibsen than Brontë.

Even less Brontë-esque is the language of this adaptation. "Edward, you said you were going to let Grace Poole go," says Jane, as no nineteenth-century woman ever could have, before breathing piously, like a modern tabloid reporter, "Surely it's only a matter of time before a tragedy occurs." This use of neologism finds its darkest hour in the psychobabble which both Rochester and Jane start to spout after Mason's interruption of the wedding, beginning with the former's explanation, "I tried the best doctors; I sought alternative methods." (Aromatherapy? Reflexology?) He rants to Jane, "You were never in love with me. . . . You're no better than Blanche Ingram. . . . I thought you were mature" (a good slur coming from a man who has just thrown her bags downstairs). Jane quickly proves herself equally fluent in New Age self-discovery-speak, riposting, "You led me to believe you were one person but you are really another."

They are even more of the twentieth century than of the nineteenth in their frank discussion of sex. Rochester pants, "You want me — I can feel your passions are aroused — Say you want me! Say it!" What Jane actually says, though, is "How can I lie with you knowing that I am not your wife?" adding, in the true spirit of an advertisement for L'Oréal hair products, "I am worth more than that." To this, Mr. Rochester reverts to the psychobabble and angrily responds, "Do you think what we have is nothing?" An even more egregious instance of such language occurs when Jane returns after the fire (of which, as in the novel, we have had no prior notice) and, finding Mr. Rochester blind, soothingly tells him, "You are not your wounds." Actually, blindness is probably grist to her mill; she is quite likely disappointed that here, as in the Zeffirelli film, his hand is not damaged too. Virtually the only thing here which is in the spirit of the original is that Mr. Rochester still bullies and hectors her.

Though Jane may sound like the veteran of some depressingly formulaic counseling, however, she does retain a surprising amount of her original grit — in some ways more so than in the Zeffirelli adaptation. Though she recoils from the religion of Mr. Brocklehurst, she tells Mr. Rochester that she has "studied the Bible since and found my own faith in the Lord." Here, she sounds a genuinely nineteenth-century note, as she does again later when she lists her accomplishments for him because "it's a fact." Unlike the Zeffirelli version, this adaptation also retains Jane's post-betrothal independence of mind on the subject of clothes and presents, and, again unlike the Zeffirelli version, we have glimpses of Jane's suffering and endurance on the moors, of her teaching career, of her attempts to learn German, and of her serious entertainment of St. John's proposal of marriage and a joint missionary career. The only counterindications are that here, unlike in Zeffirelli's film, she gains neither fortune nor family: the Rivers family are not revealed to be related to her, nor does she inherit money from a long-lost uncle. But then, we are in any case less aware of the prevalence of fragmented families: Mr. Rochester here is warm towards Adèle, whom he affectionately *tutoies,* and the presence of Bessie joins with a less powerless Miss Temple to make us feel Jane's own orphaned state less poignantly.

If the Jane of this adaptation has a better developed sense of her own ego, however, she also unquestionably has a more pronounced id. Though she has not, in this version, cut her hand on the roses, she nevertheless has a sudden horror of giving it to Mr. Rochester and shivers uncontrollably. As in the Zeffirelli adaptation, she is lit in blue at this point; she also wears a blue dress the next day and is bathed in blue light once again when she hears the noises of Bertha's attack on Mason. At first, those noises sound like her heartbeat, and this suggestion that we are in the Gothic realm of the unconscious is further reinforced when Mason exclaims, "She sucked the blood from my shoulder like a vampire," while Jane's horror is clearly signaled when she hides behind the door as Grace Poole enters to check on Mason. All in all, the treatment of the whole episode hints strongly that we may, on one level, see these events as rooted in Jane's subconscious.

This is even more true of the proposal scene, in which Ciaran Hinds exhibits a roughness quite alien to William Hurt's postfeminist nineties man. We then cut to Jane asleep, as though the scene had been her dream rather than reality — as indeed she says she fears. The same technique is applied to the tearing of the veil: Jane stares sleepily as it is ripped, and we cut straight to Mr. Rochester saying "must have been a dream, Jane," which posits for Jane a psyche strikingly similar to that of Clarissa in the 1991 BBC adaptation. Even Mr. Rochester thinks he may be dreaming when he hears Jane's voice in his blindness. In choosing how to plot the fine line which the novel treads between realism and Gothic, this adaptation has clearly veered towards the Gothic, but it has done so unsystematically and without understanding that the Gothic works best when it has something to suggest about its society as a whole, rather than as a mechanical device used in isolation, in the absence of any compelling psychological or visual agenda, and all too often as a supposed shortcut to the inner workings of the female mind. The end result of these Gothicizing details is to fragment the sense of any dominant viewpoint or style.

These two adaptations, then, encapsulate virtually opposite approaches to the issues of adapting a classic Gothic text for screen. The Zeffirelli version exemplifies the idea that a text can be changed and updated if the reshaping is performed in the context of a coherent guiding project; it offers a *Jane Eyre* retold to address the concerns of the postfeminist nineties, an age ridden with guilt and fear about its children, and it controls both its retelling and its audience's response through a strongly developed visual pattern which substitutes well for the novel's manipulative tools of tone and pace. Above all, it understands that a classic was not always a classic; once it was new and *urgent,* and in order to feel the full flavor of its power, it needs to be made so again, which is what Zeffirelli does with his use of big-name actors, such as Elle Macpherson and William Hurt, who are strongly associated with highly contemporary cultural forms, and by tapping into distinctively nineties concerns. At the same time that Zeffirelli successfully reinvents *Jane Eyre* to speak to contemporary concerns, however, he must perforce sacrifice any sense of the meanings it may have had for its original audience, amongst which are its Gothic affiliations.

The ITV adaptation, on the other hand, illustrates the dangers of treating a classic text merely *as* classic since trying faithfully to reproduce its letter inevitably ends by foreclosing on its spirit. Moreover, the novel suffers from being treated not only as a classic but also as a celebrated romance, for where the ITV adaptation does update, as in its use of the currently popular language of feeling, it does so not in the realm of issues but of emotions, which are presumably conceived of as timeless and as transcending culture, with *Jane Eyre* merely being a particularly good repository of them. Since our own culture allows for more heightened expression of emotion and of sexual feeling, the language of passion is consequently injected into the story, presumably on the assumption that it had been there latently all the time and that to allow it be more fully heard is indeed to do the book a favor. But for those who believe in the shaping influence of cultures on psyches, what the ITV adaptation thus offers tells us nothing either about Brontë's society or about our own.

A Blue Inferno: Francis Ford Coppola's *Dracula* (1992)

Bram Stoker's *Dracula* is undoubtedly one of the most famous Gothic novels of all time, not only having injected new life into the Gothic genre but also having spawned an entire new subgenre of it, vampire fiction. Nevertheless, Francis Ford Coppola's film of Stoker's novel is, like the two versions of *Jane Eyre,* only selectively and intermittently Gothic. In the first place, it is an extremely personal film: Vera Dika comments that "*Bram Stoker's Dracula* (1993) is, paradoxically, very much Francis Ford Coppola's *Dracula*" and suggests, in particular, that the decapitation of Dracula at the close recalls the decapitation of Coppola's son Gio in a boating accident.[3] In the second place, it has added a number of new concerns to those found in Stoker's original novel: it clearly, for instance, reads vampirism as a metaphor for AIDS,[4] and it is also extremely interested in film history.[5] The result is that the film often comes closer to being a parable (Kenneth Jurkiewicz calls it "a New Age parable of free will, eternal love, and second chances gratefully taken" and proposes that its message is that "[t]here's hope for everybody, . . . even for an embittered centuries-old Byronic *Übermensch* with a bad attitude and an even worse drinking problem"[6]) than to being Gothic, and indeed Fred Botting declares, "With Coppola's *Dracula,* . . . Gothic dies, divested of its excesses, of its transgressions, horrors and diabolical laughter, of its brilliant gloom and rich darkness, of its artificial and suggestive forms."[7]

Critical response to *Bram Stoker's Dracula* was generally muted. The film certainly bestowed notoriety on Gary Oldman, who played Dracula, but it also inspired a short story which was printed in a centenary collection of *Dracula* spin-offs. The author, Kim Newman, says that the premise of the story "is what it would have been like if Francis Ford Coppola had made *Dracula* as one of his good films," and it is modeled on the "process of the making of *Apocalypse Now.*"[8] Instead of Keanu Reeves as Jonathan Harker, this fictional version stars Martin Sheen (who nearly dies of a heart attack during filming, although Coppola won't stop the camera rolling for it, and who is resuscitated by the vampire heroine Kate Reed) and Marlon Brando (who does endless method-inspired renditions of the same mumbled line, "I am Dracula"); it would have been filmed on location in Romania during the days of Ceaucescu, would have gone massively over both budget and schedule, and would have bled dry all those associated with it (sometimes literally).

Implicit in the writer's rationale for this story is that *Dracula* is *not* one of Coppola's good films. It is certainly a wildly camp adaptation, so drenched in postmodern irony that it is a wonder it doesn't drown in the sea of red bubbles which insistently represent blood. It is distinguished by a bravura performance from Anthony Hopkins as Van Helsing, who, although he rarely bothers to remember to put on a Dutch accent, nevertheless can't help but act his way out of every paper bag the script puts over his head, at one point answering Mina's pious enquiry about whether dear Lucy suffered much with the brilliant "Ja, she was in great pain, then we cut off her head and drove a stake through her heart and burned it—and then she found peace." And that is just a prelude to his chatty question to Jonathan, in front of Mina, "During the course of your infidelity with those demonic women, did you for one moment taste of their blood?" This entire dialogue, needless to say, takes place around the dinner table; indeed we cut immediately from a shot of the decapitation of Lucy to one of Hopkins's Van Helsing skewering meat. So comprehensively does Hopkins steal the show that Jörg Waltje has suggested that the film should be remade with Hopkins as Dracula.[9]

The ironic, complexly referential nature of the film is clearly signaled from the opening moments, which differ sharply from the analogous section of the book. (The film in general and from the outset flaunts the massiveness of its deviations from Stoker's original: there is, for instance, no excursus to Whitby.) It begins with a voiceover uttering the words "The year 1462" and the picture of a map, evoking parodic echoes of the famous opening of one of cinema's most celebrated love stories, *Casablanca,* as well as of Spielberg's habitual opening gambit in the *Indiana Jones* films.

(Sequences set in the past also open both of Stephen Sommers's later *Mummy* films.) This is followed by a battle sequence showing black warriors silhouetted against a red sky, which not only introduces the motif of redness but also appears to pay homage to Ralph Bakshi's unfinished cartoon version of *The Lord of the Rings,* which is not inappropriate given that Tolkien's trilogy has, as I discuss in the next chapter, numerous debts to *Dracula.*

However, this section, as short as it is, also declares another allegiance which is crucially significant in plotting the film: during this battle, the defeated are impaled. Coppola thus aligns himself with some modern researchers' insistence that the historical original of Stoker's Dracula was Vlad the Impaler. This is not the first time a film adaptation has made this suggestion — Alain Silver and James Ursini observe, "Reputedly, the first such link in a film adaptation was made by the Voïvode's old enemies in the Turkish production, *Drakula Istanbulda* (1952); but that film was never released in the West"[10] — but the connection is far more insistently developed here than it seems to have been in *Drakula Istanbulda.* David Glover notes that "Jonathan's . . . seduction by the Count's three 'brides' . . . reinforces Dracula's identification with the mysterious East, for it is modeled on the conceit that the influence of Turkish culture on Vlad the Impaler, following his youthful days in Istanbul, would have led him to keep a harem" and that "[t]he sense that sexuality is being produced through race . . . gains added impetus from the scenes at the country house at Hillingham which are intercut with the Castle Dracula episodes. . . . Hillingham too is an unmistakably orientalized milieu"; he concludes, "As the script slyly suggests, the journey 'through the magnificent Carpathian Mountains' takes 'us into the heart of Transylvanian darkness' (Coppola and Hart 30), and, if this is so, then Dracula's struggle to defend the West against the 'sensual Orient' has turned him into a kind of Kurtz."[11]

Moreover, allusions to Vlad the Impaler are not confined to the exposition, but are pervasive. At one point, Van Helsing reads a medieval account of Vlad Tepes, and the woodcut illustrating it blurs into a shot of Dracula in the same pose and looking strikingly similar. More significantly, Coppola has taken from the various stories told about Vlad the Impaler the legend that his wife, wrongly believing that he had been defeated and perished, threw herself into the river below the castle and died. This, in the film, is the fate of Dracula's beloved wife, who, in a further gesture towards the massive flurry of recent research on Dracula's origins, is called Elisabeta, the name of the "Blood Countess" Elisabeth Bathory.

The backstory is summarized in *The Lord of the Rings,* dir. Ralph Bakshi (Warner Bros., 1978).

The film also flaunts its geographical and etymological knowledge when, in a rather contrived exchange, Dracula explains to Mina how "The River of the Princess" came by its name.

Princess Elisabeta's suicide will cost her her soul, the priest tells Dracula, since it will inevitably ensure her damnation. His outrage at receiving this verdict both makes him determined to rise from his grave and also gives him his agenda, which is predicated on a virulent hatred of the church and all its signs and trappings. Although his fifteenth-century self had clutched a cross on the battlefield as he registered his victory, the nineteenth-century Dracula is horrified and vitriolic at the sight of a cross hanging round Jonathan Harker's neck. Although this is in line with the original, it proves to work to very different effect here. In the novel, Dracula is clearly and unequivocally aligned with the forces of evil, and his distaste for the cross illustrates this. In the film, however, Dracula comes not only to resent the symbols of Christ but increasingly to usurp and parody him: Renfield announces, "The master will come and he has promised to make me immortal"; as Dracula utters the word *blood,* we cut to Mina and Jonathan drinking the Communion wine during their Eastern

Orthodox ceremony; and Dracula offers Mina "life eternal, everlasting love." Most notably, he dies asking, "Why hast thou forsaken me?" adding, "It has finished," and as his head falls back it clearly resembles that of Christ. Moreover, as he dies, the candles light spontaneously, and a ray of light illumines his face, clearly and unequivocally affirming the existence of a divine power and suggesting that, ultimately, Dracula is redeemed. Our sense that Oldman's Dracula may contain elements of self as well as other is paradoxically reinforced still further by the sheer outlandishness of his appearance; the swollen outline of his head makes him resemble nothing so much as the aliens beloved of science fiction whose exaggerated cranial development is a signifier of their advanced mental powers. Perhaps this picks up on what Van Helsing, in the novel, says about the likely future development of Dracula's brain, but again it works to different effect, for here the iconography works subtly to reposition him as a figure of wisdom.

This is only one of the film's careful manipulations of our attitude towards Dracula himself. Most viewers will probably go into any modern

The backstory is summarized in *Bram Stoker's Dracula,* dir. Francis Ford Coppola (American Zoetrope Productions, 1992).

adaptation of *Dracula* thinking they know all about the story line, but in this version, their security in what they think they know is rapidly eroded by the counternarrative, which is heavily influenced by the research of Radu Florescu rather than that of Bram Stoker and offered in the opening moments of the film. Indeed the striking contrasts in the sequence of past and present Draculas could well be seen as analogous to the ways in which perceptions of the novel have changed over time, especially in a film which signals so clearly its awareness of the secondary literature on the text.

Many of the changes work in Dracula's favor. Harker is a stuffed shirt who fails to notice that when Dracula looks at the portrait of Mina, his shadow starts doing different things from his physical body, and who, according to Mina, pontificates that "it is a defect of the aristocracy that they say what they please." Indeed, Harker is presented primarily as stiff, lisping, and utterly ineffectual, having to be virtually forced into giving the eager, rather hussyish Mina a kiss at parting and priggishly reminding her, "We can be *married* when I return." His passive surrender to the three vampire women goes much further here than what is coyly suggested in the novel, and he seems to have little understanding of the true nature of his fiancée. He carries with him a miniature of Mina which may well be thought fundamentally to *mis*represent her as something far more staid than we ever see, although it does reveal the deep secret of Mina's identity to the rather sharper eyes of Dracula. Suggestively, there is much less apparent disjunction between the rather wooden, two-dimensional Harker and the matching miniature of him which Mina carries. The three suitors resemble nothing so much as the Three Stooges: the scene in which they are first introduced is played virtually for farce, with Seward tripping over the rug on his way in and falling prone at Lucy's feet and all of them collectively too witless to wonder whether there is anything odd about Lucy's quasinymphomaniac flirtatiousness, with Quincy Morris in particular appearing to be virtually a mental defective. When Renfield later warns Mina, "Get away from these men," he certainly seems to have a point.

Most notably, Van Helsing is a distinctly sinister figure who wanders around quoting Othello, the mistaken murderer of a woman, by muttering "It is the cause, it is the cause, my soul" and then laughs and who declares with ludicrous flippancy, "I just want to cut off her head and take out her heart." Our first sight of him comes as he is giving a lecture in which he puns on *civilization* and *syphilization*. Since this is something about which Stoker's novel itself all too obviously dared not speak, Van

Helsing appears almost as the voice of the text's subconscious, and his utterances appear to be even further privileged when he goes on to speak in quasinarratorial voiceover. For those familiar with the novel, though, alarm bells must definitely ring when Dracula addresses Mina as Madam Mina. Since this form of address is, in the novel, the exclusive preserve of the professor, the rôles of Dracula and Van Helsing begin to blur into each other at this point, and this is even further underlined when Van Helsing, meeting Mina for the first time, also greets her as "Madam Mina" and whirls her into a dance just as Dracula did moments before. Moreover, Van Helsing seems to share with Dracula the ability to move literally in mysterious ways, disappearing by apparently miraculous means in his attempt to convince his fellow Crew of Light members of the existence of the supernatural.

One reason why we might be tempted to make judgments about the characters which are very different from those offered in the novel is that the film is so much more reliant on the effect of purely visual impressions. To some extent, of course, this is inevitable, but it is also the result of an important difference between the novel and the film: the types of technology, and particularly technologies of replication, on which they focus. It has often been remarked that *Dracula* is a novel that is very interested in technology, but the technological innovations on which it focuses are primarily auditory or text-based: Dr. Seward's phonograph, Mina's typewriter, the telegraph service. Although, as Ronald R. Thomas points out, "*Dracula*'s appearance in 1897 came less than a year after London's Empire Theater began attracting capacity crowds to its sensational new diversion—Lumière's spectacular Cinematograph,"[12] Stoker's novel has little interest in the visual, and when it does focus on the visual, it does so primarily in order to concentrate on its failures and unreliability as a guide: Dracula casts no shadow and can both successfully impersonate Harker and alter his own appearance. The film, however, has very different allegiances, which are neatly emblematized in the scene in which Mina turns away from her typewriter to look at the dirty pictures in the *Arabian Nights*. Photographs, portraits, and visual replications of all sorts offer important clues: Dracula has a photo of Renfield, who went mad in Transylvania; as Dracula greets Jonathan, we see a picture of Dracula's former self and Jonathan asks, "An ancestor? I see a resemblance"; and while Dracula looks at the photo of Mina, his shadow acts differently from his body, a phenomenon which Ronald R. Thomas suggests is "perhaps evoking the crude technology with which early films produced the special effect of shadows on the screen."[13]

Perception also lies at the heart of the relationship between Dracula and Mina. The first time he sees her, he has taken the form of an animal and says "No — do not see me"; next time, he is his old self and says, "See me — see me now." The self-reflexiveness is confirmed when he further tells her, "I am only looking for the cinematograph. . . . I understand it is a wonder of the civilized world." First mentioned, appropriately enough, in a cine advertisement, the cinematograph becomes an emblem of living art that is potently contrasted with Mina's advice, "If you seek culture then visit a museum." The film self-consciously uses a number of extremely old-fashioned visual and camera techniques to offer almost a potted history of the development of cinema.[14] It is also highly self-conscious about its own visual style, which is strikingly different not only from the flat, functionalist, black and white of these miniatures and of the map of London and the woodcut of Vlad Tepes which we are later shown, but also from that of the cinematograph itself, which shows a jerky, fully clothed love triangle on flickering blue-toned film. Dracula, Mina, and Jonathan may represent a love triangle, but whereas the cinematograph's tone is purely blue, theirs, like Jane Eyre's, is a story told in shades of red and blue — a combination which of course implies a dyadic rather than a triadic perspective (but which equally disables a monolithic one).

All the opening scenes of the film are strongly tinted red, most strikingly the red and black silhouetting of the battle. (One of the few things which Kim Newman's fictional version of Coppola's film would have retained is this red opening and the blue flame.)[15] This strong stylization and the emphasis on the visual possibilities of the medium are of a piece with the film's overall self-reflexiveness and, in particular, its anxiety to present itself as stylishly foreign. Numerous touches underline this. The red and black serve to align it with one of the most passionate nineteenth-century love stories, Stendhal's *Le Rouge et le Noir* (which, like this retelling of *Dracula* itself, climaxes in decapitation). Foreignness is even more clearly stressed by Dracula's pronunciation of his own name as "Draculya" and by the translation of some of the dialogue into Romanian and the concomitant provision of subtitles. Even when the film is not stressing its fashionable Continental affiliations, however, its visual style is insistently mannered: this, it proclaims, is no Hammer Horror, but an art film. One such touch is the initial parting between Mina and Jonathan. As we view this from a distance, the tail of a peacock spreads across the lens, and we are suddenly looking not through the eye of a camera, but through the eye of a peacock feather — which, even as we watch, changes color from blue to red. It is a small moment, but it is, I think, one which is of considerable importance because it emblematizes not only the film's visual technique but its ultimate effect. The color transition signals a transition from London to Transylvania, as well as the suggestive use of an object which is either red or blue by nature but which, in this film, suddenly finds itself taking on the opposite hue from that which it normally has. In the same way, Coppola's film refuses to find Gothic elements where they were in the original, but does introduce them in other places.

The opening scenes of the film establish a pattern of a red-tinted Transylvania and a blue-tinted London. This is first indicated when the initial strong red of the opening Transylvania scenes abruptly gives way to a blue-tinted cityscape bearing the legend "London 1897." The first person we see, Renfield, who in this version had been Harker's predecessor as Dracula's agent, is also suffused with a blue light, as is his cell, and when we next cut from Transylvania, where Jonathan reads a red-tinted letter, to London, we see Mina in, inevitably, a blue dress. Mina, however, also introduces a motif of red to the London scenes (and presumably the red letter which Jonathan has been holding in Transylvania is from her): her lipstick is a lurid pink and behind her are two blue windows, each with a red shield in the center. She also looks at a blue and red pornographic picture in an illustrated edition of the *Arabian Nights*. She says "Uh — disgustingly awful," but when Lucy comes in, she finds the book and the two girls pore over it, with Lucy exclaiming that Jonathan ought not to be in Transylvania because "He should be forcing you to perform unspeakable acts of desperate passion on the parlor floor." The girls' knowingness is further emphasized when we soon discover that Lucy has been dreaming about the *Arabian Nights* and wants Quincy Morris in between her legs, leading into the high camp scene in which her three suitors make complete fools of themselves in front of the louche and laughing Lucy.

The fact that this scene, too, is tinted a lurid red further underlines the extent to which elements of Transylvania already form an unexpected and volatile core at the heart of ostensibly respectable London society. That the converse is also true is equally clear in the earlier scene in which Harker drives through a weird blue light, with wolves' eyes flashing blue all around him and blue fire leaping from the ground, to where Dracula holds up a blue lantern against his red-sleeved arm, as well as in the later scene in which he and Jonathan sit in a red room with blue light outside and Jonathan speaks of "some blue inferno." From then on, the initial oppositions dissolve, and the mingling of red and blue becomes the keynote of the film. While Jonathan is trying to escape through water, it bubbles red, and we shift to Jack talking about Lucy's blood. Later, a red-lit Mina talks over a split screen which shows her past and present selves before we cut to a blue Van Helsing preparing for a blood transfusion. Finally, Lucy eventually dies in a red shower before lying blue in her coffin.

No sooner has the initial pattern been established, then, than it is comprehensively reversed. In the original novel, Transylvania is the scene of heartlessness and horror only; in the film, it becomes the one place where we see a genuinely loving relationship brought to fruition. *London,* rather than Transylvania, proves to harbor Gothic horrors, and this is emphasized by the fact that however suspect Van Helsing and the Crew of Light may be, it is the London-based female characters who are presented in the most unfavorable light—literally so when, after a succession of night scenes and with the almost complete darkness of Renfield's cell followed by the wildly lurid blue and red of Jonathan's near-seduction, Mina and Lucy are suddenly filmed in daylight. The film is in general highly self-conscious: sets are clearly sets; special effects—most notably Dracula's head flying off—are obviously deliberately contrived in the great tradition of horror films rather than in state-of-the-art realism. We are particularly aware of the staginess and the brash Technicolor of the scene in which Lucy and Mina go outdoors in the garden. What should be ordinary is thus rendered extraordinary, an effect that is subtly stressed when, moments later, a storm sweeps across, lighting the two women much more kindly. It therefore seems hardly any wonder that they romp in it, though the indecorousness of their doing so is powerfully underscored by rapid juxtapositioning of their abandon with shots of Dracula lying asleep on the *Demeter,* lit in blue. The scene blurs into a quick succession of rapidly alternating red and blue images, which eventually crystallize into the somnambulant Lucy, vividly streaked with red and heading into the blue outside for the structural equivalent of the Whitby episode (though there is, tellingly in view of the general Gothicization of London, no indication in the film that the girls have left London).

In each of these three cases, then, an apparently Gothicizing film of an originally Gothic text proves to have inverted entirely the polarities of the original novel. In Zeffirelli's film of *Jane Eyre,* what is frightening is not the powerlessness and isolation of Lowood School, for even there Jane can still be defiant and find kindness; nor is it even the dark attic storey, for so little effort goes into building up any suspense in that area. Rather it is the stark horror of cruelty and abuse within the family. In Robert Young's film, by contrast, it is, as in *Clarissa,* the heroine herself who is Gothicized by the insistent suggestion of a psychoanalytic approach which presents Jane rather than her surroundings as the root cause of events. Finally, the uncanny suggestion that Van Helsing and Dracula are doubles rather than opposites helps Coppola's film present its eerie revenant as pitiable and heroic, while it is the ostensibly normal London surroundings which come instead to seem sinister. Once again, cinema has used doubling, psychoanalysis, and a stress on family structures to banish the Gothic from where we might expect to find it and introduce it instead where it had not been before.

Chapter Five | GOTHIC AND THE FAMILY
The Mummy Returns, Harry Potter and
the Philosopher's Stone, *and* The Lord of
the Rings: The Fellowship of the Ring

This chapter examines three very successful films which were wholly or partially pitched at children but which nevertheless deploy distinctly Gothicizing techniques. Stephen Sommers's original *The Mummy* had made no particular attempt to appeal to children, but *The Mummy Returns* featured an eight-year-old child and was accompanied by a novelization for children as well as one for adults; since its release, the characters and stories have been still further identified as suitable material for children by the launch of a *Mummy* cartoon series and comic-book annual. *Harry Potter and the Philosopher's Stone* was, of course, marketed for children from the outset, and it was perhaps partly on its back that *The Lord of the Rings: The Fellowship of the Ring,* which could well have been thought of as an adult film, was accompanied by so much child-oriented merchandise.

All these films tell stories which might, at first glance, seem wildly unsuitable for children or indeed directly calculated to give them nightmares. Nevertheless, all proved highly popular with family audiences. I argue that one reason for this is that, as well as peddling a fantasy world designed to seem safe and nostalgically appealing to parents, these films also offer children an imaging of something of crucial importance to them, the strains and tensions of family life. For all these films' emphasis on mummies, ghosts, and wizards, the real fears being explored are about what lies at the heart of the family.

Returning to the Mummy

On her arrival at a pre-election Conservative Party rally at the Plymouth Pavilion in May 2001, former UK Prime Minister Margaret Thatcher cracked a rare joke. "I was told beforehand my arrival was unscheduled," she said, "but on the way here I passed a local cinema and it turns out you were expecting me after all. The billboard read *The Mummy Returns*."[1] Predictably, this got a laugh from her audience. What, however, did she actually mean? The word *mummy* has two senses—an affectionate diminutive of *mother* and an embalmed corpse—and, depending perhaps on one's political affiliation, either might seem to be an appropriate description of Thatcher. Both possibilities seemed latent in British press coverage of the event. The *Guardian* seemed to incline to the former in its headline, "Tory matriarch goes on stage and off message," which posited her as a kind of monstrous mother returning to smother and stymie her hapless successor, William Hague, but the *Independent* quoted an unidentified former Tory minister as saying after the election "I wish 'the mummy' had stayed in her box. Every time she pops up, she costs us votes" (9 June 2001), where the reference to "box" seems to clearly align her with a corpse. It is, perhaps, suggestive that the generally left-wing, anti-Thatcher *Guardian* should think of her as a mother, while a former Tory minister, who might reasonably be supposed to be more in sympathy with her, should think of her merely as a corpse: is the mother actually more menacing than the embalmed body?

At first sight, this ambiguity may seem to be entirely absent from the film to which Thatcher was referring, Stephen Sommers's 2001 blockbuster *The Mummy Returns*, the sequel to his 1999 hit *The Mummy*, since the mummy in question is, in both films, male: it is that of the high priest Imhotep, condemned to eternal undeath after he murdered the Pharaoh Seti I because he desired the latter's mistress, Anck Su Namun. In fact, however, it becomes increasingly clear that the ambiguity is indeed present, for there is an alternative candidate for the rôle of the returning mummy, one whom the film arguably does at least on some level find more menacing than even Imhotep: the mother.

To some extent, the ambiguity was there from the outset. The souvenir film program for *The Mummy* lists "Jerry Glover's Nearly Top Ten Mummy movies." Glover's number 6 is the 1959 *The Mummy*, which, he observes, "spawned three sequels, proving that, along with Dracula, Hammer's heart belonged to mummy" (p. 31). Forty years later, the 1999 *The Mummy* showed clear signs that its allegiance is equally split between mummies and Dracula, for those familiar with the works of Bram Stoker could hardly fail to notice that Sommers's first film was, in many respects, a composite of *Dracula* and *The Jewel of Seven Stars*. The conjunction is an interesting one in many respects. It is notable that eight out of Jerry Glover's "Nearly Top Ten Mummy Movies" center, like *Dracula* and *Frankenstein*, on male monsters, and in recent years the trend towards co-opting vampirism as a metaphor for AIDS means that it is the sexual predatoriness of men rather than women that tends to be emphasized, making Stoker's male monster a culturally useful avatar. When Stoker wrote *The Jewel of Seven Stars*, though, Queen Victoria had only just died, leaving the memory of a long matriarchy fresh in people's minds, and the alarming figure of the New Woman, to which Stoker refers directly in *Dracula*, loomed equally large in the popular consciousness. Consequently, perhaps, both his mummy and four out of the five vampires we encounter in *Dracula* (as well as the pseudo-vampire in *The Lady of the Shroud*) are female, as was the first vampire to be encountered in the original version of the novel, Countess Dolingen of Gratz. If this film wanted to explore anxieties about gender, therefore, what better way than to draw on both of Stoker's kinds of monsters, his mummy and his vampire?

Given the fact that the film's central character is a mummy, the debt to *The Jewel of Seven Stars* is unsurprising. This had already been the inspiration, as Glover acknowledges, for *Blood from the Mummy's Tomb* (1971) and *The Awakening* (1980), not to mention Jeffrey Obrow's 1997 *Bram Stoker's Legend of the Mummy* and, subsequently, David DeCoteau's *Ancient Evil: Scream of the Mummy* (2000). Some of these show more obvious signs of indebtedness than Sommers's film, but nevertheless there are clear parallels between *The Jewel of Seven Stars* and *The Mummy*. In each case, the mummy of an accursed individual who hopes for resurrection is buried in a hidden grave whose occupant is identified only as "nameless." The inscription on the tomb of Imhotep is "he who must not be named," and Evie Carnahan O'Connell comments that the intention is clearly to destroy both his body and his soul—"This man must have been condemned not only in this life but in the next" (though this detail is also found in Universal's original 1932 *The Mummy*, to which Sommers's film pays clear homage). Similarly, when Corbeck asks about Tera's tomb in *The Jewel of Seven Stars*, he is told by the locals that "there was no name; and that anyone who should name it would waste away in life so that at death nothing of him would remain to be raised again in the Other World."[2] Moreover, in both *The Jewel of Seven Stars* and *The Mummy*, cats play a part in the story—in the case of *The Mummy*, this occurs in an episodic and ultimately unsatisfactory way which, in its failure to be logically integrated into the narrative, clearly suggests that an original source text has not been fully assimilated. (There was a cat in the 1932 *Mummy*, but it was Imhotep's ally rather than his enemy.) In both Stoker's and Sommers's work, the natives show a fear which is not shared by the explorers, but which in both instances proves abundantly justified by the fact that both tombs are booby-trapped. In both texts, too, a disembodied hand moves by itself, and the identity of a daughter proves to have been fundamentally shaped by an Egyptologist father. In Stoker's novel, Margaret Trelawny proves to have been radically affected by the explorations her father was undertaking at the time of her birth, while in *The Mummy* Evie owes her very existence to her father's passion for Egypt and his subsequent decision to marry her Egyptian mother. Even her employment in an Egyptological library is due to the fact that her parents were among its most generous benefactors. Finally, in each case, the reanimation of a female mummy is partially achieved and then abruptly aborted, leading directly to the death of at least one of the main male characters: in the original ending of *The Jewel of Seven Stars*, all but Malcolm Ross died, and in *The Mummy* Imhotep is distracted by the fate of Anck Su Namun and thus fails to stop Jonathan Carnahan from reading the incantation that makes him mortal and allows Rick O'Connell to kill him. (In *The Mummy Returns*, it is of course even more obvious that Imhotep owes his death directly to Anck Su Namun.)

That the attempt to create a female monster ultimately brings about the destruction of the male monster is, however, not a characteristic of *The Jewel of Seven Stars*, in which those who die as a result of this attempted creation are those whom we have by and large identified as "good" characters. This does, however, serve as a pretty fair description of both *Dracula* and its great avatar *Frankenstein*: in *Dracula*, it is the count's vamping of Lucy which first alerts the Crew of Light to his existence, and his attempted vamping of Mina then creates a telepathic link which allows them to locate and destroy him; in *Frankenstein*, Victor's refusal to complete the female monster leads ultimately to the deaths of both himself and the Creature, not to mention Elizabeth. There are also other crossovers in *The Mummy* which weave their way between *Dracula* and *The Jewel of Seven Stars*, most notably the scene in which Imhotep enters Evie's locked room in the form of sand, a clear emblem of affiliation with the desert, before metamorphosing into a man who bends down and kisses her as she sleeps, just as Dracula does with Mina.

Equally, though, there are some elements of *The Mummy* which appear to owe their genesis to *Dracula* alone. In *The Jewel of Seven Stars*, the alien being is female and, in an obvious parody of the contemporary popularity of "mummy" striptease acts, must submit to being stripped naked by the Edwardian gentlemen who have control of her corpse. In *Dracula*, however, as in *The Mummy*, these rôles are reversed because the monster is male and is poised to prey sexually on modern females —

as is made abundantly clear by the increasing skimpiness of Imhotep's costume, which culminates in a pair of briefs and a cloak for his planned reunion with his lost love. Moreover, the capelike cloak further reinforces the echoes of *Dracula,* as does the fact that the fleeing soul of Anck Su Namun clearly resembles a bat. Equally, Beni's attempt to deter Imhotep by holding up a crucifix might serve to align him with a vampire. (This is certainly how it is presented in Max Allan Collins's official novelization of the film.)[3] The way in which Imhotep sucks people dry to rejuvenate himself also directly parallels the way in which the count's blood-drinking causes him to appear significantly younger when Jonathan Harker sees him in London, and indeed the curse on Imhotep's tomb explicitly affirms that he will return initially as an "Un-dead." The shared name of Jonathan Harker (in *Dracula*) and Jonathan Carnahan (in *The Mummy*) functions as a further link between the two texts, as does Imhotep's ability to command the elements and predatory lower life-forms. Similarly, the idea of using a modern woman to resurrect an ancient one may be central to *The Jewel of Seven Stars,* but the specifically erotic inflection provided by the fact that in *The Mummy* it is not the dead woman herself but her long-lost lover who wishes to effect the resurrection is more reminiscent of Coppola's *Dracula* than of Stoker's mummy fiction. Also strongly echoing the basic situation of *Dracula* is the dearth of women in *The Mummy* and the subsequent fierceness of the competition over them.

Most interestingly, both texts share a fascination with Jewishness. As many critics have noticed, *Dracula,* with its bloodsucking, gold-grubbing, hook-nosed monster, is a clearly anti-Semitic text. *The Mummy,* meanwhile, shows strong debts not only to Stoker but to Steven Spielberg's *Raiders of the Lost Ark,* whose plot centers on the recovery of the Hebrew Ark of the Covenant. This is perhaps most obvious in the depiction of the hero, which is also where *The Mummy* departs most sharply from Stoker. Stoker's heroes, with the notable exception of Rupert Sent Leger in *The Lady of the Shroud,* tend to be found wanting in moments of crisis; all too often, they are still worrying about what they should do long after they have lost the moment when they could have done anything at all. In this respect, Rick O'Connell, who is single-handedly five times more effective than the entire Crew of Light put together (not to mention the negligible Frank Whemple in the 1932 *Mummy*), clearly owes much less to Stoker than to Indiana Jones, of whom he is pretty obviously a direct descendant.

There are a number of points of marked similarity between *The Mummy* and the Indiana Jones trilogy: the long-lost Egyptian city, locat-

able only with an antique map, which houses fabulous treasures; the transformation in the appearance of the hero, from archaeologist to college
professor in the case of Indiana Jones and from legionnaire to wild man
and back again in the case of Rick O'Connell; the repeated hair's-breadth
escapes from danger; and the hero's ultimate disdain of personal profit.
(Though Rick's and Evie's camels are in fact loaded with treasure stashed
in the saddlebags by Beni, which presumably finances the splendor of
their house in *The Mummy Returns,* they are unaware of it at the time.)
There is also the fact that Evie, like Marion in *Raiders of the Lost Ark,* has to
make up to her captor to distract his attention from the actions of her true
love; there is the presence of hideous supernatural peril and the parallels
between *The Mummy*'s Ardeth Bay and his followers and the hereditary
guardians of the holy place in *Indiana Jones and the Last Crusade;* and
at the end of both *The Mummy* and *Raiders of the Lost Ark,* the villain's
soul is borne away to Hell. Even Imhotep's nonchalant crunching of the
beetle which enters his face through the hole in his cheek could be seen as
a reprise of the moment in *Raiders of the Lost Ark* when a fly crawls across
the cheek of the French archaeologist Belloc while he is speaking and disappears into his mouth without him apparently noticing. (This moment
has been airbrushed out of the video version, but was clearly visible in the
original film.)

In the Jewish Spielberg's *Raiders of the Lost Ark,* however, the villains
are Nazis, whom Indiana Jones, though not himself Jewish, detests. By
contrast, *The Mummy* is not without its share of Jewish actors—Oded
Fehr plays Ardeth Bay and Rachel Weisz plays Evelyn (Evie)—but they
play Arab characters (Ardeth Bay is a Tuareg and Evelyn is half-Egyptian),
and though the mummy (unlike Dracula) has no fear of the cross or of the
image of Buddha, he spares Beni and indeed gives him gold when he bran-
dishes the Star of David and utters what Imhotep terms "the language of
the slaves" (Hebrew—which Beni conveniently happens to know). Later,
what finally returns Imhotep to mortality is Evie's utterance of a word
which sounds suspiciously like "Kaddish," and one might also note the
film's distinct animus, in the presence of the emblematically named Win-
ston, against the redundancy of the British air force, who have nothing
better to do than fool around drunkenly and futilely in the Middle East—
with, perhaps, the possible implication that this was effectively what they
were doing when they later presided over the birth of the state of Israel.
In this respect, the conjunction of *Dracula* with *The Jewel of Seven Stars*
allows not only for a convergence of vampires and mummies, but also for
another convergence which the film seems to find ideologically interest-

ing, that of Egypt with Israel. (It is notable that the character equivalent to Beni in the 1932 *Mummy*, who is also identified as a hereditary slave of the Egyptians, was Nubian.)

Even more anxiety-ridden than the film's depiction of racial and national identities, however, is its depiction of gender. Although O'Connell is far closer to the classically heroic status of Indiana Jones than to the beleaguered masculinity of Stoker's heroes, there are nevertheless also distinct differences from the Indiana Jones films in general, and from *Raiders of the Lost Ark* in particular. In the first place, in *The Mummy* it is the heroine, not the hero, who is knowledgeable about Egypt, able to decipher hieroglyphic inscriptions and correct the obnoxious Beni's translation of Imhotep's ancient Egyptian. When Jonathan Hyde's Egyptologist dismisses his rivals' expedition on the grounds that its leader is a woman and therefore incapable of knowing anything, the camera immediately cuts to Evie explaining precisely what she knows. Conversely, although Brendan Fraser (who plays O'Connell) remarks in the film program that his character is "sometimes the brain and sometimes the brawn in a situation" (p. 11), the element of brawn is far more pronounced, not least in the fact that whereas college professor Indiana Jones always preferred to try his hand with a rope, falling back on a gun principally for the sake of a gag—as in the famous scene in *Raiders of the Lost Ark* where, confronted with a crack swordsman, he shoots him—O'Connell shoots (usually with two guns) at everything, whether it is animate or not. (At one point, Evie, being led to be sacrificed, hears a gunshot outside and says happily "O'Connell!" Quite.) Even when he is standing against a wall at which bullets are being shot at regular intervals, Evie has to tug him out of what will obviously be the trajectory of the next one. His resolute preference for not using whatever intelligence he may possess seems part of a reversal of roles which is completed when, in a direct inversion of a scene from *Raiders of the Lost Ark*, the buildup to a kiss between hero and heroine is interrupted by one of them passing out—only this time it is the heroine, not the hero, who loses consciousness, and it is through drunkenness, not excessive fatigue.

In one way, what seems to be at work here is simply a cultural shift which has ensured that the feistiness of *Raiders of the Lost Ark*'s Marion has been replaced by quietist post-feminist gender rôles—it is notable that Evie, unlike Marion, cannot hold her drink and falls over when she tries to learn to throw punches. (Indeed one might notice that the Indiana Jones films themselves discarded Marion and in fact never settled on a heroine, with Kate Allen's Marion giving way without explanation or comment to Kate Capshaw's Willie Scott in the second and no heroine at all in the third since Alison Doody's Dr. Elsa Schneider turns out to be a villainess). Thus, though Evie may be clever, she is quite incapable of looking after herself (she even has an accident in her own library) and is totally reliant on O'Connell to save her at regular intervals—which of course he duly proceeds to do. Indeed one might well conclude that the film's ultimate moral is that while half-naked hussies will attract only losers, nice girls who dress decently will always find themselves properly taken care of.

However, there are equally clear traces of a counternarrative at work. In this respect, the most interesting figure is Evie's feckless brother, Jonathan (John Hannah). The first time we see him is when Evie, alone in the Egyptological museum, hears a noise. Clearly scared, she goes to investigate and is horribly startled by Jonathan popping up out of a sarcophagus. Quietly but implicitly, Jonathan is thus initially identified with a mummy, though he himself seems to seek to undo this immediately by addressing Evie as "Old Mum." In the next sequence, Jonathan and Evie visit an imprisoned O'Connell, whose pocket Jonathan had previously picked. Reaching through the bars, O'Connell punches Jonathan and kisses Evie, actions which, amongst other purposes, seem clearly to interpellate them in their respective gender rôles. Jonathan, however, does not stay put in his because not only does he prove to need rescuing by O'Connell nearly as often as Evie does, he also puts himself in her place in other ways: when O'Connell, having seen off Imhotep, asks Evie, "Are you all right?", it is Jonathan who answers "Well . . . not sure." Not for nothing does he refer to O'Connell at one point as "the man" (assuming as he does that O'Connell's injunction to stay put and keep out of danger applies to him as well as to Evie). Most notably, when O'Connell sets off to rescue the parasol-carrying Egyptologist from Imhotep, he tells Jonathan, Henderson, and Daniels to come with him and Evie to stay in safety. The three men, however, are all too scared to come, while Evie is equally adamant that she won't stay behind. Not until O'Connell scoops her up in a fireman's lift, tosses her on the bed, and locks the door on her are gender rôles restored—but even then it is visibly at the price of conceding that however firmly they may thus be instantiated, the majority of the film's characters don't actually conform to them.

Moreover, intertextual echoes may well mean that for some members of the audience at least, even O'Connell's position is not fully assured. When he appears long-haired and unkempt in a Cairo prison, Brendan Fraser is obviously reprising his rôle as the eponymous hero in the 1997 Disney film *George of the Jungle,* while Evie's "What's a nice place like this doing in a girl like me?" recalls the chat-up line which George proposes to use on Ursula, "What's a nice girl like you doing in a plane like this?" In one sense, George is, of course, the ultimate wild man, over whom all of Ursula's girlfriends swoon when they see him running with a horse, but he does also appear in a dress and, at the outset, has no concept of gender at all, referring to the hyperfeminine Ursula as a "fella." Since Ursula dislikes her official fiancé and runs off instead with the socially unacceptable outsider George, the possible intertext with *The Mummy* is doubly interesting here.

In *The Mummy Returns,* the note of uncertainty thus introduced is further developed, and new areas of anxiety are highlighted. *The Mummy Returns* opened, at least in the UK, to a barrage of distinctly lukewarm reviews which stressed the incoherence of its plot. The *Independent* reviewed it twice in two days and hated it both times, with Anthony Quinn demanding on 18 May 2001, "Are you following all this? I don't think the filmmakers could care less if you do or not. . . . There's nothing so old-fashioned as plot development here, just a pile-up of set-pieces"; Peter Preston in the *Observer* asked, "What's going on here? Silly question, one beyond any computer's figuring. . . . Summon the Raiders of the Lost Plot. Nothing in Stephen Sommers's screenplay makes, or is intended to make, any sense" (20 May 2001), while Xan Brooks in the *Guardian* more succinctly advised, "Forget trying to follow the plot" (18 May 2001). Even Barbara Ellen in the *Times,* who had a soft spot for it, suggested retitling it *Indiana Jones and the Script of Doom* (17 May 2001).

There definitely are uncertainties about its plot. "Why?" asks Imhotep when the Scorpion King hoists up the curator, and one can think of few better questions. What is the curator's motivation? Why does he need Imhotep to fight the Scorpion King? What happens to Evie's previously mortal wound when she is resurrected? What is the nature of the apparent feud between Ardeth Bey and Lock-Nah? Who is Patricia Velazquez's character before the soul of Anck Su Namun takes possession of her? Is Rick really a Medjai, and if so, does it matter? Where exactly would Anubis, a jackal, wear a bracelet? Perhaps most puzzlingly, who on earth are the pygmies? The only possible explanation for them seems to come from Rick's remark at the beginning about the shortness of Napoleon, together with production designer Allan Cameron's observation in *The Mummy Unwrapped* that design for the film relied heavily on a volume of Egyptian sketches produced for Napoleon.

A far deeper fault line, however, runs through the second film, and that is its representation of its characters. In the preview of *The Mummy Returns* included in the "ultimate edition" of *The Mummy,* director Stephen

Sommers observes that his paramount aim in making the sequel was to retain as many of the same characters as possible but to make their relationships "more intertwining." He has certainly reprised for all he is worth: the Cairo Museum in the first film is replaced by the British Museum in this one; the O'Connell's son, Alex, collapses pillars in a domino-like fashion just as Evie did the bookshelves; and Alex can't read the last word of the incantation just as Jonathan couldn't in the first film (and it's the same word). So close are the similarities, indeed, that Anthony Quinn in the *Independent* complained, "This didn't look like a sequel. This looked like a remake. . . . [T]his is the worst case of *déjà vu* I've ever had in a cinema" (18 May 2001). The debt to Indiana Jones, too, is not only revisited but extended, with the lamplit digging scene directly pastiching that in *Raiders of the Lost Ark* and the presence of Alex invoking the spinoff series *Young Indiana Jones*, particularly in the scene in which he runs through the ruins of a temple, with gunfire all around him, looking like a miniature version of his father in the legionnaire sequence of the first film. (This element is even more pronounced in the spinoff novelization *Revenge of the Scorpion King*, billed as the first of "The Mummy Chronicles," in which Alex, now 12, bands together with the Jewish refugee Rachel to prevent Hitler completing a deal with Anubis.)

There are changes, though. Perhaps the most noticeable of these is that almost as strong as the influence of the Indiana Jones trilogy is that of the Star Wars films, most particularly *The Phantom Menace*, which opened the same summer as the original *Mummy* and was thus its direct comparator and rival. Nicholas Barber in the *Independent on Sunday* (20 May 2001) scathingly listed just a few of the similarities:

> *The Phantom Menace* introduced a mop-topped blond boy to the cast; *The Mummy Returns* does the same. *The Phantom Menace* used racial caricatures; *The Mummy Returns* has dozens of desert-folk machine-gunned and burned alive. And just as *Star Wars* had an archetypal fairy-tale clarity that was subsequently obscured by portentous backstory and pseudospiritual mumbo jumbo, *The Mummy Returns* is clogged up with complicated exposition and flashbacks that serve no purpose except to lay foundations for another sequel. It even blabs on about the sacred "Medjai" warriors—couldn't Sommers have come up with a name that didn't share four letters with Jedi?

Other elements of similarity between the two films could also be pointed out. The final battle of *The Mummy Returns*, in which the warriors of Anubis disappear at the death of the Scorpion King, clearly echoes the final fight of *The Phantom Menace,* in which the droids drop when the mother ship is disabled (and in each case the large-scale fight is taking place in the open air while the crucial smaller one is in a confined space). When the first vision generated by the bracelet of Anubis fades away, there is a noise just like that of a light saber. There are also echoes of the earlier Star Wars films. The new character Izzy closely parallels Lando Calrissian from *The Empire Strikes Back:* both are black (something to which Izzy draws attention by referring to Rick as "the white boy"), both are introduced by the hero to the heroine as an old acquaintance but immediately react in an apparently hostile way, and both supply an aircraft. Thus Rick, having started his career in the first film as Harrison Ford in the Indiana Jones trilogy, seems now to have been reinvented as Harrison Ford in the Star Wars trilogy, a parallel that is made even clearer when Ardeth, having identified Rick as a Medjai and Evelyn as the reincarnation of Nefertiri, tells him that it is his preordained rôle to protect a royal woman, just as Han Solo protects Princess Leia.

Most significantly, the incorporation of motifs and borrowings from the Star Wars series has helped *The Mummy Returns* become something which *The Mummy,* by and large, was not: Gothic. This element is clearly present in *Star Wars* Episodes Three and Four, in which the ostensible opposition of Darth Vader and Luke Skywalker rapidly gives way to a paired and conflicted relationship in which one sees the other in the mirror. In *The Mummy,* however, oppositions stay, by and large, opposed. There are one or two moments of doubling—Imhotep staring after his own soul-self as it is borne away to hell, the twinned books, Beni facing the mummy for the first time with matching expressions on their faces— but, in general, the film occupies a terrain in which the bad are simply bad and the good are simply good.

In the second film, however, identities and affiliations prove much less stable: it is after all, as Max Allan Collins's novelization declares, an expedition for Evie "to discover not the history of the pharaohs, but the meaning of her own dreams" (pp. 16-17). We may, for instance, be disconcerted to find Ardeth Bay in the company of the baddies, and although we may guess that his motive is to keep an eye on them, Rick's first response is to smash him against the wall and demand to know where Evie is. Most notably, although actions are directly repeated from the first film, as with the reading of the incantation and the demolishing of the pillars, *they are not performed by the same person,* as though identities are shifting. Other doublings and pairings are also apparent: we learn for the first time that

Evie was Nefertiri in a previous life (a doubling which is strongly reminiscent of that of Margaret and Tera in *The Jewel of Seven Stars*), while Meela is Anck Su Namun reincarnated and Rick's tattoo seems to identify him as actually one of the Medjai (though this, unless it is leading up to a further sequel, proves to be a bit of a narrative red herring, complicated by the fact that the novelization for children describes the tattoo as proving that he is "a Masonic Templar"[4] and the novelization for adults calls him a "Knight Templar,"[5] even though common elements to both, which do not appear in the film, clearly indicate that both of these descriptions were based on the shooting script).

The most notable instance of these doublings and slippages takes us back to Margaret Thatcher's joke. When Evie goes with Imhotep in the first film, she turns back to Rick and says, "If he makes me into a mummy, you're the first one I'm coming after." In one way, the meaning of this remark and of the surrounding sequence is obvious: she loves Rick and is hoping he will rescue her before Imhotep can kill her. But it is also shadowed by other meanings. In the first place, what would she be "coming after" O'Connell for—because she loves him, or because, having been made into a monster herself, she would seek him as prey? There would certainly be a direct Stokerian precedent here in a precisely parallel situation, Lucy's attempted vamping of Arthur. More troublingly is the fact that, from the first time he sees her, Imhotep identifies Evie with his lost love, Anck Su Namun. Every time he meets her subsequently, he tries to kiss her (and on one occasion succeeds). He is therefore clearly established as an alternative suitor. Of course there might well seem to be no contest: O'Connell is dashing, handsome, honorable, and alive, whereas Imhotep passes through a variety of stages of decay and proposes to kill her. Nevertheless, a different interpretation is offered in Max Allan Collins's novelization of the film.

Collins—who, suggestively, also directed and novelized *Mommy* (1995) and *Mommy's Day* (1997), in which an apparently perfect mother is revealed to be evil—seems to incriminate Evie several times. Developing the idea sketched in the sequence in which she tells O'Connell and the Americans, "Let's be nice, children. If we're going to play together we must learn to share," he has her thinking "Men were such children" (p. 142). He also makes Jonathan ask the Americans after the blinding of Burns, "Going back home to mummy?" (p. 166). This again develops on a much fainter hint in the film, when Jonathan explains to Rick the meaning of a preparation chamber—"Mummies, my good son. This is where they made the mummies"—where sons and mothers are forced uneasily but briefly into conjunction. Most suggestively, Collins invents for the sleeping Evie a dream sequence in which she is having

> nearly delirious images of herself and O'Connell fleeing from the mummy across the ruins of the City of the Dead, only at times she was fleeing from Rick and holding on to the mummy's hand . . . it was all very troubling, which was why she was moaning, even crying out in her fitful sleep. (p. 188)

For Collins, Imhotep here is less a monster than the handsome prince awakening Snow White (p. 189). And after all, Rick has already had to demand of Evie, "You dream about dead guys?"

Can this really be true? When Evie says to O'Connell, "If he makes me into a mummy, you're the first one I'm coming after," can her words, at any level, really be gesturing at an alternative possibility in which it is Imhotep who becomes her successful suitor, going so far as to impregnate her, and O'Connell whom she would seek to destroy? On the level of common sense, this is patently absurd. However, on the darker levels of the subconscious, perhaps the film does not find its heroine so biddable as it might like — it is certainly not hard to read her slamming of the suitcase on Rick's hands as a snapping *vagina dentata,* while the scarabs which emerge from mouths clearly recall the *Alien* films, with their clear interest in the monstrous-feminine — nor is its mummy quite so repellent as one might expect. In *The Mummy Unwrapped,* producer Sean Daniel refers to him as "an extremely dangerous and extremely handsome man," and Pete Hammond, who is introduced with an ambiguity which is itself interesting as "film analyst," opines that "people want to believe in a life after death situation" and thus sees the figure of the mummy as representing, however bizarrely, a wish fulfillment rather than a threat. Certainly when Ardeth and Dr. Bey explain that Imhotep must still love Anck Su Namun after three thousand years, Evie observes, "[T]hat's very romantic," and in one sense, so it is. It is of course unusual for a mummy fiction to include a romance element at all (though it is true that both *The Jewel of Seven Stars* and the 1932 *Mummy* do, both are very nugatory), and, given that and our resulting paucity of narrative expectations, we might well expect the initial concentration on the romance of Imhotep and Anck Su Namun to continue to be the focus of interest and to be viewed more sympathetically than it ultimately is: we certainly could not predict at that stage that the initial kiss between Imhotep and Anck Su Namun would ultimately be replaced by that between Rick and Evie at the close. And though Ardeth Bay obviously regards Imhotep as evil, we are not necessarily inclined to take his word for it since, in the first place, others of the Medjai have already tried to stab Evie, and, in the second, Ardeth Bey was actually the alias used by Imhotep himself in the 1932 *Mummy*. And it is also noticeable that *The Mummy Returns* certainly seems to find Imhotep so insufficiently scary that it feels obliged to supplement the menace he offers with that provided by the Scorpion King (who, in another instance of these films' perverse ability to find their villains rather than their hero attractive, in fact upstages Imhotep so much that he stars in his own spinoff, *The Scorpion King* [2002], in which he is featured as the hero).

In one way, however, the addition of the Scorpion King to the lineup of villains in *The Mummy Returns* proves unnecessary because there is already an extra threat present in the second film, coming from Evie. However faint the hint of menace playing over her in the first film, it is far more clearly marked in the second (and was also sharply present in the 1932 *Mummy,* in which Helen Grosvenor, pathologized from the outset by being under the care of the doctor, fed bromide when she puts on her makeup and tries to join Imhotep, and explicitly associated with the adulterous temptress Helen of Troy, is a reincarnation of Anck Su Namun). Indeed, while the second film's treatment of O'Connell stays much the same, the characterization of Evie has been fundamentally reconceived: despite her hopelessness during the boxing lesson in the first film, in which she displayed an inability to cope so profound that she even had to ask a blind man for help, she is now a superbly accomplished fighter who rescues Jonathan from Anck Su Namun, she no longer needs her glasses, and she wears trousers. Most strikingly, towards the end of *The Mummy Returns,* there is an entirely unprepared-for narrative twist: Anck Su Namun, on her way into the temple, turns and stabs Evie in the stomach, inflicting a wound from which Evie shortly after dies, only to be restored to life by Alex reading the incantation from the Book of Amun-Ra. Since Evie's death proves to be only temporary, the event may seem to have little narrative significance, but its thematic resonances are great. In particular, for the first time, it is not O'Connell, but Alex, her son, who rescues her. For him, at least, *Evie* is the mummy who returns.

Is she so for the rest of us? Is *Evie,* in some bizarre sense, the monster we most fear? Anck Su Namun's choice of the stomach as the site of attack is certainly highly suggestive. (Rick, by contrast, is habitually attacked in the neck — the botched hanging at Cairo prison, the Medjai grabbing him round the neck on the burning ship, Imhotep's attempt to throttle him — almost as though he were the victim of a vampire.) In the first film, both

Imhotep and Anck Su Namun herself die from precisely similar wounds to the stomach (in her case twice), so Evie is thus linked with them, as she is when she is seen as Nefertiri, wearing a mask just as Imhotep does before he is fully regenerated, and when Anck Su Namun pacifies a group of gun-wielding men just as Evie herself did in the first film. Moreover, Meela adopts pseudomaternal behavior towards Alex, and Max Allan Collins's novelization even suggests that Imhotep does so too:

> And Imhotep, grinning, almost as if proud of the boy, wagged a finger down at Alex.
> "Naughty, naughty," he said, and held out his hand.
> Swallowing, reluctant, Alex got to his feet, brushed off his short pants, and took the mummy's hand. (p. 169)

A mummy thus merges with a mummy (and we might note that when Meela stabbed herself in the stomach and then revived, she came back with a completely different personality, which would leave open the possibility that the same might happen to Evie). The thrust can also be read as a direct blow to the womb, with Anck Su Namun, childless and with no sign of any other relatives, pitted deliberately against Evie, wife, mother, sister, and daughter both to Seti and to her Carnahan parents (with the name, according to the novelization, deliberately invoking a blend of Carter and Carnarvon; in addition, the first name of Evie's father is specifically given in the book as Howard, and he is said to have discovered the tomb of Tutankhamun). It would be easy to see this act as motivated primarily by the childless woman's envy of the mother, while it would be equally possible to see it as configured by the fact that, in the story as it is now told, Anck Su Namun is also the replacement for Evie's/Nefertiri's mother, who is never mentioned, and thus her stepmother. (O'Connell, too, is now identified as motherless: both the children's and the adult novelization have him referring to having received his tattoo in an orphanage in Hong Kong, though in the movie he appears to say "Cairo," while *Revenge of the Scorpion King* is equally the revenge of Rachel for the death of her mother at the hands of the Nazis, immediately after which Alex uncovers a cache of weapons and shouts "We've hit the mother lode!"[6])

This film, then, appears to regard mothers and motherhood with some trepidation, and one reason for this may well be because it is fairly obviously based on Elizabeth Peters's series of pseudo-Victorian detective stories featuring Amelia Peabody Emerson. Peters's books are the source of the names O'Connell and Evelyn, and they repeatedly make the point that motherhood can be at least as much of a trial as a pleasure, as when the heroine notes, "All in all it had been a delightful existence, marred by only one minor flaw. That flaw was our son, Walter Peabody Emerson, known to friends and foes alike by his sobriquet of 'Ramses' "; when the child agrees to stay behind while she and her husband go to Egypt, she exclaims, "I had not ventured to hope, much less pray, for such bliss."[7] This animus towards motherhood appears to have leached into Sommers's films along with the borrowed names. "Run, you sons of bitches!" screams Henderson in *The Mummy* to O'Connell and Jonathan, casually indicting all mothers as he flees. "Mother!" screams the Cockney lackey in *The Mummy Returns* when he first sees Imhotep. "Mummies!" says Rick in the first film disgustedly, adding "I hate mummies!" in the second. This is unfortunate since Evie's dying words, "Look after Alex. . . . I love you," in a sense constitute him as a mummy. Moreover, he is at first prostrated by grief, and, though he goes to fight Imhotep and the Scorpion King, he is soon knocked to the ground again and raised only by the unexpected sound of her voice. The effect is that of a resurrection from the dead, something which is repeated when Evie pulls him up from the abyss: in one sense, then, it is now he who has returned from a symbolic grave. That his reprieve is, however, conditional is clearly indicated by the fact that the classic hand-over-the-edge shot here has a suggestive variation in that the first thing we notice is his wedding ring: the suggestion is clearly that Evie comes and pulls him up because they are properly married, whereas Anck Su Namun leaves Imhotep to die because they aren't.

Rick's survival, then, is contingent on his status as a family man. But, as he himself says, "Sometimes it's hard being a dad," and the film does indeed make us clearly aware of the pressures of having children (not least since Jonathan, to whom Rick says sternly, "I thought I said no more wild parties?" in effect functions as a substitute teenager, while Collins's novelization makes quite clear the extent to which the pygmy mummies are also conceived of as hideously threatening children [p. 228]). Indeed the very casting of Brendan Fraser as Rick creates ripples since, two years before *The Mummy*, he had appeared in Ross Marks's *Twilight of the Golds* (another film with a highly conflicted view of Jewishness), playing a gay man whose sister is appalled to discover that the son she is carrying is likely to share his sexuality: in the end, she keeps the child, but the decision breaks up her marriage. (Not to mention Fraser's even more recent appearance as Ian McKellen's object of lust in Bill Condon's 1998 *Gods and Monsters*, in which he once again sports a tattoo which allows another man to guess his past and appears with Kevin J. O'Connor, who was to play Beni in *The Mummy*.) In *The Mummy Returns,* Alex's repeated "Are we there yet?" seems only partly parodic, he and Jonathan both groan whenever Rick and Evie kiss (and it is also during a kiss that Alex manages to get himself kidnapped), and it is in fact only when Rick and Evie are without Alex that they are actually able to reprise the first film. The first two dangers Rick faces in the film come from his own family: Alex creeps up behind him, and Evie throws a snake just as he enters. Most notably, although the second film seems to be deliberately less frightening than the first, it still received a 12 certificate, meaning that if you actually have a child like Alex, you can't go to see it without a babysitter. Gothic is often predicated on the loss of a parent; here, though, the ultimate, darkest fantasy may well be the loss of a child. It is played out in safety (you can, of course, retrieve your own offspring from the babysitter later) but, just briefly, you can acknowledge that the rôle of mummy is the enemy and kill it.

Harry Potter and the Philosopher's Stone

On the weekend that *Harry Potter and the Philosopher's Stone* (known as *Harry Potter and the Sorcerer's Stone* in the U.S.) was released in Britain, a colleague and I were both involved in organizing children's birthday parties. My son was turning nine; my colleague's godson was four. My colleague reported that at the four-year-old's party, all the children were agog for Harry Potter merchandise and showing each other what they had, though none, of course, had read the books. My son, who had read all the books several times, was anxious to see the film, which he quite enjoyed, but would not have been seen dead in possession of any of the associated merchandise, an attitude shared by all the friends of the same age who attended his party. It seemed as though the books and the products existed essentially in isolation from each other, appealing to quite different clientèles.

Harry Potter and the Philosopher's Stone might well seem to form something of a halfway house between these two positions. Trumpeted for its fidelity to the book, it was nevertheless always going to find it hard to please diehard aficionados and ran the risk of falling into the same trap as the Branagh *Hamlet,* offering everything and thus delivering nothing. In fact, though, it did diverge from the book in a number of ways. For one thing, the film is clearly Gothic. Obviously, this element is already strongly present in the book, but it is considerably more developed in the film, for the book is also interested in other things, such as jokes, the house points system (elements of this remain in the film, but there is no hint of the disastrous consequences to Harry of the deduction of one hundred and fifty points from Gryffindor over the Norbert incident), and Quidditch—which is again played down in the film, with only one match rather than the full series being shown. The film thus omits or minimizes the non-Gothic elements and replaces them with Gothic ones. From the moment that the lightning scar on Harry's forehead comes alive to generate the title sequence, lightning is a recurrent feature of the film and indeed becomes effectively a synecdoche for magic. Thunder and lightning lash the island before Hagrid appears (and since there is no explanation of how or why they have come to be on the island, it is thus strongly identified as a place of magic). Lightning flashes behind Hagrid as he breaks down the door; during the flashback of Lily's death, lightning flashes around the Potters' house in an obvious borrowing of classic Gothic iconography; later, it plays around the Halloween pumpkins and is also seen outside when Quirrell comes in. Finally, it flashes in the aftermath of the troll sequence. (Lightning is also drawn on in *Harry Potter and the Chamber of Secrets,* although only when we are about to learn that Hermione has been petrified.) Equally typical of the Gothic is the use of sharply foreshortening or of distorted camera angles, as when the camera looks down at Harry as he enters Olivander's and unwraps the broomstick and at Quirrell as he enters the Great Hall to warn Dumbledore about the troll; conversely, it looks sharply up at both the troll and Snape on his first appearance, while during the Quidditch match it veers wildly in both directions. The shifting staircases are deeply Gothic, as of course is the architecture of Gloucester Cathedral, where much of the film was shot; so too is Voldemort's hood, the disembodied hand carrying the lantern which we see when Harry is wearing the invisibility cloak (and which is so obviously reminiscent of a hand of glory), the vampiric iconography of Voldemort drinking the blood of the unicorn, and the fact that because Quirrell faces Harry, Voldemort speaks as if out of the mirror.

It is partly as a result of this Gothicization that the film is more insistently about identity than the book is and that it takes a far darker view of the possible overtones than is found in the original text, where wizardry offers a welcome escape from the Dursleys (although it is true that similarly dark hints about the weight of the past cluster ever more thickly in the later books). In one of its few complete departures from the book, there is a startling initial misrecognition by Hagrid, who takes Dudley to be Harry and is surprised that he is so fat. Dudley duly protests, "I'm not Harry," upon which Harry steps forward out of the shadowed alcove in which he has been completely concealed and says "I am." To this, Hagrid replies, "Well of course you are." He then proceeds to tell Harry that he is a wizard, but Harry demurs, "I can't be a wizard—I'm just Harry," and Hagrid replies, "Well, 'just Harry' . . ." There is a complex series of nuances here. Given that he is totally hidden, Harry does not have to come forward; his doing so therefore seems to stand as a deliberate claiming of his identity, which has an obvious extradiegetic resonance given the much-publicized search for a boy to play Harry. The further qualification that he is "just Harry" is simultaneously self-denigratory and affirmatory: if nothing else, he is at least Harry. Hagrid's two responses complicate things still further. "Well of course you are" sounds as much like a reassurance as a recognition, and the tone of the "just Harry" suggests that he is far more than "just Harry" at the same time that the phrasing unmistakably evokes "just William," suggesting that Harry is more than "just Harry" not only because he is to be the hero of this story but also because he stands so recognizably in a long line of heroes of other stories. So, who is Harry, and is his identity actually as dual as that of the film and its merchandise?

This question is made all the more urgent by a number of other subtle changes. Dudley is not only menaced by the escaping snake but actually ends up behind the glass himself, which, together with Harry's ability to communicate with the snake, subtly riddles the distinction between animal and human. This scene also has another effect: as we later discover in *Harry Potter and the Chamber of Secrets*, Harry is able to communicate with snakes only because he is a parselmouth. When this is revealed, there are other people listening, so it is made clear that the words which Harry speaks to the snake are not in English but in parseltongue. In the film, however, he speaks in English to the snake, and though it is clear that this had to happen in order to avoid giving away a crucial element of the plot, it does nevertheless confirm the extent to which we are viewing events strictly from Harry's perspective: we experience him as speaking in English at this point because that is how he experiences it himself. The removal of any explanation for Snape's behavior makes his motivation completely incomprehensible to anyone who has not read the book and thus renders his identity an impenetrable puzzle. Most notably, in the book, Aunt Petunia reveals that she has always known that Harry must be a wizard because "How could you not be, my dratted sister being what she was?"[8] In the film, this is subtly but significantly altered to "*who* she was" (my emphasis), which significantly increases the sense of concentration on individual rather than collective identities.

Most notable of all, of course, is the delayed revelation of Harry's uniqueness and identity. Unlike the novel, which begins in the resolutely ordinary world of the Dursleys, the film opens with magic and, indeed, Harry never leaves the magical world once Hagrid has made his initial entrance, although in the book he returns to live with the Dursleys for several weeks before finally leaving for Hogwarts. However, although we know about magic from the outset, Harry himself has no idea how he fits into this world. Instead of being told his whole history by Hagrid at their first meeting, Harry is forced to wait for this knowledge until after his visit to Diagon Alley, when he independently guesses that his parents were killed by the man who gave him the scar. The effect of this is twofold, though it will be fully felt only by the rare viewer who does not already know the story: Harry is confirmed as distinguished not only by his past history, but also by his intelligence and intuition. Moreover, the deferred explanation of Harry's history is balanced and echoed by the deferred introduction of his archenemy, Draco Malfoy. Since the episode in Madam Malkin's robe shop is entirely absent from the film, the whole burden of making Malfoy suitably repulsive falls on his brief encounter with Harry immediately before they are sorted into houses. The few lines which he is given might well have struggled to bear the weight of generating the appropriate amount of dislike for him, except that, strikingly, they have been so exclusively focused on issues of identity. Malfoy's first gambit is to identify Harry: "So it's true! . . . Harry Potter has come to Hogwarts." His second is introduce Crabbe and Goyle, mentioning each by name, and his third is to identify Ron as a Weasley, which leads up to his crowning strategy of offering to teach Harry how to tell the right sort of wizarding family from the bad. Clearly Malfoy's reliance on a model of identity based on heredity and nature is being implicitly pitted against one founded on ideas of personal choice and nurture.

This is certainly an important concern in the book, in which Malfoy, who already knows what house he will be in, disapproves of the very concept of acquired knowledge: "I really don't think they should let the other sort in, do you? They're just not the same, they've never been brought up to know our ways."[9] Malfoy judges people by their surnames: the wizarding world is, it seems, so small that one can identify a member of it by name alone, and he and Ron do indeed prove on the train to have heard about each other's families, just as Hagrid will later be able to identify Ron as a Weasley on sight, on the basis of his red hair. Malfoy's very formulation undoes the basis of his own argument, though, when he pinpoints the nature of his objection to Muggle-borns as being that "they've never been brought up to know our ways"; here he is effectively conceding that nurture has a rôle to play and that wizarding is not innate but must be learned. The books themselves, of course, later resoundingly underscore the superiority of nurture over nature by the neat device of having the twin sisters Padma and Parvati Patil placed in different houses, Padma in Ravenclaw and Parvati in Gryffindor, something which looks for all the world like a direct rejoinder to the numerous studies which have attempted to use twins to show the importance of nature.

Malfoy signals his commitment to ideas of heredity and nature by his proclaimed preference for Slytherin, the house of which all his family have been members. The house for which he expresses particular dislike is, interestingly, not Gryffindor, which we later come to identify as the natural opposite of Slytherin, but Hufflepuff (p. 60). However, Hagrid, whom we have already learned to like, assures Harry that even though the students of Hufflepuff may not be the brightest, they are preferable to those of Slytherin, a house whose very name suggests effortless entry and which is, we subsequently learn, populated primarily by students belonging precisely to the same hereditary caste as valorized by Malfoy, while the meritocratically selected Muggle-borns, such as Justin Finch-Fletchley in Hufflepuff and Hermione Granger in Gryffindor, gravitate to the other three houses.

It is suggestive that Malfoy dislikes Hufflepuff in particular. This cannot be because it is associated particularly with Muggle-borns: there are plenty of these in Gryffindor too (as well as Hermione, Dean Thomas arrives that year, and Colin Creevey joins them the next), and there are also purebloods in Hufflepuff—the Hufflepuff Quidditch Seeker Cedric Diggory, who comes to such prominence in *Harry Potter and the Goblet of Fire*, has a father who works in the Ministry of Magic. Moreover, the fact that the Sorting Hat debates between Gryffindor and Slytherin as possible houses for Harry suggests some sort of similarity or affinity between the two. The Hat even comments on the quality of Harry's mind (p. 90), as though Ravenclaw might briefly have been considered as a possibility, but not, apparently, Hufflepuff.

The reason for this seems to be that Hufflepuffs do indeed appear to be generally slow on the uptake. In *Harry Potter and The Prisoner of Azkaban*, Fred is adamant that Cedric's silence is the result of his having nothing to say (p. 127), and in *Harry Potter and the Chamber of Secrets*, Justin Finch-Fletchley is completely taken in by Lockhart (p. 73), while Ernie Macmillan and Hannah Abbott are easily seduced into believing that Harry must be the heir of Slytherin (p. 149). Hufflepuffs do have compensating qualities, however: they are loyal and hardworking, with their determined nature suggested by their emblem of the badger and its associated connotations of "badgering someone," just as their comic aspect is encapsulated in the very name Hufflepuff.

Malfoy's scornful dismissal of the Hufflepuffs therefore raises the issue of the relative merits of acquired versus innate knowledge since Hufflepuffs rarely know how to do anything instinctively, but are prepared to work at it. Once Harry is at Hogwarts, there seems to be (both literally and metaphorically) a level playing field. Despite a wizarding background, Ron Weasley has no advantage over Harry and certainly none over Hermione because, as Hagrid has reassured Harry, "[e]veryone starts at the beginning at Hogwarts" (p. 66), mimicking, of course, the experience of the reader. Even Ron Weasley, from a long-established wizarding family and with a father working at the Ministry of Magic, cannot use the combination of a magic wand and a spell he learned from one of his brothers to turn Scabbers yellow. Indeed, the sheer difficulty of finding one's way around Hogwarts means that everyone's attention must initially be focused on knowledge acquisition, with Muggle-borns and wizard-borns being equally disadvantaged.

Nature, then, is pitted against nurture in both book and film, but the combat is rather different in the two. In particular, the film has two crucial episodes which differ subtly but significantly from their analogues in the book. The first is when the Sorting Hat so decisively assigns a group identity to the new students. This comes as a complete surprise to those new to the story since there has been no previous mention of the house system, and the absence of the Sorting Hat's song means that, with the exception of Slytherin, to which Ron gives Harry a whispered introduction, we have no concept of what the other houses stand for and thus of the nature of the identity being conferred on Harry—but whatever this identity is, it is obviously one which he cannot contest or shape. Equally, another identity which he seems to have formed entirely for himself proves to have been partially predetermined by heredity when Hermione informs him that his father was a Seeker before him and so "it's in your blood." This directly parallels the information supplied in the book by Professor McGonagall, but in the film Hermione's remark leads Ron to comment, "She knows more about you than you." Here the second "you" is poised in tantalizing syntactical ambiguity: the obvious reading is that it is the subject of an implied "do"—"She knows more about you than you [do]"—but it can also eerily suggest a division of Harry into two "you's," as is certainly the case later in the film when, in a powerful image of uncanny doubling,

Harry sees himself in the mirror of Erised having his shoulder gripped by his mother. In the Gothic vault, the mirror shows what isn't there — and in each case the presence or legacy of the parents seems disturbing as well as reassuring.

It is the final confrontation with Voldemort which really puts identities and the weight of heredity to the test. Ron's decision to be a knight in the chess game is clearly presented as a deliberate identity choice rather than anything predetermined by the nature of the gaps on the board, and his self-sacrifice is indeed in the highest traditions of chivalry. This sets the stage for Harry's assertion of himself. But in another departure from the book, Voldemort makes him a remarkable offer: "Do you want to see your parents—together—we can make it happen." Just like that "you" of Hermione's, the "together" here is ambiguously poised. On one level, it seems to represent a suggestion that Harry and Voldemort might join forces, but it is also impossible to overlook the cliché of reuniting parents which has been one of the most pervasive cultural legacies of the growth in divorce, as in Disney's *The Parent Trap*. At this point, the film suddenly seems less like a glimpse into the unique and narratively self-sufficient world of Harry Potter than cultural pastiche, gesturing to the actual resurrection of the mother in *The Mummy Returns*. (This film is also evoked when Quirrell's face crumbles and when the book which Harry takes from the restricted shelf billows out at him like the head of Imhotep.)

There is even ambiguity about whether Harry might have accepted Voldemort's offer to reunite him with his parents. He goes so far as to take the stone out of his pocket and look at it longingly, but then he shouts "Liar!"—a refusal, to be sure, but one which does not entirely preclude the possibility that he might have accepted the offer if he had *not* thought it a lie. The final frames of the film keep up the proliferation of meanings even as they move towards ostensible closure: As Harry lies in his sickbed talking to Dumbledore, the actual nurse in the sickroom is eerily echoed by the identically dressed nurse in the painting who is attending to a different sickbed which might perhaps suggest Nicolas Flamel's deathbed. There is also a final displacement in that the photograph album, which in the book is given to Harry while he is still in sick bay, is here moved to become the grand climax of events. This is of course a fitting finale for the film in that film is in itself a collection of moving images, but it also eerily emblematizes the way in which doubled images may produce doubled meanings, which proliferate in ways other than the official.

In the case of this particular film, the proliferating meanings work, ultimately, to produce a story with a rather different emphasis from that found in the original book. When the first wave of merchandising appeared, it included T-shirts bearing the name "Voldemort." This appeared completely wrongheaded since evil is in no way glamorous in the Harry Potter books. But evil *is* typically glamorous in the Gothic, and that, in the end, is also one effect of the film, even if not the whole effect. Not only is Malfoy less repulsive than he ought to be, but Snape too is problematic (and though it may well be that Snape is ultimately rehabilitated, there is no hint of that in the books until the very end of *Harry Potter and the Goblet of Fire*). First, the casting of Alan Rickman in the rôle of Snape invites one to expect the kind of scene-stealing performance he supplied as the Sheriff of Nottingham in *Robin Hood: Prince of Thieves,* and second, the complete absence of any explanation of his motivation for saving Harry at the Quidditch match simply leads us to distrust our own sense of the differences between good and evil in this world. Add to that the dramatic effect of the revelation of what lies behind Quirrell's turban and Harry's apparent hesitation about accepting his offer, and the boundaries between good and evil have indeed become blurred here in a way that they were not in the book. The effect is, indeed, Gothic, but it is Gothic in a way which means that we see far more clearly than in the book that Harry's heritage is perhaps the darkest of the shadows that lie in weight for him.

The Lord of the Rings: The Fellowship of the Ring

There are a number of striking parallels between *Harry Potter and the Philosopher's Stone* and *The Fellowship of the Ring* (films which originally opened less than a month apart). Large parts of both are played out in subterranean spaces and Gothic buildings; each has a white-bearded, benevolent, elderly wizard and a hideous, terrifying troll; and both feature a character on whom the burden of his past and heredity weighs heavily and proves to be an increasingly dominant factor in his future. (In *Harry Potter and the Chamber of Secrets,* the similarities multiply still further since the computer-generated image of Dobby so strongly resembles Gollum.) Finally, both films are fundamentally Gothicized in a way that the books on which they were based were not, and in both cases the Gothicizing effects play most insistently around issues of identity.

Although generally faithful to the original book, Peter Jackson's film of J. R. R. Tolkien's *The Lord of the Rings: The Fellowship of the Ring* also introduces a new and essentially Gothicizing emphasis. Jackson's film is openly Gothic in its visual style and, ultimately, in its approach to its characters. The dwarves' city looks like a Gothic cathedral, and we are very aware of the way in which the landscape is littered with ruins like Amon Sûl and the watchtower that the fellowship passes later. The film also has other Gothic connotations: for instance, the clawed point of the Nazgûl's armored shoe echoes medieval armor, and there is the added frisson of the fact that Pippin knocks a body into the well in Moria rather than just a stone. There are clear echoes of *Star Wars*, as well, most notably in the way that the whole army falls over when Sauron's hand is cut off. There also seems to be a deliberate contrast with *Star Wars* when Elrond tells Aragorn that he is the last of his bloodline, as opposed to the revelation at the equivalent moment in *Star Wars* that Luke has a sister. Sauron himself crumbles in a way that recalls the *Mummy* (and *The Mummy Returns* also features the army-falling-over scene), while Elrond's face is the only bare one in the battle just as Rick's is at beginning of *Mummy*. The face of the Uruk-hai emerging from mud also echoes the materialization of Imhotep from the sand in *The Mummy*.

It is true that this emphasis was not entirely alien to the original, for Tolkien's novel is heavily indebted to *Dracula*. Gollum is clearly vampiric: "The Woodmen said that there was some new terror abroad, a ghost that drank blood. It climbed trees to find nests; it crept into holes to find the young; it slipped through windows to find cradles." [10] This is even more strongly marked in *The Two Towers*, in which Gollum's descent down the Emyn Muil so insistently recalls Harker's view of Dracula crawling down the walls of his castle:

> I saw the whole man slowly emerge from the window and begin to crawl down the castle wall over that dreadful abyss, *face down*, with his cloak spreading out around him like great wings. . . . I saw the fingers and toes grasp the corners of the stones, worn clear of the mortar by the stress of years, and by thus using every projection and inequality move downwards with considerable speed, just as a lizard moves along a wall. [11]

Compare the equivalent passage from *The Lord of the Rings*:

> Down the face of a precipice, sheer and almost smooth it seemed in the pale moonlight, a small black shape was moving with its thin limbs splayed out. Maybe its soft clinging hands and toes were finding crevices and holds that no hobbit could ever have seen or used, but it looked as if it was just creeping down on sticky pads, like some large prowling thing of insect-kind. And it was coming down head first, as if it was

smelling its way. Now and again it lifted its head slowly, turning it right back on its two small pale gleaming lights, its eyes that blinked at the moon for a moment and then were quickly lidded again. (*Two Towers,* p. 272)

When Gollum catches Sam, "sharp teeth bit into his shoulder" (*Two Towers,* p. 274), and when he thinks of harming Frodo, his fingers reach towards his neck (*Two Towers,* p. 299), so we are again reminded of vampires. Similarly, Strider says of the Riders, "[A]t all times they smell the blood of living things, desiring and hating it" (*Fellowship,* p. 255); Éowyn tells the Nazgúl, "[L]iving or dark undead, I will smite you" (*Return,* p. 137); and the hill-trolls "would bite the throats of those that they threw down" (*Return,* p. 203). There are also strong resemblances between *The Lord of the Rings* and Stoker's later novel *The Lady of the Shroud:* Rupert reading the signs in the camping place prefigures Aragorn on Weathertop, the kidnapped Teuta is whipped on by Turks just as the kidnapped Pippin and Merry are by orcs, Rupert jumps out of a tree like an eagle just as Gandalf does, and the aeroplane circling the Silent Tower to bring off the Voivode foreshadows both the Nazgúl and the rescue of Gandalf from the top of Orthanc.[12]

Tolkien's original novel also shares with *Dracula,* and indeed with Stoker's work in general, a clear interest in evolutionary theory and above all in degeneration. Hobbits "have dwindled, they say, and in ancient days they were taller" (*Fellowship,* p. 18). The steed of the Nazgúl also shows clear signs of evolutionary change:

[I]f bird, then greater than all other birds, and neither quill nor feather did it bear, and its vast pinions were as webs of hide between horned fingers; and it stank. A creature of an older world maybe it was, whose kind, lingering in forgotten mountains cold beneath the Moon, out-stayed their day, and in hideous eyrie bred this last untimely brood, apt to evil . . . (*Return,* p. 135)

Men now live less long than they once did, and at the close of the epic cycle, the entire Third Age passes away, taking with it forever many forms of life once familiar in Middle Earth, which effectively become extinct.

But if the original book revisits *Dracula,* the film equally clearly revisits *Frankenstein,* and although both *Dracula* and *Frankenstein* are Gothic, they are so in very different ways, so the film's switch in orientation ultimately introduces a very different emphasis from that found in Tolkien.

Like *Frankenstein,* this is unmistakably a story about the difficulties of family life. This idea is introduced early, when Bilbo says "these confounded relatives," and because there is no mention, as there is in the book, of the specific relative whom he clearly means (Lobelia Sackville-Baggins), it sounds simply as if he is referring to relatives in general. There is much emphasis on heredity — Isildur says, "All those who follow in my bloodline shall be bound to its fate," and it is clear that Aragorn's relationship with Isildur weighs heavily on him. Indeed, Elrond seems to indicate that Aragorn is a voluntary exile — "He turned from that path long ago. He chose exile" — and Boromir has heard of him, suggesting that he is not so much a lost king as one who has deliberately absented himself. The extent to which Aragorn feels himself a prisoner of his own ancestry is made even clearer when Arwen asks him "Why do you fear the past?" beside the statue of Isildur and he says "The same blood flows in my veins. . . . The same weakness." (Though it is notable that Isildur doesn't look like Aragorn, which suggests that his fears may well prove unfounded, presumably coming from his own apprehension of his situation rather than from any external cause.) Indeed the film's official website made Aragorn even more of an outcast than he is in the book, describing him as "a human reared by elves" and thus suggesting that, if this is to be read in the light of *Frankenstein,* Aragorn narrowly misses being the Monster.

Also as in *Frankenstein,* that which is artificial is clearly pitted against that which is natural. The loathsome and sinister Orthanc is obviously manmade, a point underlined when we cut from it to growing sheaves of corn. To similar effect, Sauron tells Saruman to "build me an army," and we cut to a shot of trees being felled. Most notably, Saruman explains to the Uruk-hai that orcs originated from tortured elves, though we are also told, "By foul craft Saruman has crossed orcs with goblin men." (Lest we be tempted to disbelieve him, the film even works to create some similarities between these two apparently antithetical races: orcs have long hair and pointy ears and use bows and arrows — all just like the elves.) This essentially presents the Uruk-hai as representing the same sort of monstrous parody of the birth process as that offered by the Monster, while their hatred of the elves invites comparison with the Monster's animus against the similarly more favored William. And as in *Frankenstein,* there are, apart from a hobbit woman seen in the opening sequence, no living mothers here, nor even mention of any dead ones; for instance, there is no reference to Celebrian, mother of Arwen, or to Gilraen, mother of Aragorn (though her tombstone is shown in the extended version subsequently released on video and DVD).

Analogous to the difference between the novel's debt to *Dracula* and the film's debt to *Frankenstein* is the difference between the New Zealand of the film and the Africa which is a hidden but powerful influence on the novel. Even greater than Tolkien's debt to Stoker is his debt to Haggard (who was also a strong influence on Tolkien's fellow Inkling C. S. Lewis). In Haggard's *She and Allan* (1921), Allan and his party follow the Amahagger through a marsh in which there is foul gas and strange lights like will-o'-the-wisps, as in the Dead Marshes of Mordor; later, smoking pipes, they look at the mountain which is their goal.[13] In *Ayesha* (1905) there is a chapter headed "The White Witch," which occurs immediately after Allan and his party are carried to safety after an emissary rescues them from an attack by black men, rather as Frodo and his companions arrive at Rivendell after Glorfindel rescues them from the Black Riders.[14] Shelob's foul-smelling cave (*Two Towers*, p. 408) is of course a Haggard staple; Aragorn's length of lineage recalls that of the Leo Vincey of *She*, who can similarly trace his male ancestry back thousands of years, while Arwen's immortality parallels Ayesha's length of years. In *She*, Holly longs for his own rooms, just as Bilbo does, noting that Leo's "reference to chapel made me reflect, with a sort of sick longing, on my comfortable rooms at Cambridge. Why had I been such a fool as to leave them? This is a reflection that has several times recurred to me since, and with ever-increasing force."[15] There is an impregnable mountain city resembling Gondolin (*She*, pp.124–125); She, like Galadriel, has water in which the future can be seen (p. 149); and Job, like Sam, fusses about hot water (p. 164) and, also like Sam, sees his family in Ayesha's mirror (p. 208). Finally, Leo, Holly, and Job pass through "the Land of Shadow" (p. 277) to a Mordor-like region of desolation around a volcano (p. 298). In *King Solomon's Mines*, Allan, like Bilbo at the beginning of *The Hobbit*, is fifty-five when the story begins; there is wonderful mail like mithril, and the exiled king Ignosi and his mother prefigure Aragorn and Gilraen, while Foulata's medicine seems to be administered and to work like kingsfoil.[16]

There are also echoes of that other writer influenced by Stoker and Haggard, Buchan. Aragorn summons the dead by the Black Stone (*Return*, p.181), which is the name of the conspiracy in *The Thirty-Nine Steps;* and Earendil travels "where grey the Norland waters run" (*Fellowship*, p. 309), while the greater part of Buchan's *The Island of Sheep* is set on the Norland islands. Like both Haggard and Buchan, Tolkien tends to project the characteristics of Scotland onto his remote landscapes: he writes of "the dark mass of Mount Mindolluin, the deep purple shadows of its high glens" (*Return*, p. 20), and there is an obvious link between the Stewarts of Scotland and the Stewards of Minas Tirith. There is also a less happy echo of South Africa in the clear resemblance between Dunharrow under the Dwimmorberg and the concentration camps which Buchan helps to set up after the Boer War (*Return,* pp. 76–77). In Buchan's short story "The Frying-Pan and the Fire," we find the "glen of the Hollin,"[17] and in *Huntingtower,* Mrs. Morran's cottage "had a green door and a polished brass knocker," like Bilbo's. Dickson the grocer buckling on his pack, taking his pipe on a journey, and contemplating burglary also recall Bilbo, and again it is jewels which are at stake and which Dickson must conceal on his person. At the climax of *Huntingtower,* we are told, "The garrison had entered the Dark Tower."[18] In Buchan's *Witch Wood,* there is a "mirk wood" with a "muckle spider's wab" and only one road through it, and David is called a "halfling" and sets riddles.[19] In *The House of the Four Winds,* Juventus, like the Dark Lord, have an open eye as their symbol (it is directly compared to the swastika), and Glynde appears in their midst at the inn without their being aware of him because the landlord is a friend of his, just as Aragorn does.[20]

Both Haggard and Buchan insistently connote Africa, consequently bringing with them strong echoes of the theories of fixed racial identities to which post-Darwinian scientific racism had given rise. New Zealand has no such clearly packaged set of meanings, though it is increasingly famous as the home of "Kiwi Gothic," a genre to which Jackson's earlier work could well be said to belong (certainly his first film *Bad Taste* and his 1996 "mockumentary" *Forgotten Silver* both seem to be distinctively about New Zealand, as does *Heavenly Creatures*). A staple of "Kiwi Gothic" is violence within the family (*Heavenly Creatures* features matricide), and to the extent that New Zealand was a popular destination for emigrants, it could also be seen as representing the possibility for breaking away from existing families and from ancestral ties. If Africa speaks of long-distant origins, then, New Zealand might well be thought to speak of both more recent and even present family structures.

The Fellowship of the Ring is certainly riddled with questions about the rôles of individuals both inside and outside the family. Above all, there are the characteristically Gothic motifs of uncertain identity and uncanny doubling: when Frodo looks in the mirror of Galadriel, the first thing he sees is Legolas. At Rauros, in the first major departure from text, many more characters than in the original are tested and apparently found wanting, in line with Galadriel's prophecy to Frodo that the Fellowship will turn one by one. This happens first with Aragorn, when Frodo recoils from him, seeming to think that he is Boromir, although in a further reversal of expectations Aragorn then proceeds to resist the ring. Next comes the sequence in which Frodo refuses to join Merry and Pippin—who then similarly prove themselves by acting as decoys. This, however, is merely the extreme example of a phenomenon which is present throughout the film. Galadriel and Gandalf are both distinctly menacing—in the first exchange between Gandalf and Frodo, which is our introduction to both characters, Gandalf seems grim and Frodo unsure, and then Gandalf sits by the fire muttering "my precious" for all the world as if he were Gollum instead of himself. A similar effect is created in the sequence where we first see the Black Rider and then cut to Frodo returning to Bag End; it clearly looks as though the hobbit-hole has been broken into, and we are invited to expect that there will be a Black Rider lurking inside—but instead the intruder turns out to be Gandalf. Moreover, the entire trick is repeated when we hear a disturbance outside. This time it must surely be the Black Rider—but in fact, it is Sam. Similar techniques come into play when we are introduced to Aragorn: before we grasp that the hobbits have been taken to safety, we see the Riders poised over the beds in which they are apparently sleeping and then cut directly to Aragorn so that it looks as though he has colluded with them. Most notably, of course, Arwen is first encountered with her sword at Aragorn's throat.

It is not only individual identity which is uncertain, moreover, but gender identity. When Pippin rises up from his fall holding a broken carrot, we should begin to guess that this is a film in which masculinity is fundamentally imperiled. (The carrot could also be seen to some extent as standing in for Aragorn's sword, which is initially broken in the novel but is fully functional from the outset here.) As Elrond (played with delicious irony by Hugo Weaving, famous for his rôle in *Priscilla, Queen of the Desert*) declares, "Men are weak. The race of men is failing." The elves certainly teeter dangerously on the edge of camp (and fall well over it in Lothlorien). Indeed campiness is implicit everywhere: as well as being indelibly associated with Weaving's public profile, it also features strongly in that of Orlando Bloom, whose film debut was in *Wilde,* as one of Wilde's boys,[21] a fact which was naughtily invoked by Ian McKellen in much of the publicity work he did for the film, perhaps most notably in an interview in the *Observer* in which he declared:

> So we even had the situation where gays were saying to Peter: 'You *are* going to understand that Sam and Frodo are in love, you know;

they're always hugging and kissing and sleeping together' — and you've got to say, yeah, but you can go too far. Sex really isn't on the agenda in Middle-Earth. . . . Although I was suggesting to Peter yesterday he should insert some love interest for Gandalf in a later one. He suggested Galadriel. . . . I said, no, I was thinking more of someone like Legolas.[22]

However, it is not Gandalf and Legolas whom the film comes closest to presenting as a gay couple, but Aragorn and Boromir. From the moment we register the initial antagonism between them, their relationship follows the classic courtship trajectory, tracing a growing intimacy and culminating finally in a kiss. When Boromir tells Aragorn, "They took the little ones," and Aragorn responds by promising to protect "[o]ur people," they sound for all the world like the joint heads of a family, and it is also notable that they are often photographed in the same shot (this being, presumably, because the similarity of size made this an easy option, with no need for the complicating factor of scale doubles). It may well seem suggestive, too, that the putting of the ring on the finger, with its obvious heterosexual overtones, becomes here the forbidden thing; this, together with the enhanced and more aggressive rôle given to Arwen and the astonishing androgyny of Cate Blanchett's Galadriel, may well seem to suggest that traditional modes of masculinity are indeed deeply embattled here and that, as so often in Kiwi Gothic, the fundamental question is that which Frodo asks of Aragorn, "Can you protect me from yourself?" Like *The Mummy Returns* and *Harry Potter and the Philosopher's Stone*, then, *The Lord of the Rings: The Fellowship of the Ring* ostensibly offers escapist fantasy and is packaged as suitable for family entertainment, but, also like them, it raises some extremely disturbing questions about families, their effects, their dynamics, and the extent to which they recognize and accommodate the real range of human identities. Far from being in retreat, as some of the earlier chapters may have suggested, the Gothic is alive and well; but it has fled from its original lairs, which have now been definitely marked as uncanny, to resurface, even more uncannily, at the heart of "family entertainment."

Modern society has developed an obsession with the idea of "stranger danger" and, fearing a pedophile on every street corner, is now reluctant to let its children out alone. In these films, though, the real danger to children and to those represented as infantilized or small proves to lurk, frighteningly, much closer to home. It is true that in *The Mummy Returns* a child is indeed abducted by a stranger, but it is a stranger who eerily parallels the child's own mother. In *Harry Potter and the Philosopher's Stone,* the monster looks out of the mirror, and in *The Fellowship of the Ring,* it is his own companions whom Frodo comes ultimately to fear. These three films, ostensibly for children, thus prove to contain some of the darkest and deepest fears of all the Gothic films I have examined.

CONCLUSION

*I*n this book, I have tried to trace a trajectory in the deployment of the Gothic on screen. It is only partially a chronological one: though it is true that the first chapter deals with the earliest text I consider (*Hamlet*) and the last with the most recent (*The Mummy Returns* and the Harry Potter books), there is no similar sequencing at work in terms of the dates of the adaptations I discuss, and the presence or absence of the Gothic on screen is not, in fact, a matter of chronology or even of historical moment. Nor is its presence or absence the result of the preferences of particular directors: although I discuss two films by Zeffirelli and two by Kenneth Branagh, they fall into very different categories. Instead the extent of a film's Gothic qualities seems, as I have argued throughout the book, to be a product of the original nature of the text being adapted.

The "formula" whose existence I have tried to establish is a simple one. In the first place, if a written text originally had Gothic attributes or was written as a conscious contribution to the Gothic tradition, it is impossible to adapt it for the screen in a fully Gothicized mode. Even where a Gothic element does remain in the adaptation, it is Gothic in a different way from the original text; to reiterate, I assume in this book that the three key characteristics of the Gothic are doubling, a psychoanalytic perspective, and an emphasis on family tension, and my point is that no Gothicized film of a Gothic text picks the same characteristic to emphasize as the original text did. Even when it comes to the more contingent and peripheral indications of the Gothic, such as castles, ruined mansions, vulnerable heroines, and sinister elderly men, films of Gothic texts noticeably fail to reproduce these in the way that they found them.

In the case of *Hamlet,* the three films which I discuss in the first chapter all offer completely different takes on this most notable harbinger of the Gothic genre proper. Zeffirelli's film retains the trappings of the historical period most closely associated with the Gothic, but has nothing of its troubled, probing spirit. Conversely, Branagh's version, while opening the settings to an almost unimaginable scale, nevertheless offers so many doublings and psychologically suggestive deflections of focus and attention that it is a truly Gothic film, and so, albeit in a different way, is Almereyda's ostensibly spankingly up-to-date, technological vision.

Together, these three films not only represent opposing ends of the Gothic spectrum, but also sum up the whole argument of this book: that the Gothic is inescapably dual, and that its soul is rarely, if ever, to be found in the same place as its body. This is even truer of the groups of films which I discussed in chapters two and three. In the second chapter of the book, I looked at screen adaptations of four novels which were all, in their different ways, quite antithetical to the ethos and representational practices of the Gothic, but which have all been thoroughly Gothicized in their transition to the screen. In *Clarissa* and *The Time Machine,* this is done overwhelmingly by emphasis on dreams; in the two Jane Austen adaptations I discussed, the Gothicizing effect is achieved by a rearrangement and reassigning of character traits which destabilizes the idea of coherent personality so important to Austen's narrative ethos and leaves us in a Gothic world of lurching and unpredictable urges rather than in Austen's shaped and rational one. Conversely, in the third chapter I discussed four texts which in their original forms were either written within the Gothic tradition or, in the case of *'Tis Pity She's a Whore,* can be clearly seen as foreshadowing it. When they are translated to the screen, however, all trace of the Gothic is drained away, and we are left instead with exactly the kind of systematic investigations of social, familial, and political structures which we might have expected to find in Jane Austen.

The adaptations I discussed in the fourth chapter operate in a rather different way, but nevertheless ultimately support the overall thesis of the book. Both *Jane Eyre* and *Dracula* were originally written wholly or partially in the Gothic mode, and they remain in many ways Gothic on screen—but the elements which are Gothic on screen are not the same as those which were Gothic in the original books. In the original novel of *Jane Eyre,* the source of greatest terror is, notoriously, the madwoman in the attic. But Zeffirelli's film of the book does not even try to find Bertha Mason frightening; instead, it focuses its imaginative energies on child abuse and on the warped psychologies of those who perpetrate it. In Taylor's *Jane Eyre,* this process is taken even further, because the prevalence of the language of therapy means that it is *everyone*'s psychology, even that of the most normal-seeming people, which is estranged and potentially pathologized. Finally, in Coppola's *Dracula,* as in Zeffirelli's *Jane Eyre,* it is not the monster who is frightening, but the repressed, hypocritical society which comes together only in its wish to destroy him.

The pathology of the ostensibly normal is even more at the forefront in the three films I discussed in the last chapter, *The Mummy Returns*, *Harry Potter and the Philosopher's Stone*, and *The Lord of the Rings: The Fellowship of the Ring*, for the imagination of each is most strongly fired by the home. This might appear to be a wildly counterintuitive claim in the light of all these films' epic scale, formidable special effects, and apparent interest in action rather than emotion, but nevertheless what lies at the heart of all of them is an acute interest in the domestic, in both the importance and difficulty of families. It is at the heart of the *heimlich* that the energies of the *unheimlich* ignite, and it is in the setting of what seems the strangest—the corridors of Hogwarts, the mines of Moria—that we find what is most uncannily familiar. Once again, the Gothic proves to be a visitor which surfaces when least expected. What all these films prove is, as we might have expected from this most haunted and contradictory of modes, that the Gothic is never identical with itself. Most absent when most conspicuously present, it is also most present only when most conspicuously absent.

This is perhaps most strikingly shown by a film whose very title announces that it tackles the question of the Gothic head on. Ken Russell's *Gothic,* made in 1986, is a clear illustration of the ways in which the energies of the Gothic are sparked most strongly by the familiar and often by what is literally within the family. The film centers on an evening and night at the Villa Diodati, after the poet Shelley has arrived with his mistress Claire Clairmont to visit Lord Byron, who is self-exiled to a villa in Switzerland with only an elderly butler and his Italian-born doctor, John Polidori, for company. Amidst a variety of louche and reckless behavior, including at least a gesture towards virtually every possible sexual coupling of those assembled, the party stages a séance and apparently calls to life a monster which runs amok through the villa for the rest of the night. As sights of horror multiply, there is no shortage of reminders both of the concretely real and monstrous—perhaps most notably Byron's bloodstained mouth as his head comes up from performing oral sex on Claire—and also of the fact that this is the night which spawned two of the most famous Gothic horror stories ever told, *Frankenstein* and (indirectly, through Polidori's vampire novel) *Dracula.* Indeed the closing shot shows a drowned baby slowly morphing into the classic image of Boris Karloff as Frankenstein's Monster.

Nevertheless, it is interiority that is most frightening in this film. It is made abundantly clear that the creature which the party conjures up is born from their own imaginations, just as the reason that Claire goes into a fit as she imagines childbirth is that she is indeed pregnant. When Claire proposes that they each tell a ghost story, Polidori maliciously stabs at Byron by asking, "What about a dark English nobleman who draws women to him, sucks their blood, and discards them empty?" and Byron equally maliciously ripostes, "Oh yes. Or an obscene Italian doctor raised by the Benedictines who turns to sin and buggery?" Equally, it is clear that the genesis of Mary Shelley's monster novel lies in the death of her baby and in her future husband's interest in lightning and scientific experiment. Once more, it is the domestic which gives rise to the Gothic.

When the Gothic began as a genre, it was located primarily in Italy and dealt with the habits of those who were different from its original readers in nationality and, above all, in religion. Now, it finds its most urgent energies in the home, in the presence of those most like, and most nearly related to, those who read and watch it. It is unsurprising, therefore, that its most recent place of residence should be in children's movies, where it speaks so powerfully to fears about the abuse and indeed the general oversexualizing of our children. It may be safe to get back into the water, but what about the bath?

$\mathcal{N}$OTES

Introduction

1. Robert Miles, *Gothic Writing 1750–1820: A Genealogy* (London: Routledge, 1993), p. 2.

2. Fred Botting, *Gothic* (London: Routledge, 1996), p. 1.

3. Linda Bayer-Berenbaum, *The Gothic Imagination: Expansion in Gothic Literature and Art* (London and Toronto: Associated University Presses, 1982), p. 25.

4. David J. Skal, *Hollywood Gothic: The Tangled Web of* Dracula *from Novel to Stage to Screen* (London: André Deutsch, 1990), p. 12.

5. Markman Ellis, *The History of Gothic Fiction* (Edinburgh: Edinburgh University Press, 2000), p. 13.

6. I am aware that William Patrick Day draws a distinction between the two, in that he opines "The important differences between the nature of the Gothic's therapeutic functions and those of psychoanalysis lie in the fluidity of the Gothic vision and its faith in the powers of imagination and pleasure" (*In the Circles of Fear and Desire: A Study of Gothic Fantasy* [Chicago: The University of Chicago Press, 1985], p. 189). However, it is not so much the terms of the affiliation but its existence which matters for my purposes.

Chapter One

1. Philippa Sheppard, "The Castle of Elsinore: Gothic Aspects of Kenneth Branagh's *Hamlet*," *Shakespeare Bulletin* 19.3 (Summer 2001), pp. 36–39, p. 37.

2. Robert Hapgood, "Popularizing Shakespeare: The artistry of Franco Zeffirelli," in *Shakespeare, the Movie: popularizing the plays on film, tv and video*, edited by Lynda E. Boose and Richard Burt (London: Routledge, 1997), pp. 80–94, p. 83.

3. For analysis of this, see for instance Barbara Hodgdon, "The Critic, the Poor Player, Prince Hamlet, and the Lady in the Dark," in *Shakespeare Reread: The Texts in New Contexts*, edited by Russ McDonald (Ithaca: Cornell University Press, 1994), pp. 259–294, pp. 282–283.

4. Hapgood, "Popularizing Shakespeare," p. 88.

5. For comment on this aspect of the film, see Lynda E. Boose and Richard Burt, "Totally Clueless? Shakespeare goes Hollywood in the 1990s," in *Shakespeare, the Movie,* pp. 8–22, pp. 9–10.

6. Samuel Crowl, "Flamboyant realist: Kenneth Branagh," in *The Cambridge Companion to Shakespeare on Film,* edited by Russell Jackson (Cambridge: Cambridge University Press, 2000), pp. 222–238, p. 224.

7. Sheppard, "Castle of Elsinore," p. 36.

8. *The Readiness Is All: The Filming of Hamlet,* BBC2, first shown 15 February 1997. The interview is reproduced on the programme's website at http://www.bbc .co.uk/education/bookcase/hamlet/dream.shtml

9. http://www.tnt-tv.com/specials/hamlet

10. Courtney Lehmann and Lisa S. Starks, "Making Mother Matter: Repression, Revision, and the Stakes of 'Reading Psychoanalysis Into' Kenneth Branagh's Hamlet," *Early Modern Literary Studies* 6.1 (May 2000) 2.1–24, 4. Online: http:// www.shu.ac.uk/emls/06-1/lehmhaml.htm

11. Sheppard, "Castle of Elsinore," p. 37.

12. See for instance Desson Howe in *The Washington Post,* 24 January 1997 (available online at http://www.washingtonpost.com/wp-srv/style/longterm/ movies/review97/hamlethowe.htm).

13. *The Readiness Is All: The Filming of Hamlet.*

14. See for instance Laura Mulvey, *Visual and Other Pleasures* (Bloomington: Indiana University Press, 1989), Judith Mayne, *Cinema and Spectatorship* (London: Routledge, 1993), and Christian Metz, *The Imaginary Signifier: Psychoanalysis and the Cinema* (Bloomington: Indiana University Press, 1977).

15. *The Readiness Is All: The Filming of Hamlet.*

16. Russell Jackson says that what is happening here is that "an incident described in the dialogue is enacted for the camera," which is cumbersome but strictly accurate; the lack of any more pat phrase shows the unusual nature of what Branagh is doing here ("From play-script to screenplay," in Jackson, ed., *Cambridge Companion,* pp. 15–34, p. 27).

17. William Shakespeare, *Hamlet,* edited by Harold Jenkins (London: Methuen, 1980), I.iii.104. All further quotations from the play are taken from this edition and references are given in the text.

18. Carol Chillington Rutter, "Looking at Shakespeare's women on film," in Jackson, ed., *Cambridge Companion,* pp. 241–260, p. 253.

19. William Shakespeare, *Love's Labour's Lost,* edited by John Kerrigan (Harmondsworth: Penguin, 1982), IV.iii.288 ff.

20. Richard Corliss, "The Whole Dane Thing," *Time* 149:2 (13 January 1997), available online at http://www.time.com/time/magazine/1997/dom/970113/cinema .the_whole.html

21. Joe Baltake, *Bee Movie Critic,* 24 January 1996; reprinted at http://www .movieclub.com/reviews/archives/96hamlet/hamlet.html

22. *Hamlet—to cut or not to cut?*, BBC2, first shown 5 February 1997.

23. J. Lawrence Guntner, *"Hamlet, Macbeth* and *King Lear* on film," in Jackson, ed., *Cambridge Companion,* pp. 117–134, p. 122.

24. William Shakespeare, *Richard III,* edited by E. A. J. Honigmann (Harmondsworth, England: Penguin, 1968), I.i.28.

25. Tanja Weiss provides a table of the shots in this sequence which clearly shows the extent to which it is a four-way rather than a two-way scene (*Shakespeare on the Screen: Kenneth Branagh's Adaptations of* Henry V, Much Ado About Nothing *and* Hamlet [Frankfurt am Main: Peter Lang, 1999], p. 160).

26. http://www.tnt-tv.com/specials/hamlet/

27. Kenneth Branagh, *Hamlet, by William Shakespeare: Screenplay, Introduction and Film Diary* (London: W. W. Norton, 1996), p. 162.

28. *Hamlet—to cut or not to cut?*

29. See James Hirsh, "The 'To Be or Not To Be' Scene and the Conventions of Shakespearean Drama," *Modern Language Quarterly* 42:2 (1981), pp. 115–136.

30. Lehmann and Starks, "Making Mother Matter," p. 10.

31. For comment on this, see for instance Mark Thornton Burnett, "The 'Very Cunning of the Scene': Kenneth Branagh's *Hamlet," Literature/Film Quarterly* 25:2 (1997), pp. 78–82.

32. See for instance Christopher Small, *Ariel Like a Harpy: Shelley, Mary and Frankenstein* (London: 1972), p. 37; Mary K. Patterson Thornburg, *The Monster in the Mirror: Gender and the Sentimental/Gothic Myth in Frankenstein* (Michigan: UMI Research Press, 1984; reprinted, 1987), p. 102; and Anne K. Mellor, *Mary Shelley: Her Life, Her Fiction, Her Monsters* (London and New York: Routledge, 1988), p. 38.

33. William Shakespeare, *Othello,* edited by E. A. J. Honigmann (Lerder: Thomas Nelson, 1997), III.iii.400–401.

34. Burnett, "The 'Very Cunning of the Scene,' " p.80.

35. See for instance Harry Keyishian, "Shakespeare and movie genre: The case of *Hamlet,"* in Jackson, ed., *Cambridge Companion,* pp. 72–81, p. 80.

36. For comment on Zeffirelli's setting, see for instance Ace Pilkington, "Zeffirelli's Shakespeare," in *Shakespeare and the Moving Image,* edited by Anthony Davies and Stanley Wells (Cambridge: Cambridge University Press, 1994), pp. 163–179, pp. 165 and 173–174.

37. On the use of water imagery in the film, see for instance Philip Armstrong, *Shakespeare in Psychoanalysis* (London: Routledge, 2001), pp. 216–217.

Chapter Two

1. See for instance E. Ann Kaplan, *Woman and Film: Both Sides of the Camera* (London: Methuen, 1983), especially p. 30 ff, Annette Kuhn, *Women's Pictures: Feminism and the Cinema* (London: Routledge, 1982), especially pp. 63–64,

and Laura Mulvey, *Visual and Other Pleasures* (Bloomington: Indiana University Press, 1989), pp. 25–26.

2. Samuel Richardson, *Clarissa,* edited by Angus Ross (Harmondsworth, England: Penguin, 1985), p. 883. All page references are to this edition.

3. Slavoj Žižek, *Enjoy Your Symptom!: Jacques Lacan in Hollywood and Out* (London: Routledge, 1992), p. 158.

4. Terry Eagleton, *The Rape of Clarissa* (Oxford: Basil Blackwell, 1982), p. 63.

5. Jane Austen, *Sense and Sensibility,* edited by Tony Tanner (Harmondsworth: Penguin, 1969), p. 93. All further quotations from the novel are taken from this edition and references are given in the text.

6. For critical comment on this, see for instance Margaret Kirkham, *Jane Austen: Feminism and Fiction* (Brighton, England: The Harvester Press, 1983), p. 141; Anne Ruderman, "Moral Education in Jane Austen's *Emma*," in *Poets, Princes, and Private Citizens: Literary Alternatives to Postmodern Politics,* edited by Joseph M. Knippenberg and Peter Augustine Lawler (London: Rowman & Littlefield, 1996), pp. 271–288, p. 272; and Inger Sigrun Thomsen, "Words 'Half-Dethroned': Jane Austen's Art of the Unspoken," in *Jane Austen's Business: Her World and Her Profession,* edited by Juliet McMaster and Bruce Stovel (Basingstoke, England: Macmillan, 1996), pp. 17–29, p. 97.

7. Kristin Flieger Samuelian, " 'Piracy Is Our Only Option': Postfeminist Intervention in *Sense and Sensibility,*" *Topic* 48 (1997), pp. 39–48, p. 40.

8. Samuelian, "Piracy," p. 41.

9. On the blurring of Brandon with Willoughby, see also Cheryl L. Nixon, "Balancing the Courtship Hero: Masculine Emotional Display in Film Adaptations of Austen's Novels," in *Jane Austen in Hollywood,* edited by Linda Troost and Sayre Greenfield (Lexington: University of Kentucky Press, 1998), pp. 22–43, p. 39, and Nora Nachumi, " 'As If!': Translating Austen's Ironic Narrator to Film," in *Jane Austen in Hollywood,* pp. 130–139, pp. 132–133.

10. Susie Mackenzie, "Angel with Horns," *Guardian Weekend* (3 January 1998), pp. 10–16, pp. 10 and 16.

11. Samuelian, "Piracy," p. 42.

12. Emma Thompson, *Jane Austen's Sense and Sensibility: The Screenplay and Diaries* (London: Bloomsbury, 1995), p. 179.

13. Samuelian, "Piracy," pp. 42–43.

14. On the ways in which the two sisters seem at times almost to reverse roles in the film, see Rebecca Dickson, "Misrepresenting Jane Austen's Ladies: Revising Texts (and History) to Sell Films," in *Jane Austen in Hollywood,* pp. 44–57, p. 51.

15. John R. Greenfield, "Is Emma Clueless? Fantasies of Class and Gender from England to California," *Topic* 48 (1997), pp. 31–38, p. 32.

16. See D. W. Harding, "Regulated Hatred: An Aspect of the Work of Jane Austen," *Scrutiny* 8 (March 1940).

17. H. G. Wells, *The Time Machine,* edited by John Lawton (London: J. M. Dent, 1995), p. 19. All further quotations from the book are taken from this edition and references are given in the text.

18. For comment on this, see John Huntington, *The Logic of Fantasy: H. G. Wells and Science Fiction* (New York: Columbia University Press, 1982), p. 45, and Paul K. Alkon, *Science Fiction Before 1900: Imagination Discovers Technology* (New York: Twayne, 1994), p. 50.

19. Quoted in Elaine Showalter, *Sexual Anarchy: Gender and Culture at the Fin de Siècle* (London: Bloomsbury, 1990), p. 9.

20. For discussion of the black presence in fin-de-siècle England, see for instance Ziggi Alexander and Audrey Dewjee, "Black Politicians," in *The Edwardian Era,* edited by Jane Beckett and Deborah Cherry (London: Phaidon Press, 1987), pp. 24–25.

Chapter Three

1. See Rowland Wymer, " 'The Audience Is Only Interested in Sex and Violence': Teaching the Renaissance on Film," in *Working Papers on the Web* 4 (September 2002). Online: http://www.shu.ac.uk/wpw/renaissance/wymer.htm

2. There is no possessive apostrophe in the title of the film. On the reasons for its omission, see Ben Spiller, " 'Today, Vindici Returns': Alex Cox's *Revengers Tragedy,"* *Early Modern Literary Studies* 8.3 (January 2003). Online: http://www.shu.ac.uk/emls/08-3/spilreve.html

3. For comment on this, see for instance Terri Clerico, "The Politics of Blood: John Ford's *'Tis Pity She's a Whore,"* *English Literary Renaissance* 22.3 (1992), pp. 405–434.

4. Angela Carter, "John Ford's *'Tis Pity She's a Whore,"* in *Burning Your Boats: The Collected Short Stories* (London: Chatto & Windus, 1995).

5. See Lisa Hopkins, "Incest and Class: *'Tis Pity She's a Whore* and the Borgias," in *Incest and the Literary Imagination,* edited by Elizabeth Barnes (Gainesville: University Press of Florida, 2002), pp. 94–113.

6. On the doubleness of the monster and Victor, see for instance Safaa El-Shater, *The Novels of Mary Shelley* (Salzburg: Salzburg Studies, 1977), p. 18; Tim Marshall, "*Frankenstein* and the 1832 Anatomy Act," in *Gothick Origins and Innovations,* edited by Allan Lloyd Smith and Victor Sage (Amsterdam: Rodopi, 1994), pp. 57–64, p. 60; Mary Poovey, *The Proper Lady and the Woman Writer* (Chicago: University of Chicago Press, 1984), p. 126; and William Veeder, *Mary Shelley and Frankenstein: The Fate of Androgyny* (Chicago: University of Chicago Press, 1986), p. 91.

7. Mary Elizabeth Braddon, *Lady Audley's Secret* [1862] (London: Virago, 1985), p. 366.

Chapter Four

1. Ace Pilkington, "Zeffirelli's Shakespeare," in *Shakespeare and the Moving Image,* edited by Anthony Davies and Stanley Wells (Cambridge: Cambridge University Press, 1994), pp. 163–179, p. 164.

2. The ITV version also has only one Rivers sister, but there it is Mary who is axed and Diana who remains.

3. Vera Dika, "From Dracula—with Love," in *The Dread of Difference,* edited by Barry Keith Grant (Austin: University of Texas Press, 1996), pp. 388 and 399.

4. See for instance Dika, "From Dracula—with Love," pp. 394–395, and Michael Kline, "The Vampire as Pathogen: Bram Stoker's *Dracula* and Francis Ford Coppola's *Bram Stoker's Dracula,*" *West Virginia University Philological Papers* 42/43 (1997/1998), pp. 36–44.

5. For comments on this, see Jörg Waltje, "Filming *Dracula:* Vampires, Genre, and Cinematography," *Journal of Dracula Studies* 4 (2002), pp. 24–33, p. 29.

6. Kenneth Jurkiewicz, "Francis Coppola's Secret Gardens: *Bram Stoker's Dracula* and the Auteur as Decadent Visionary," in *Visions of the Fantastic,* edited by Allienne R. Becker (London: Greenwood Press, 1996), pp. 167–172, p. 170.

7. Fred Botting, *Gothic* (London: Routledge, 1996), p. 180.

8. Kim Newman, "Coppola's Dracula," in *The Mammoth Book of Dracula,* edited by Stephen Jones (London: Robinson, 1997), pp. 109–155, p. 109.

9. Waltje, "Filming *Dracula,*" p. 33.

10. Alain Silver and James Ursini, *The Vampire Film from* Nosferatu *to* Interview with the Vampire, 3rd edition (New York: Proscenium, 1997), p. 155.

11. David Glover, "Travels in Romania: Myths of Origins, Myths of Blood," *Discourse* 16 (1993), pp. 126–144, pp. 132 and 133.

12. Ronald R. Thomas, "Specters of the Novel: *Dracula* and the Cinematic Afterlife of the Victorian Novel," *Nineteenth Century Contexts* 22.1 (2000), pp. 77–102, p. 92.

13. Thomas, "Specters of the Novel," p. 90.

14. For comments on this, see Francis Ford Coppola and James V. Hart, *Bram Stoker's Dracula: The Film and the Legend* (London: Pan, 1992), p. 52.

15. Newman, "Coppola's Dracula," p. 110.

Chapter Five

1. *The Guardian,* 23 May 2001, p. 1.

2. Bram Stoker, *The Jewel of Seven Stars,* introduced by David Glover (Oxford: Oxford University Press, 1996), p. 96. All further quotations from the novel are from this edition and references are given in the text.

3. Max Allan Collins, *The Mummy* (London: Ebury Press, 1999), p. 156. All

further quotations from the novelization are from this edition and references are given in the text.

4. John Whitman, *The Mummy Returns* (London: Bantam Books, 2001), p. 63.

5. Max Allan Collins, *The Mummy Returns* (New York: Berkley Boulevard, 2001), p. 96.

6. Dave Wolverton, *Revenge of the Scorpion King* (London: Bantam, 2001), pp. 71 and 72.

7. Elizabeth Peters, *The Snake, the Crocodile and the Dog* (London: Constable & Robinson, 1992), pp. 6 and 21.

8. J. K. Rowling, *Harry Potter and the Philosopher's Stone* (London: Bloomsbury, 1997), p. 44. All further quotations from the book are from this edition and references are given in the text.

9. Rowling, *Harry Potter and the Philosopher's Stone*, p. 61.

10. J. R. R. Tolkien, *The Fellowship of the Ring* [1954] (London: Grafton, 1991), p.87. Quotations from the other two volumes are from the same series. See also Gwenyth Hood, "Sauron and Dracula," in *Dracula: the Vampire and the Critics*, edited by Margaret L. Carter (Ann Arbor, Mich.: UMI Research Press, 1988), pp. 215–230.

11. Bram Stoker, *Dracula*, edited by A. N. Wilson (Oxford: Oxford University Press, 1983), p. 34.

12. Bram Stoker, *The Lady of the Shroud* [1909] (London: Alan Sutton, 1994), pp. 100, 154, and 157.

13. H. Rider Haggard, *She and Allan* [1921] (London: Macdonald, 1960), pp. 112–113 and 126.

14. H. Rider Haggard, *Ayesha* (London: Ward Lock & Co., 1905), p. 134.

15. H. Rider Haggard, *She* [1887] (Harmondsworth: Penguin, 1994), p. 60.

16. H. Rider Haggard, *King Solomon's Mines* [1885] (Harmondsworth: Penguin, 1994), pp. 144, 139, and 223.

17. John Buchan, "The Frying-Pan and the Fire," in *The Best Short Stories of John Buchan, vol. 1,* edited by David Daniell [1980] (London: Panther, 1984), p. 202.

18. John Buchan, *Huntingtower* [1922] (Far Thrupp: Alan Sutton, 1993), pp. 6, 27, 49, and 105.

19. John Buchan, *Witch Wood* [1927] (Edinburgh: Canongate, 1988), pp. 114, 19–20, and 143–144.

20. John Buchan, *The House of the Four Winds* [1935] (London: J. M. Dent, 1984), pp. 58 and 86.

21. Brian Sibley, *The Lord of the Rings: Official Movie Guide* (London: Harper-Collins, 2001), p. 44.

22. Euan Ferguson, "A world under his spell," *The Observer Review* (17 February 2002), p. 5.

*W*ORKS CITED

Alexander, Ziggi, and Audrey Dewjee. "Black Politicians." In *The Edwardian Era.* Edited by Jane Beckett and Deborah Cherry. London: Phaidon Press, 1987.

Alkon, Paul K. *Science Fiction Before 1900: Imagination Discovers Technology.* New York: Twayne, 1994.

Armstrong, Philip. *Shakespeare in Psychoanalysis.* London: Routledge, 2001.

Austen, Jane. *Sense and Sensibility.* Edited by Tony Tanner. Harmondsworth, England: Penguin, 1969.

Baltake, Joe. *Bee Movie Critic.* Online: http://www.movieclub.com/reviews/archives/96hamlet/hamlet.html

Bayer-Berenbaum, Linda. *The Gothic Imagination: Expansion in Gothic Literature and Art.* London and Toronto: Associated University Presses, 1982.

Boose, Lynda E., and Richard Burt. "Totally Clueless? Shakespeare goes Hollywood in the 1990s." In *Shakespeare, the Movie: Popularizing the plays on film, tv and video.* Edited by Lynda E. Boose and Richard Burt. London: Routledge, 1997.

Botting, Fred. *Gothic.* London: Routledge, 1996.

Braddon, Mary Elizabeth. *Lady Audley's Secret* (1862). London: Virago, 1985.

Branagh, Kenneth. *Hamlet, by William Shakespeare: Screenplay, Introduction and Film Diary.* London: W. W. Norton, 1996.

Buchan, John. "The Frying-Pan and the Fire." In *The Best Short Stories of John Buchan, vol. 1.* Edited by David Daniell. London: Panther, 1984.

———. *The House of the Four Winds* [1935]. London: J. M. Dent, 1984.

———. *Huntingtower* [1922]. Far Thrupp, England: Alan Sutton, 1993.

———. *Witch Wood* [1927]. Edinburgh: Canongate, 1988.

Burnett, Mark Thornton. "The 'Very Cunning of the Scene': Kenneth Branagh's *Hamlet.*" *Literature/Film Quarterly* 25:2 (1997): 78–82.

Carter, Angela. "John Ford's *'Tis Pity She's a Whore.*" In *Burning Your Boats: The Collected Short Stories.* London: Chatto & Windus, 1995.

Clerico, Terri. "The Politics of Blood: John Ford's *'Tis Pity She's a Whore.*" *English Literary Renaissance* 22.3 (1992): 405–34.

Collins, Max Allan. *The Mummy.* London: Ebury Press, 1999.

———. *The Mummy Returns.* New York: Berkley Boulevard, 2001.

Coppola, Francis Ford, and James V. Hart. *Bram Stoker's Dracula: The Film and the Legend.* London: Pan, 1992.

Corliss, Richard. "The Whole Dane Thing." *Time* 149:2 (13 January 1997).

Crowl, Samuel. "Flamboyant realist: Kenneth Branagh." In *The Cambridge Companion to Shakespeare on Film.* Edited by Russell Jackson. Cambridge: Cambridge University Press, 2000.

Day, William Patrick. *In the Circles of Fear and Desire: A Study of Gothic Fantasy.* Chicago: The University of Chicago Press, 1985.

Dickson, Rebecca. "Misrepresenting Jane Austen's Ladies: Revising Texts (and History) to Sell Films." In *Jane Austen in Hollywood.* Edited by Linda Troost and Sayre Greenfield. Lexington: University of Kentucky Press, 1998.

Dika, Vera. "From Dracula—with Love." In *The Dread of Difference.* Edited by Barry Keith Grant. Austin: University of Texas Press, 1996.

Eagleton, Terry. *The Rape of Clarissa.* Oxford: Basil Blackwell, 1982.

Ellis, Markman. *The History of Gothic Fiction.* Edinburgh: Edinburgh University Press, 2000.

El-Shater, Safaa. *The Novels of Mary Shelley.* Salzburg: Salzburg Studies, 1977.

Ferguson, Euan. "A world under his spell." *The Observer Review.* 17 February 2002.

Glover, David. "Travels in Romania: Myths of Origins, Myths of Blood." *Discourse* 16 (1993): 126–144.

Greenfield, John R. "Is Emma Clueless? Fantasies of Class and Gender from England to California." *Topic* 48 (1997): 31–38.

Guntner, J. Lawrence. "*Hamlet, Macbeth* and *King Lear* on film." In *The Cambridge Companion to Shakespeare on Film.* Edited by Russell Jackson. Cambridge: Cambridge University Press, 2000.

Haggard, H. Rider. *Ayesha.* London: Ward Lock & Co., 1905.

———. *King Solomon's Mines* [1885]. Harmondsworth, England: Penguin, 1994.

———. *She* [1887]. Harmondsworth, England: Penguin, 1994.

———. *She and Allan* [1921]. London: Macdonald, 1960.

Hamlet—to cut or not to cut? BBC2, first shown 5 February 1997.

Hapgood, Robert. "Popularizing Shakespeare: The artistry of Franco Zeffirelli." In *Shakespeare, the Movie: Popularizing the plays on film, tv and video.* Edited by Lynda E. Boose and Richard Burt. London: Routledge, 1997.

Harding, D. W. "Regulated Hatred: An Aspect of the Work of Jane Austen." *Scrutiny* 8 (March 1940).

Hirsh, James. "The 'To Be or Not To Be' Scene and the Conventions of Shakespearean Drama." *Modern Language Quarterly* 42:2 (1981).

Hodgdon, Barbara. "The Critic, the Poor Player, Prince Hamlet, and the Lady in the Dark." In *Shakespeare Reread: The Texts in New Contexts.* Edited by Russ McDonald. Ithaca, New York: Cornell University Press, 1994.

Hood, Gwenyth. "Sauron and Dracula." In *Dracula: The Vampire and the Critics.* Edited by Margaret L. Carter. Ann Arbor, Mich.: UMI Research Press, 1988.

Hopkins, Lisa. "Incest and Class: *'Tis Pity She's a Whore* and the Borgias." In *Incest and the Literary Imagination*. Edited by Elizabeth Barnes. Gainesville: University Press of Florida, 2002.

Huntington, John. *The Logic of Fantasy: H. G. Wells and Science Fiction*. New York: Columbia University Press, 1982.

Jackson, Russell. *The Cambridge Companion to Shakespeare on Film*. Edited by Russell Jackson. Cambridge: Cambridge University Press, 2000.

———. "From play-script to screenplay." In *The Cambridge Companion to Shakespeare on Film*. Edited by Russell Jackson. Cambridge: Cambridge University Press, 2000.

Jurkiewicz, Kenneth. "Francis Coppola's Secret Gardens: *Bram Stoker's Dracula* and the Auteur as Decadent Visionary." In *Visions of the Fantastic*. Edited by Allienne R. Becker. London: Greenwood Press, 1996.

Kaplan, E. Ann. *Woman and Film: Both Sides of the Camera*. London: Methuen, 1983.

Keyishian, Harry J. "Shakespeare and movie genre: The case of *Hamlet*." In *The Cambridge Companion to Shakespeare on Film*. Edited by Russell Jackson. Cambridge: Cambridge University Press, 2000.

Kirkham, Margaret. *Jane Austen: Feminism and Fiction*. Brighton, England: The Harvester Press, 1983.

Kline, Michael. "The Vampire as Pathogen: Bram Stoker's *Dracula* and Francis Ford Coppola's *Bram Stoker's Dracula*." *West Virginia University Philological Papers* 42/43 (1997/1998): 36–44.

Kuhn, Annette. *Women's Pictures: Feminism and the Cinema*. London: Routledge, 1982.

Lehmann, Courtney, and Lisa S. Starks. "Making Mother Matter: Repression, Revision, and the Stakes of 'Reading Psychoanalysis Into' Kenneth Branagh's Hamlet." *Early Modern Literary Studies* 6.1 (May 2000): 2.1–24.

Mackenzie, Suzie. "Angel with horns." *Guardian Weekend* (3 January 1998): 10–16.

Marshall, Tim. "*Frankenstein* and the 1832 Anatomy Act." In *Gothick Origins and Innovations*. Edited by Allan Lloyd Smith and Victor Sage. Amsterdam: Rodopi, 1994.

Mayne, Judith. *Cinema and Spectatorship*. London: Routledge, 1993.

Mellor, Anne K. *Mary Shelley: Her Life, Her Fiction, Her Monsters*. London and New York: Routledge, 1988.

Metz, Christian. *The Imaginary Signifier: Psychoanalysis and the Cinema*. Bloomington: Indiana University Press, 1977.

Miles, Robert. *Gothic Writing 1750–1820: A Genealogy*. London: Routledge, 1993.

Morgan, Jack. *The Biology of Horror: Gothic Literature and Film*. Carbondale: Southern Illinois University Press, 2002.

Mulvey, Laura. *Visual and Other Pleasures*. Bloomington: Indiana University Press, 1989.

Nachumi, Nora. " 'As If!': Translating Austen's Ironic Narrator to Film." In *Jane*

Austen in Hollywood. Edited by Linda Troost and Sayre Greenfield. Lexington: University of Kentucky Press, 1998.

Newman, Kim. "Coppola's Dracula." In *The Mammoth Book of Dracula.* Edited by Stephen Jones. London: Robinson, 1997.

Nixon, Cheryl L. "Balancing the Courtship Hero: Masculine Emotional Display in Film Adaptations of Austen's Novels." In *Jane Austen in Hollywood.* Edited by Linda Troost and Sayre Greenfield. Lexington: University of Kentucky Press, 1998.

Peters, Elizabeth. *The Snake, the Crocodile and the Dog.* London: Constable & Robinson, 1992.

Pilkington, Ace. "Zeffirelli's Shakespeare." In *Shakespeare and the Moving Image.* Edited by Anthony Davies and Stanley Wells. Cambridge: Cambridge University Press, 1994.

Poovey, Mary. *The Proper Lady and the Woman Writer.* Chicago: University of Chicago Press, 1984.

Richardson, Samuel. *Clarissa.* Edited by Angus Ross. Harmondsworth, England: Penguin, 1985.

Rowling, J. K. *Harry Potter and the Philosopher's Stone.* London: Bloomsbury, 1997.

Ruderman, Anne. "Moral Education in Jane Austen's *Emma.*" In *Poets, Princes, and Private Citizens: Literary Alternatives to Postmodern Politics.* Edited by Joseph M. Knippenberg and Peter Augustine Lawler. London: Rowman & Littlefield, 1996.

Rutter, Carol Chillington. "Looking at Shakespeare's women on film." In *The Cambridge Companion to Shakespeare on Film.* Edited by Russell Jackson. Cambridge: Cambridge University Press, 2000.

Samuelian, Kristin Flieger. " 'Piracy is our Only Option': Postfeminist Intervention in *Sense and Sensibility.*" *Topic* 48 (1997): 39–48.

Shakespeare, William. *Hamlet.* Edited by Harold Jenkins. London: Methuen, 1980.

———. *Love's Labour's Lost.* Edited by John Kerrigan. Harmondsworth, England: Penguin, 1982.

———. *Othello.* Edited by E. A. J. Honigmann. Lerder, England: Thomas Nelson, 1997.

———. *Richard III.* Edited by E. A. J. Honigmann. Harmondsworth, England: Penguin, 1968.

Showalter, Elaine. *Sexual Anarchy: Gender and Culture at the Fin de Siècle.* London: Bloomsbury, 1990.

Sibley, Brian. *The Lord of the Rings: Official Movie Guide.* London: HarperCollins, 2001.

Silver, Alain, and James Ursini. *The Vampire Film from Nosferatu to Interview with the Vampire.* 3rd ed. New York: Proscenium, 1997.

Skal, David J. *Hollywood Gothic: The Tangled Web of* Dracula *from Novel to Stage to Screen.* London: André Deutsch, 1990.

Small, Christopher. *Ariel Like a Harpy: Shelley, Mary and Frankenstein.* London: 1972.

Spiller, Ben. " 'Today, Vindici Returns': Alex Cox's *Revengers Tragedy,*" *Early Modern Literary Studies* 8.3 (January 2003). Available online at http://www.shu.ac.uk/emls/08-3/spilreve.html

Stoker, Bram. *Dracula.* Edited by A. N. Wilson. Oxford: Oxford University Press, 1983.

———. *The Lady of the Shroud* [1909]. London: Alan Sutton, 1994.

———. *The Jewel of Seven Stars* [1903]. Oxford: Oxford University Press, 1996.

The Readiness Is All: The Filming of Hamlet. BBC2; first shown 15 February 1997.

Thomas, Ronald R. "Specters of the Novel: *Dracula* and the Cinematic Afterlife of the Victorian Novel." *Nineteenth Century Contexts* 22.1 (2000): 77–102.

Thompson, Emma. *Jane Austen's Sense and Sensibility: The Screenplay and Diaries.* London: Bloomsbury, 1995.

Thomsen, Inger Sigrun. "Words 'Half-Dethroned': Jane Austen's Art of the Unspoken." In *Jane Austen's Business: Her World and Her Profession.* Edited by Juliet McMaster and Bruce Stovel. Basingstoke, England: Macmillan, 1996.

Thornburg, Mary K. Paterson. *The Monster in the Mirror: Gender and the Sentimental/Gothic Myth in Frankenstein.* Michigan: UMI Research Press, 1984.

Tolkien, J. R. R. *The Fellowship of the Ring* [1954]. London: Grafton, 1991.

Veeder, William. *Mary Shelley and Frankenstein: The Fate of Androgyny.* Chicago: University of Chicago Press, 1986.

Waltje, Jörg. "Filming *Dracula:* Vampires, Genre, and Cinematography." *Journal of Dracula Studies* 4 (2002): 24–33.

Weiss, Tanja. *Shakespeare on the Screen: Kenneth Branagh's Adaptations of* Henry V, Much Ado About Nothing *and* Hamlet. Frankfurt am Main: Peter Lang, 1999.

Wells, H. G. *The Time Machine.* Edited by John Lawton. London: J.M. Dent, 1995.

Whitman, John. *The Mummy Returns.* London: Bantam Books, 2001.

Wolverton, Dave. *Revenge of the Scorpion King.* London: Bantam Books, 2001.

Wymer, Rowland. " 'The Audience Is Only Interested in Sex and Violence': Teaching the Renaissance on Film." In *Working Papers on the Web* 4 (September 2002). Available online at http://www.shu.ac.uk/wpw/renaissance/wymer.htm

Žižek, Slavoy. *Enjoy Your Symptom!: Jacques Lacan in Hollywood and Out.* London: Routledge, 1992.

*I*NDEX